OUT OF THE JUNGLE

Thaddeus Russell

OUT OF THE JUNGLE

Jimmy Hoffa and the Remaking of
the American Working Class

Alfred A. Knopf

New York

2001

THIS IS A BORZOI BOOK
PUBLISHED BY ALFRED A. KNOPF

Grateful acknowledgment is made to the following for permission to use pictures
in the photo insert, as indicated: photo of Sidney Hillman, copyright
© Hulton-Deutsch/Corbis; photo of John L. and Dennie Lewis, copyright
© Underwood & Underwood/Corbis; all other photos, Bettmann/Corbis.

Library of Congress Cataloging-in-Publication Data
Russell, Thaddeus.
Out of the jungle: Jimmy Hoffa and the remaking of the American working class /
Thaddeus Russell.
p. cm.
ISBN 0-375-41157-7 (alk. paper)
1. Hoffa, James R. (James Riddle), 1913–1975.   2. Labor unions—United States—
Officials and employees—Biography.   3. International Brotherhood of Teamsters,
Chauffeurs, Warehousemen, and Helpers of America.   I. Title

HD6509.H6 R87 2001
331.88'11388324'092—dc21
[B]   2001029927

Manufactured in the United States of America
First Edition

For Lisa

CONTENTS

ACKNOWLEDGMENTS

Although in a formal sense I began working on this project six years ago, its real beginning came in 1984, when Antioch College allowed a part-time employee of a cookie store with a mediocre high school record a chance to change his life. During my first quarter at Antioch, I luckily chose to take a course taught by Al Denman. Al was the best teacher I had ever encountered, and he inspired me to make a life in the world of ideas. My growing interest in history and in an academic career was encouraged by a trio of historians at Antioch: Bob Fogarty, Lester Lee, and Tom Martin. The small-scale but vigorous intellectual culture in Yellow Springs also profoundly shaped my ideas. Through marathon sessions in the Caf, North Hall, and the Saloon, I received a first-rate political education and invaluable friendship from Mike Diamond, Michael Glavin, and Joe Lowndes. And without the sacrifice and support of Margo Lee, my first two years of graduate school and therefore this book would not have been possible.

My transformation at Antioch allowed me to sneak into the graduate program in history at Columbia, but I would not have lasted long there were it not for the support of several members of the faculty. I will always be grateful to Betsy Blackmar, Richard Bushman, Eric Foner, and Jim Shenton for taking a chance on me and for teaching me everything I know about American history. My tutor, comrade, and friend Josh Freeman gave me tough but encouraging feedback on the Hoffa project from its earliest stage as a jumble of ideas to its final form. Alan Brinkley has done more for me than I could have imagined. Since my first day in Fayerweather Hall, Alan has been a wise and generous mentor, an incisive and empathetic editor, and a model of intellectual integrity.

Acknowledgments

Fellow graduate students at Columbia made the isolation of scholarly life bearable. Special thanks go to Mike Flamm for being the first person to encourage me to take on Hoffa as a dissertation topic. Fellow Teamsterologist Aaron Brenner took me under his wing during my first weeks in graduate school and became a good friend, challenging interlocutor, and basketball nemesis. I was lucky that John Stoner, who has been a close and loyal friend since we were both babes in the woods of Morningside Heights, had the courage or foolishness to share a dingy apartment with me during a lengthy research junket in Michigan.

On an earlier research trip I learned how dependent on the kindness of strangers I would be when I arrived at the State Historical Society of Wisconsin to examine the official papers of the International Brotherhood of Teamsters. In the folder containing the records of Local 299 I found two pieces of paper, one being an invitation to a banquet. Without the help of several scholars and librarians the story of Hoffa's years in Detroit would still be largely untold. Melvyn Dubofsky, Tom Sugrue, Bridgett Williams-Searle, and David Witwer offered useful advice when I was groping my way through the early stages of research. Nelson Lichtenstein met me when I was in preschool and again when I was beginning my dissertation. Since our second introduction, he has been an invaluable resource, an astoundingly attentive reader, and an encouraging and generous advisor.

My buddy Mike Smith at the Archives of Urban and Labor Affairs at Wayne State has been a rock since my very first adventure in Detroit. My thanks go to Nancy Bartlett, Fran Blouin, Bill Wallach, and the staff of the Bentley Historical Library in Ann Arbor for awarding me the Mark C. Stevens Researcher Travel Fellowship and for meeting my endless photocopying requests. Martin Tuohy at the Chicago branch of the National Archives was tremendously helpful in tracking down court documents. The wonderful people I met in Brazil, Indiana, especially the staff of the Brazil Public Library, helped unlock the mysteries of Hoffa's hometown. Pat Zacharias saved me from hundreds of hours of dreaded microfilm work by allowing me access to the *Detroit News* library. Sarah Potter bailed me out with last-minute research assistance, and my brother Jacob Russell retrieved an important oral history that I had overlooked in Boston.

I owe special thanks to the people who generously granted me interviews during my trips to Michigan. Tom Downs, Bobby Holmes, and Leonard Shaffner invited me into their homes and provided both important information and helpful interpretations of past events. Robert Farrell of the National Automobile Transporters Association was a vital source for piecing together the early history of Local 299. George Geller was my key to the world of the Detroit Teamsters, and in the course of a fascinating conversation over pasta primavera at Mario's he gave me the idea for the title of the book. Rolland and Marilyn McMaster spent the better part of a weekend hosting me at their beautiful horse farm, and Rolland's memories gave life to many parts of the early chapters.

My editors at Knopf, Ash Green, Asya Muchnick, Jonathan Fasman, and Melvin Rosenthal, saved me from many embarrassing mistakes and made the process of converting a dissertation into a book relatively painless.

They didn't know it at the time, but every one of the students in my section of Introduction to Contemporary Civilization at Columbia during the 1997–98 academic year helped me work through the ideas in this book, so I feel obligated to acknowledge them all by name: Sandie Arnold, Stephanie Camp, Kenny Deutsch, Alicia Dooley, Josh Dybnis, Seth Glucksman, Ross Goodman, Tanjila Islam, Gavan Kwan, Zoe Leibowitz, Eric Leskly, Erica Lutzker, Jennifer Newman, Jaye Pace, Jonathan Parrott, Eric Peel, Susan Phung, Elissa Refold, James Renovitch, Michael Richard, Mike Schiraldi, Pearl Wang, Frances Webb, Bettina Welsch, Gavin Williams, and Leslie Zivin.

My father, Robert Russell, an avid and astute reader of history, was the first person to read the entire manuscript. Not only did he catch several important errors, but his enthusiasm for my work did more for me than he probably knows. In the fall of 1988, my mother, Leslye Russell, suggested that I look at the interunion rivalry between the Teamsters and the United Farm Workers as a possible topic for my senior thesis at Antioch. It was a typically brilliant suggestion. She had a great deal of knowledge about the conflict, since John Larson, her husband and my stepfather, had worked inside Teamsters Local 70 in Oakland in behalf of the UFW. Though I eventually developed different ideas than theirs about the labor movement, my work is guided by our shared interest in the efforts of ordinary people to improve their lives. The incredible warmth and generosity of my parents-in-law,

Acknowledgments

Barbara and Mark Hacken, have helped sustain me and my work through good times and bad.

Finally, the writing of this book coincided with and was shaped by a painful but ultimately liberating revolution in my personal and political life. Three people deserve special credit for taking me there and getting me through it.

I met Jonathan Cutler when I had just started to conceive the project and was struggling to break out of an ideological prison I had built for myself. Jonathan rocked my world and freed my mind. If there is a more brilliant or original social thinker in my generation, I don't know who it is. Jonathan's ideas about the labor movement—which are in themselves monumental but which make up only a small part of what I have learned from him—inspired many of the arguments in this book.

I don't know whether Kate Bar-Tur knows anything about Jimmy Hoffa, the Teamsters, or labor history, but she not only forced me to think seriously about my relationship with my work, she also saved my life.

After writing the first two chapters, I took time off to marry Lisa Jane Hacken. This proved to be the best thing I could have done for the book and its author. Certainly Lisa deserves my gratitude for editing every significant piece of my writing, for waiting patiently for me to return from research trips and long nights at the computer, and for listening with that enormous heart of hers to my anxieties, but simply waking up next to me every morning deserves more thanks than I can give.

Thaddeus Russell
New York City
March 2001

OUT OF THE JUNGLE

Introduction

Jimmy Hoffa's judgment may have been unduly dismissive, but the record of his life, his career, and his union does raise questions about the work of labor historians, especially what has been called "the new labor history." Since the 1960s, a generation of scholars dissatisfied with the old labor history's narrow focus on the institutional features of trade unions has produced a mountain of literature on American workers, their consciousness, their identities, their politics, and their various communities and organizations. Out of this scholarship has come a set of highly influential conclusions about labor's history in this country, and, by implication, its future as well. The story of Jimmy Hoffa and the Teamsters, however, stands in mocking defiance of those conclusions.

The practitioners of the new labor history in the United States have produced countless studies of the unions of the Congress of Industrial Organizations (CIO), which emerged out of the American Federation of Labor (AFL) in 1935, but only a pitiful few on the affiliates of the AFL after the split.[2] In fact, a new student of the field looking through the labor history section on the shelves of the typical research library might not know that the AFL and its constituent unions continued to exist after 1935. This disparity is particularly curious when one considers that even at the height of the CIO's growth, the AFL was three times larger in membership, and that on its own terms the AFL could be considered the most successful working-class organization in American history, having dramatically improved the material conditions of

3

tens of millions of workers—female and male, skilled and unskilled, agricultural and industrial, native-born and immigrant, black, white, Latino, and Asian.[3]

No AFL union was larger or more successful than the International Brotherhood of Teamsters (IBT). By the end of Hoffa's career, the membership of the IBT stood at more than two million—making it the largest labor union in the history of the United States—and nearly all of those members enjoyed wages, hours, and working conditions far superior to those of workers in similar occupations before the growth of the union.[4] Yet no academic historian has written a study of the Teamsters union or of its most important leader, Jimmy Hoffa.

Hoffa's Teamsters defy the new labor history in other, more important ways as well. While scholars of the 1960s generation have attempted to find within the labor movement a purpose other than "delivering the goods," the Teamster locals in Detroit and later the international union under Hoffa's leadership adhered to a strictly economic mission, and scorned the attempts of radicals and "labor statesmen" to bring worker organizations into the political and managerial classes. Perhaps new labor historians have shunned the Teamsters because the union supplies substantial evidence to support the claim made by Selig Perlman that American workers in an organization devoid of radical intellectuals would choose the "pure and simple" objective of material improvements over grander aspirations of social transformation.[5] Similarly, the rapid growth and material accomplishments of the Teamsters under Hoffa's leadership present new labor historians with the troubling fact that much of this success was caused not by the "industrial democracy" they endorse but by the compelling power of competition both within the IBT and from rival unions. Moreover, where Hoffa and the Teamsters failed to deliver the goods, anticompetitive forces were largely responsible.* Of course, it should be expected that contemporary labor historians would avoid a market analysis since, as has been noted even by scholars sympathetic to the cause, virtually all share some sort of anti-market political orientation.[6]

---

*Since an essential function of trade unions is to limit competition between workers within the labor market, the argument presented here differs substantively from libertarian and "neo-liberal" endorsements of universal competition. The competition described in this study was between and within trade unions for representation of workers, not between workers for jobs.

4

The existing literature on Hoffa and the Teamsters has done little to correct the deficiencies of labor history. Most of it was produced by journalists and government investigators bent on exposing Hoffa's immorality and is therefore preoccupied with his illicit dealings with underworld figures. Only two biographies of the Teamster leader have been written by academic scholars: an important work concentrating on Hoffa's collective bargaining techniques that was published in 1965 by the economists Ralph and Estelle Dinerstein James, and a 1991 biography by Arthur A. Sloane, a professor of industrial relations, that relies on secondary research. But even the study by the Jameses, who enjoyed exclusive access not only to Hoffa himself but to many IBT records that have subsequently been destroyed, leaves much of his story either obscured by mythology or utterly mysterious. While much is known about his later career and eventual disappearance in 1975, the literature provides only a cursory record of Hoffa's twenty years with the Detroit and Michigan Teamsters before his rise to the IBT presidency in 1957. And since the chroniclers of Hoffa and the Teamsters have not been historians, the changing social context of his life has been largely ignored.[7]

This study attempts not only to fill in gaps in the historical record but also to examine Hoffa historically. Here Hoffa and his union are shown as products of a multitude of social forces—both material and ideological—that emerged and evolved during his lifetime. This is, therefore, more an examination of those social forces than it is of Hoffa himself, and in this way it breaks not only from conventional biographical forms but also from the strict institutional approach of the old labor history. This anti-biography borrows from the innovations of contemporary labor historians in many other ways as well. The culture, community life, and ethnic, racial, and gender identities of the Detroit Teamsters are treated as determinative, not decorative, in their history. As will be seen in the following pages, it is impossible to fully understand Hoffa's union without understanding the complex web of relationships, stretching from local bars to the White House, from which it developed.

But perhaps the most important point of agreement between this work and recent scholarship is the causal agency that both grant to ordinary workers. As the following pages will show, one of the most significant determinants of the course of Hoffa's career was the desire of his union's members for material improvements in their lives and their willingness to act on that desire. Ironically, though, when applied to Hoffa and the Teamsters, the methodology of the new labor history yields starkly different conclusions from those reached by its creators.

As this narrative will demonstrate, the public Jimmy Hoffa was produced by an unregulated and amoral political economy. In Hoffa's "Depression City," small businesses—like most trucking firms—could be terrorized into submission to the union, police and politicians could be bought, saloons became the locus of social activity, and criminals left unemployed by the repeal of Prohibition furnished a ready source of useful services.[8] For Hoffa personally, the unfortunate consequence of building a labor organization in this environment was the constant threat to his power from rivals within the Teamsters and from other unions. This meant a grim life for Hoffa, but because it forced him to be accountable to the interests of the members, for them it proved to be a boon.

With the rise of the New Deal and the CIO in the 1930s and the wartime state in 1941, Hoffa's primitive world of unfettered competition and desire was confronted by concerted attempts, from the streets of Detroit to the national capital, to impose civilization on that world and to remake its working class into a responsible citizenry. The CIO's campaign to unify the labor movement within a monolithic and disciplined industrial organization and to share power in a managed economic system—the product of a semi-socialist idea that later came to be called "corporatism"—merged with efforts by state and federal governments to tame and regulate the conflict between labor and capital. After World War II, the managerial and self-regulating impulses of corporatist union leaders found common cause with crusades by government reformers to bring social responsibility and ascetic morality to the labor movement. However, the intrusions by these civilizers into Hoffa's jungle—many of which benefited Hoffa personally—produced dubious results for the working class itself. It is hoped, therefore, that for those of us who study the history of workers, and, more important, for workers themselves, the narrative that follows will at least raise questions about the ideal of worker self-management that has fired the imagination and guided the efforts of so many labor historians.

One

American Soil

Bourgeois society stands at the crossroads, either transition to socialism or regression into barbarism.—FRIEDRICH ENGELS[1]

When James Riddle Hoffa was born in Brazil, Indiana, on February 14, 1913, American socialism had reached its apex. Just twelve years after its founding, the Socialist Party could boast of a membership of more than 100,000, the election of 1,200 party members to public offices across the United States, and the ongoing publication of more than 300 periodicals. Most impressive was the widespread popularity of another native of west-central Indiana, Eugene Debs, who received more than 900,000 votes as the party's nominee in the 1912 presidential election. But over the next several years, during Hoffa's childhood, the United States provided a stark answer to the query posed by Friedrich Engels at the close of the nineteenth century. Jimmy Hoffa's America crucified Eugene Debs and set fire to his world.[2]

In the fall of 1925, Debs wrote a letter to his local newspaper in Terre Haute bitterly lamenting the fate of both his hometown and his country. Debs had returned to live in Terre Haute after his release from the Atlanta Federal Penitentiary, where he had served three and a half years for violation of the Espionage Act—the penalty for having given a series of antiwar speeches during World War I. The leader of the Socialist Party of America saw a new world when he moved back to the town of his childhood. The party he had spent much of his life building was nearly destroyed, the victim of government repression

7

and a postwar right-wing resurgence. Most painfully, he saw that America, and even Terre Haute, had been fully transformed by modern industrial machinery. Aged and depleted from his years in prison, Debs lacked the energy and spirit to renew the fight for socialism but held out hope that others might take up the work of redeeming what he saw as a fallen America. Gone were the "simplicity and beauty" of pioneer life in the Wabash Valley, he wrote to the *Terre Haute Tribune*. "This is predominantly a business age, a commercial age, a material and in a larger sense a sordid age, but the moral and spiritual values of life are not wholly ignored by the people." Having never moved from Christian socialism to the "scientific" doctrine of his immigrant comrades, Debs looked not to objective conditions for salvation but to what he believed to be the God-given moral sensibility of human beings. "Sentiment, without which men are lower than savages, is still rooted in and flowers in the human soul and makes possible the hope that some day we shall seek and find and enjoy the real riches of the race."[3]

The socialist utopia that Debs imagined closely resembled his own memories of the "beloved little community" of Terre Haute during his youth, "where all were neighbors and friends." While this surely was a romanticized description, the small Indiana city in the late nineteenth century did offer sources of inspiration for a communitarian such as Debs. Established at the intersection of the Wabash River and the National Road and promoted as a railroad link between the eastern markets and St. Louis, until the turn of the century Terre Haute developed slowly enough to allow it to remain an exemplar of small-town American republicanism. Despite the presence of the Terre Haute and Indiana railroad and the Vigo Iron Company, the predominantly native-born and Protestant white population enjoyed the close social relations of a decentralized economy. Most businesses employed only a handful of people, and even the railroad maintained a personalized work environment by limiting its hiring to familial and friendship networks. Workers were more likely to identify with their employers than to feel class antagonism towards them. Added to this was a pervasive Christian evangelicalism, handed down from the Second Great Awakening, that imbued the community with the ethics of self-sacrifice and social responsibility.

As an adult in a rapidly changing world, Debs was motivated by a longing for his "beloved little community" and a fear that it would be buried under the advance of industrial capitalism. But unlike most workers who shared these feelings, Debs's intellectual training enabled him to articulate them. His father, the product of a wealthy Alsatian family, introduced him to the works of the greatest French writers and social theorists, including Voltaire, Rousseau, and Victor Hugo. From his early immersion in Enlightenment thought Debs developed a view of the world as a single community, which, paired with the lessons of Terre Haute's culture of social obligation, created in him a sense of responsibility for the entire human race. He aspired to be a manager of others, to correct the human impulses that threatened social harmony. A teenage friend expected him either to become the owner of a large business or to join the railroad and "step into a Master Mechanics job in charge of all the engine men." Indeed, as a leader of the Brotherhood of Locomotive Firemen—whose motto was "Benevolence, Sobriety and Industry"—Debs viewed the trade union as an instrument of moral discipline. "It is no small matter to plant benevolence in the heart of stone, instill the love of sobriety into the putrid mind of debauchery, and create industry out of idleness," he wrote in 1881. "These are our aims, and if the world concedes them to be plausible, we ask that they find an anchoring place in its heart."

As smokestacks grew higher, railroad lines stretched longer, and moral depravity sank deeper in Terre Haute and the rest of America, Debs's inclinations naturally turned him toward socialism. Flowing directly from his yearning for the classless Christian community of his imagined youth and his ambition to oversee it, Debs's socialism shared the basic principles of socialists around the world, but it bore his own distinctive mark. Within a collectively managed political economy, workers would organize, discipline, and regulate themselves and thereby "work out their own salvation, their redemption and independence." But to transform workers into responsible social managers, socialism would have to be above all a moralizing mission. "What is Socialism?" Debs rhetorically asked a crowd of party members. "Merely Christianity in action." And who would bring it about? "The martyred Christ of the working class."[4]

Twenty years later, in prison, his movement crushed, his health shattered, and the world outside lost to capitalism, Debs wrote a letter to a friend that described a troubling dream he had had: "I was walking by the house where I was born—the house was gone and nothing left but ashes. All about me were ashes. . . . The house was gone—and only ashes—Ashes!"[5]

Rising from those ashes was not the phoenix of socialism or a new Christ of the working class, but something else altogether. The fuel for the railroad engines and blasting furnaces that incinerated Debs's Terre Haute came from coal mines a few miles away, in the towns where Jimmy Hoffa spent the first eleven years of his life.

In the late nineteenth century, Clay County accounted for more than half of Indiana's coal production. Much of that coal was put on railroad cars in Brazil, the county's seat and largest town, and shipped sixteen miles west to Terre Haute. In 1910 John Cleveland Hoffa and Viola Riddle Hoffa moved to Brazil from nearby Cunot, a farming town where Viola was raised. The relocation was necessary for John, since the headquarters of his employer, Ben Mershon, an independent coal prospector, was in Brazil. John Cleveland Hoffa was a member of the third generation of Hoffas in Indiana. His German ancestors had immigrated to Pennsylvania, then moved west along the National Road, ultimately settling in Indiana in the early nineteenth century. John and Viola, who was of Irish descent, moved themselves and their newborn daughter, Jenetta, into a house in "Stringtown," the neighborhood in Brazil with the highest concentration of miners. In the front room of the house, Viola gave birth to their second and third children: William Henry in 1911 and James Riddle, on St. Valentine's Day, 1913.[6]

By 1913 Brazil had reached its peak as a boomtown. After a geology survey in 1871 revealed that the land around the town contained two trillion tons of coal, the little stopover along the National Road took off. Within three years Brazil's population grew from a few hundred to a few thousand, and by the time of Jimmy Hoffa's birth it topped out at 11,000. Like most fast-growing mining towns during this period, Brazil was a world apart from Debs's Terre Haute. The prospects for upward mobility and workers' identification with employers had been greatly diminished by the concentration of the mining industry into the hands of a few companies. State regulations and contracts won by the United Mine Workers of America (UMW) had raised wages and improved working conditions for coal miners, but the deep-shaft mines surrounding Brazil were still deadly. Explosions, fires, and cave-ins were commonplace, as were less spectacular fatalities caused by intense heat, poisonous vapors, pneumonia, and black lung.

The culture of Brazil expressed the pain and desperation created by its economy. Violence, suicides, drunkenness, prostitution, and gambling were common features of everyday life. In the 1910s, Brazil featured one saloon for every 500 residents. Most were concentrated on Meridian Street, a few blocks from the Hoffas' home, which was known as "Bloody Row" for the frequency of its drunken brawls and homicides. Battles between white and black miners were especially vicious in a town that had attracted significant numbers of African Americans from the South. The rest of Stringtown was dotted with brothels and gambling houses, including one operated by Hoffa's uncle and namesake, James.[7]

Of course, all this sinning prompted a great amount of repentance. Like other Indiana coal towns, Brazil had almost as many churches as saloons. One of the largest was the First Christian Church, which the Hoffas attended every Sunday. Their participation, however, came more from a sense of obligation than from belief. "We weren't a very religious family," Hoffa later recalled. This attitude is evident in his bored, mechanical account of a typical Sunday morning:

> Dressed starch-white-clean, we trooped off to the Christian Church of Brazil to attend a rather formal service patterned after the eastern Congregational Church order of worship. The standard operating procedure was to begin with the singing of a hymn, followed by a prayer, with the congregation still standing, then the singing of the doxology, 'Praise God from whom all blessings flow. . . .' Then came the reading of the Scripture lesson, to which, ultimately, the sermon made reference. That was followed by a choral selection and the offertory, the taking of the collection.

Through indifference, both Hoffa and his brother, who later followed him into the Teamsters, escaped the Christian sense of duty that had defined Eugene Debs's life:

11

Mother went home after church services, but we had to remain for Sunday school, a session lasting nearly an hour in which we learned the meaning of some passage in the Bible, customarily based on a little "Reader" that was handed to us each week by our Sunday-school teacher. . . .

All told it made for about two and a half hours of inactivity, and I am grateful that neither Billy nor I was ever graded for our attentiveness or application to the subject matter under consideration.[8]

Hoffa's father spent much of his time traveling to surrounding counties on prospecting trips with Mershon. One day in 1920 he returned early from one of these trips, disoriented and exhausted. About a week later he died of unknown causes, just short of his fortieth birthday. Viola Hoffa was now forced to support the family, which had added a fourth child, Nancy, in 1915. She washed and ironed laundry for coal miners, cleaned houses in the town's wealthy neighborhood, and cooked in a restaurant, but the amount of money she received for these jobs was too small to sustain five people. By 1920, wages in Brazil had begun to decline, especially for women. The town's economic growth ebbed during the war as several of the local mines were found to be "worked out." Hoffa's mother decided to move the family to Clinton, located eleven miles north of Terre Haute on the Wabash River, which had surpassed Brazil as the boomtown of the region and where several relatives from the Riddle family lived.[9]

Clinton was even further removed than Brazil from Debs's vision of producer republicanism. In 1920, the town's thirty-two mines were producing nearly two million tons of coal annually but not much republicanism. Like Brazil, Clinton had grown quickly, fallen under the domination of a few companies, and suffered all the social destruction attendant upon coal mining. But Clinton's population was far different from Brazil's, and light-years from Debs's Protestant, Anglo-Saxon neighborhood. The separation between workers and employers was especially pronounced. Beginning at the turn of the century, family networks brought thousands of Italian immigrants to work in the mines. They filled the north side of the town, creating the largest concentration of Italians in Indiana. Viola Hoffa moved her family into a small house near her sister's home on North Third Street, in the heart of "Little Italy." There, with the help of the three children, she operated the "Hoffa Home Laundry," washing and ironing the coal-blackened clothes of mine workers. Jimmy and Billy picked up bundles of laundry from customers, gathered wood to fire the laundry tubs standing in the yard, delivered the clean clothes, and collected the money.

Having moved to Clinton the year Prohibition was put into effect, the Hoffas saw the birth and growth of an industry that became second only to coal in the area. In the 1920s, Clinton quickly gained notoriety as one of the bootlegging centers of Indiana, with illegal stills in the surrounding forests supplying the speakeasies in Little Italy and other towns in the coal belt. The Hoffas also witnessed the transformation of Clinton into one of the roughest towns in the Midwest, where violence often moved out of the mines and into the town's streets. Police raids on bootleggers frequently resulted in shoot-outs, federal attacks against the town's sizable Socialist Party branch were equally fierce, and strikes called by the United Mine Workers were typically met with armed resistance from scabs and cops. Stirred into this explosive mix were various Italian criminal organizations and a highly visible local chapter of the Ku Klux Klan, which held marches down the main streets in Little Italy to intimidate the Catholic, "un-American" immigrants.[10]

For four years, the Hoffa family managed to eke out an existence in their turbulent neighborhood, but by 1924 Clinton's economic base had begun to wither. The mechanization of mining and a declining demand for coal closed several mines, depressed wages, and squeezed the already meager profits of the Hoffa family business. Viola was forced to move again, and this time she chose the biggest boomtown in the Midwest. In 1924 the family packed up, left the relatives, and headed for Detroit.[11]

The Hoffas were among thousands of migrants then arriving in the Motor City from the South and Midwest. They were brought there by the dramatic growth of the automobile industry, which by 1924 was churning out several thousand new cars each day and paying some of the highest wages in the country. The city's population, which surged above one million in the 1920s, was increasingly made up of African Americans and "hillbillies" from the American hinterland as well as immigrants from all over Europe. Detroit's neighborhoods changed

13

virtually overnight, as one ethnic group replaced another through this period of extraordinary growth. Most of these newcomers were single men who planned to stay only a few years, save money, and return home. The 1920 Census recorded 87,000 more men than women, or 119 men to every 100 women, living in Detroit. Among the country's seventy largest cities, only Akron, Ohio, contained a greater gender imbalance. Many of these single men were clustered around the factories in the industrial area of the Lower West Side, the neighborhood where the Hoffas settled. Eleven-year-old Jimmy Hoffa had arrived in a volatile and highly masculine world.[12]

The Hoffas rented a flat in a house on Merritt Street that was occupied by three other families. Their immediate neighborhood at the time was made up mostly of native white rural refugees and German immigrants, many of whom were employed in the various nearby automobile plants, machine shops, and lumberyards. Viola Hoffa worked in the few industries that were open to women. She first took a job in a laundry as a clothes presser, then heard that General Motors was hiring women at its massive new Ternstedt parts plant near the Hoffas' house. For four years she worked at Ternstedt alongside thousands of other women, most of them Polish and Hungarian immigrants, performing repetitive work on pieces of machinery as they moved past her on the assembly line. From there she moved to somewhat less dehumanizing work as a radiator cap polisher at the Fisher Fleetwood plant. The wages Viola earned in the jobs consigned to women at the bottom of the automobile industry forced her children to work to supplement the family income. Not yet a teenager, Jimmy Hoffa worked after school and on weekends doing odd jobs for the C. F. Smith grocery store and other retail shops in the neighborhood.[13]

After completing the ninth grade at the Frank C. Neinas School, Hoffa spent the summer working in grocery stores to help support the family. When the school year began he walked to Western High School to enroll, but before his name was called he turned and headed back home. He had decided to end his schooling so that he could fully enter the world of work. Lacking Debs's love for book-learning, Hoffa felt no ambivalence about his decision. "It didn't seem right to have to spend so much time at inconsequential pursuits before being able to get down to man's business," he recalled later. "And it was man's business that interested me, not kid's." Hoffa's first experience in "man's business" was as a stock boy at Frank and Seder's Dry Goods and General Merchandise store. He earned two dollars a day and proudly handed over the money to his mother at the end of each week.[14]

The death of his father had created in Hoffa a fierce sense of obligation to provide for his family, but the conditions of his life prevented that feeling of responsibility from extending beyond his home. Many years later, Hoffa described his social philosophy:

> Every day of the average individual is a matter of survival. If by chance he should go from home to work and have an accident, lose an arm or an eye, he's just like an animal wounded in the jungle. He's out. Life isn't easy. Life is a jungle. . . . Ethics is a matter of individualism. What may be ethical to you may be nonethical to someone else. . . . But my ethics are very simple. Live and let live and those who try to destroy you, make it your business to see that they don't and that they have problems.[15]

The course of Hoffa's life, and the fate of much of the American labor movement, would largely be determined by his struggles with the heirs of Eugene Debs who sought to impose order, morality, and an ethos of collective responsibility on the jungle.

Two

Jungle Unionism

In the conditions of the proletariat, those of old society at large are already virtually swamped. The proletarian is without property; his relation to his wife and children has no longer anything in common with the bourgeois family relations; modern industrial labor, modern subjection to capital, the same in England as in France, in America as in Germany, has stripped him of every trace of national character. Law, morality, religion are to him so many bourgeois prejudices, behind which lurk in ambush just as many bourgeois interests.—KARL MARX AND FRIEDRICH ENGELS, *MANIFESTO OF THE COMMUNIST PARTY*[1]

The Great Depression cut through Detroit like a scythe. In the year following the stock market crash of 1929, employment in automobile and other manufacturing plants in southeastern Michigan dropped by more than 20 percent. The crisis in the basic industries quickly spread to ancillary businesses. By the end of 1930, at least one-third of Detroit's workforce was unemployed, the highest rate of any major city in the United States.[2] The competition for the remaining jobs reduced many workers to a nearly animal existence. A social worker gave this account of the scene:

> The lines at the city welfare stations are not the only ones. More of the automobile workers were to be found among the men and women shuffling dejectedly at the public and private employment offices, and again all of them at one time or another in those lines which run into the thousands before the gate or any of the large plants which are hiring help, and in lesser numbers,

before the door of any plant whether it is hiring or not . . . they may spend the night in line waiting to be let in through the gates to the employment offices in the morning. In freezing weather they build fires to warm themselves, and what with the wet and the strain, there are occasional fracases to get up front and a rush when opening time comes.[3]

At about the time this report was written, the seventeen-year-old Hoffa quit his job at Frank and Seder's for what he believed to be a more secure position unloading crates of produce from railroad cars at the Kroger's warehouse on Green and Fort Streets, near the Hoffa household in the southwest corner of the city.[4] Hoffa got the job through neighbors who were employed in the warehouse and through connections he had made while working during summers in Kroger grocery stores.[5]

The Kroger job paid 32 cents an hour, but Hoffa and the other dock loaders were compensated only for the hours they actually spent working, which was often less than half the time they were forced to spend at the warehouse. Even at those wages, Hoffa was lucky to get the job, as the warehouse was daily encircled by legions of Detroit's newly unemployed hoping to find work on the loading docks.[6] As he later described it, he and his co-workers disliked the wages and hours, but especially resented the "outrageous meanness" of the produce foreman.[7] Through the fall of 1930 and the spring of 1931, the workers endured the abuse and dictatorial commands of "The Little Bastard," afraid to rebel against him for fear of joining the workers fired daily. Unfortunately, no documentation of the ensuing events at Kroger's exists outside the recollections of the participants. What is verifiable is that Detroit in 1931 was one of the worst places to begin a career as a union leader.

Following a decade of decline, trade unionism reached its nadir during the first three years of the Depression. Mounting unemployment reduced the number of union members in the United States by more than 469,600—a decline of nearly 14 percent—in the period from 1929 to 1933. With the industrial reserve army waiting around every corner, organizing campaigns were rarely attempted and usually failed miserably when they were.[8] During this period, worker militancy, measured by the percentage of the workforce involved in a strike or lockout, reached its lowest point since the 1880s.[9] The Bureau of Labor Statistics recorded exactly nine strikes in Michigan in 1931 and only two in Detroit.[10] As Hoffa himself acknowledged, "A chance to earn some money to buy bread and pay part of the rent outweighed any notions of loyalty to the downtrodden working class, and the poor creatures eagerly took jobs to break strikes—either the easy way or the hard way."[11] The Kroger's foreman used this leverage to eliminate any source of worker rebellion. Workers were discharged for offenses large and small, or simply to make room for friends and relatives of the managers.[12]

Given these conditions, it is difficult to explain why Hoffa and a small band of conspirators began a clandestine organizing drive in the spring of 1931 among the 175 workers in the produce section of the warehouse. Some commentators have argued that Hoffa's early obligation to support his family fomented his aggressiveness. Yet he certainly wasn't the only worker of his generation who faced such adversity. Or perhaps it was the presence of Sam Calhoun, a former member of the Brotherhood of Railway and Steamship Clerks, whom Hoffa credited with fostering the idea of unionizing among the warehouse employees.[13] But while Calhoun certainly helped prod the inexperienced workers into taking action against the company, the presence of any one man could not have been determinative. Rather, for Hoffa and many others, organizing was an act of simple desperation; he and his co-workers banded together "out of a need for self-preservation."[14] They feared the foreman's ax even without a union, and the Depression had considerably dimmed the prospects of finding better jobs elsewhere. "We concluded that organization offered the only sensible course left open to us . . . if we didn't organize, we knew, our lives would continue to be miserable; one by one we would be fired for no reason."[15] Whatever its cause, the circumstances of the Kroger's rebellion indicate that the agitators possessed an uncommon belligerence that distinguished their subsequent careers as union leaders.

Resentment toward the foreman came to a head in May, after he fired two workers for no apparent reason. When a carload of strawberries arrived on a warm evening, the loaders looked to Hoffa for a cue. According to his own account, Hoffa set down a crate and walked away from the loading line. The rest of the loaders then followed suit, leaving the crates of highly perishable fruit on the platform.[16]

After a hostile stand-off, the night supervisor met with the strikers. Hoffa presented a list of grievances and demanded a meeting with management.[17]

The strikers formed a committee that was led by Calhoun and included Hoffa, Jim Langley, Frank Collins, and Bobby Holmes. Langley was another émigré from rural Indiana and a close friend of the Hoffa family. Collins was a product of a working-class Irish neighborhood on the West Side, and Holmes had immigrated from Yorkshire, England, where he worked in the coal mines as a member of the Yorkshire Mine Workers' Association.[18] After several days of negotiations with a group of managers, the strikers won a one-year agreement that contained certain provisions for job security, work rules, and the guarantee of a half-day's pay. Perhaps most important, management agreed to recognize the strikers' negotiating committee as the collective bargaining representative for the 175 workers.[19]

During the confrontation with management, the impromptu Kroger's union became an official labor organization after drafting bylaws and electing Calhoun as president, Hoffa as vice-president, and Holmes as secretary-treasurer.[20] Seeking organizational solidity, Calhoun secured a federal charter from Frank Martel, president of the Detroit Federation of Labor, the local affiliate of the American Federation of Labor.[21] But when the contract with Kroger's management expired in 1932, the company refused to renew the agreement with what was now the new AFL Local No. 19341. Dispirited and pessimistic about its chances in a second recognition fight, the dock loaders continued to work without a contract.[22]

In 1934, an organizer with the International Brotherhood of Teamsters visited the dock and instructed the workers that since they loaded and unloaded trucks, they properly belonged within the Teamsters' jurisdiction. The Teamster organizer also promised them strike benefits if they chose to take on the company again.[23] In response to Martel's urging, the Kroger's warehousemen voted to affiliate with the Commission House Drivers, Warehouse, Produce and Fish Employees Local 674 of Joint Council 43 of the IBT.[24] What the Teamster organizer did not tell them was that the local was on the verge of bankruptcy. Soon after the Kroger's workers affiliated, Local 674 lost a last-ditch strike and then its charter with the international union. Once again Hoffa and his co-workers were without a union.[25] But the eagerness of the Detroit Teamsters to recruit the unskilled dock loaders at Kroger's indicates that the local union was moving away from the IBT's traditional exclusivity, which limited its membership to drivers in specialized "crafts" such as coal, ice, milk, and bread delivery. Teamsters General President Dan Tobin had been a leader in the fight against industrial organization in the AFL and had insisted that the IBT restrict itself to its traditional craft jurisdictions. The unskilled Kroger's dock loaders were precisely the kind of workers that Tobin considered "rubbish" unworthy of a Teamster button.[26] It was this shift in the union's membership that laid the groundwork for the rise of Hoffa and the decline of the Teamsters' bourgeois respectability.

In 1935 the fortunes of the Kroger's dock loaders began to turn. Hoffa was fired for dropping a crate of vegetables on the loading dock.[27] The next day he received a call from Ray Bennett, an organizer with Joint Council 43, who asked him to take a job as a business agent with Local 299, the general truck drivers' union.[28] Bennett, like many of the Detroit Teamster officers, was an ambitious former "hillbilly" who found in the union a vehicle for raising himself out of the rural poverty into which he was born. He had joined the Teamsters as a coal driver but found greater opportunity as a staffer with the union. He took a job as a business agent with the coal drivers' Local 247, then worked his way up to the presidency of the local before being named a "General Organizer" by the international union. His principal responsibility for the IBT was to bring new members and promising young organizers into the Detroit locals. In the 1930s, Teamster organizers under Bennett were given no salary but were paid a percentage of the dues from every new member they signed. Yet with job prospects still bleak in Detroit and the labor movement beginning to show some life in 1934, Hoffa quickly accepted Bennett's offer.[29]

The Rise of Industrial Civilization

The long decline of the American labor movement ended in 1934. In that year nearly 1.5 million workers engaged in work stoppages, and ferocious class warfare engulfed three major cities. The passage during the previous year of the National Industrial Recovery Act (NIRA), with its section 7(a) promising the federal government's protection of workers seeking to unionize, sparked uprisings in industrial centers across the country. In Toledo, Ohio's "Little Detroit," striking workers at the Auto-Lite automotive parts plant who had lost patience with bureaucratic delays by the National Labor Board waged war with National Guardsmen. The strike spread to other AFL unions, culminating in a rally of some 40,000 workers in the city's central square. Faced with an entire city in revolt, the Auto-Lite management capitulated to a wage increase above the NIRA's auto industry code and agreed to recognize the AFL federal local as the exclusive bargaining agent of the workers.[30]

The two other general strikes in 1934 featured Teamsters as principal participants. Teamster members in San Francisco joined the longshoremen's union in leading a general strike that paralyzed the Bay Area's waterfronts and provoked deadly clashes with police. The strike succeeded in replacing the hated "shape-up" system—in which workers were selected each day from crowds on the docks by often corrupt bosses—with a hiring hall controlled by the union.[31] In Minneapolis, Trotskyist-led Teamsters Local 574 crippled the state's trucking industry and brought the city's commerce to a halt. After a month of violence involving thousands of Teamsters, sympathetic workers, National Guardsmen, and thugs hired by the right-wing Citizens Alliance, the employers conceded to the union's major demands, including substantial wage increases and recognition of the union as bargaining representative for "inside" workers as well as truck drivers.[32]

This eruption of worker militancy was first confronted with violence by local governments, then channeled into a safer and more sophisticated system of regulated industrial relations at the federal level. By establishing legal mechanisms through which workers would form unions and redress grievances, the National Labor Relations Act (NLRA) of 1935 was intended to remove "sources of industrial strife and unrest by encouraging practices fundamental to the friendly adjustment of industrial disputes." The act identified as some of these disruptive sources "certain practices by some labor organizations, their officers, and members [which] have the intent or the necessary effect of burdening or obstructing commerce by preventing the free flow of goods in such commerce through strikes and other forms of industrial unrest."[33] It created the National Labor Relations Board (NLRB) to oversee elections for union representation and arbitrate grievances over alleged unfair practices by unions or management. The right to engage in collective bargaining was guaranteed, but the state would ensure that this right would be exercised in accordance with the interest of maintaining a stable polity. Labor was required to sacrifice its ability to gain its objectives through disruption and to adopt a share of social responsibility. Put another way, the NLRA was designed to bring class conflict out of the jungle and into civilization.[34]

Industrial union leaders such as Sidney Hillman and Walter Reuther, who joined the labor movement in order to act on their broader social visions, came to embrace state-regulated collective bargaining as a necessary component of a planned economy.[35] However, these leaders found that workers were often unwilling to restrain their desires for the sake of such a system. And the workers of Minneapolis, San Francisco, and Toledo must have been aware that their victories were won without their rights being exercised or protected. The Detroit Teamsters noticed that they too were winning in the jungle, and, lacking the corporatist vision of a well-ordered society of mutual sacrifice, chose to avoid civilization altogether.[36]

Creative Destruction

When Hoffa joined the staff in 1935, Joint Council 43 was one of the newest metropolitan councils in the IBT, having been established only a few years earlier. It was made up of Local 299, headed by Joseph Campau, president, and Al Milligan, secretary-treasurer, and Locals 51 (bakery drivers), 155 (milk drivers), 243 (furniture van drivers), 247 (coal haulers), and 285, a semiautonomous local of Jewish laundry drivers under the leadership of Isaac Litwak, a Russian immigrant who had been imprisoned by the Czarist police for his revolutionary activities.[37] Litwak was exceptional among Detroit Teamster officers as an immigrant, as a Jew, and as a union leader who viewed labor as part of a broader movement for social justice. The Joint Council was headed by Sam Hurst, a former bakery driver who also held the presidency of Local 51.[38] Hurst's timid leadership allowed more ambitious officers to run their locals with virtual autonomy. It also made the youthful and freewheeling Joint Council 43 unusual within the IBT, which was composed mostly of long-standing local baronies dominated by autocratic leaders with deep roots in their cities' labor and political cultures.[39]

Hoffa's Local 299 was one of the greenest in the Joint Council. In 1935 it had only 400 members in good standing and even fewer dollars in its treasury.[40] The local had been established in 1933 to organize truck drivers not covered by the jurisdictions of the other locals in the joint council. Despite Tobin's instructions to shun intercity ("over-the-road") freight drivers, whom he considered to be unruly, proletarian "trash," Local 299 found it impossible to resist the opportunity presented by the rapidly expanding automobile transport industry that shipped cars from Detroit's manufacturing plants to dealers across the country.[41] In the early 1930s, carhaul trucking firms made major inroads into the industry that had been dominated by the railroads since the beginning of mass automobile production. In 1930, motor trucks delivered fewer than 200,000 new automobiles; by 1935 more than two million cars were shipped over roads. As a new industry with relatively small capital requirements, carhauling in the 1930s, like most interstate trucking, was a highly competitive field made up mostly of small firms.[42] The average number of employees per firm in southeastern Michigan in 1934 was just under nineteen.[43]

Desperate to add dues-paying members in order to stave off bankruptcy, Local 299's organizers eagerly set upon Detroit's fastest-growing trucking business. Their plan to build the local, implemented by Campau, Milligan, and lead organizer Al "Pop" Squires, was largely unaffected by the passage of the NIRA or the NLRA. Rather than devoting their time to signing up workers and petitioning for representation elections, they preferred a two-step strategy that was far more effective against the small and scattered carhaul companies. The local's business agents first approached the owner of a firm and told him that if he did not enroll his employees with the union his trucks would be bombed. Next, if the employer refused to capitulate, they bombed his trucks. In the mid-1930s the local gained a reputation as the most violent, lawless union in an unusually violent, lawless city.[44] Despite its public-relations problems, the strategy worked. In September 1934 a group of carhauling companies succumbed, signing an agreement that granted the "so-called Teamsters' Union" sole bargaining rights over their employees.[45] A month later the local demonstrated a more traditional form of militancy when it called a strike of its entire membership against the employers' association. The leaders of the union hoped the walkout would produce benefits that would gain the loyalty of the newly conscripted members.[46] Despite a series of arrests and a Wayne County deputy sheriff's threat to the strikers that his men would "shoot first and ask questions afterwards," the union held out for four weeks and ultimately won a 10 percent wage increase with all twenty-six carhauling firms in the Detroit area.[47]

Hoffa's first assignment with 299 was to secure the organization of the Kroger's warehousemen, who were directed to the truck drivers local because a warehouse local had not been established by the Joint Council. Shortly after Hoffa's firing, Kroger's management transferred Calhoun, Collins, Holmes, and Langley to the company's Merritt Street warehouse, which they began organizing in 1935 with the assistance of Hoffa and Squires, who had been reassigned by Bennett from the coal drivers local to help build 299. In 1936 the "Strawberry Boys" won recognition and affiliated with Hoffa's local.[48] In March of the following year the Kroger's Teamsters received their own charter as the Food, Beer and Beverage Handlers Union Local 337, which for several decades operated as an auxiliary of Local 299.[49]

While helping to reorganize Kroger's, Hoffa began assisting Squires in the guerrilla campaign to sign up the remaining carhaulers. Through 1935 and 1936, with the local still on the verge of bankruptcy, 299 continued to carry out its strategy of threats and bombings and began blowing up employers' homes as well. But while successful in winning representation contracts, the unorthodox organizing campaign created new problems for the local. Late in 1935 all the officers of the joint council and Local 299 were brought into the Detroit federal building for questioning by agents of the FBI.[50] In addition, local newspapers gave the Detroit Teamsters their first notoriety with a series of articles on the bombings. Worse still, most of the local's 800 members, who had been brought into the union involuntarily, refused to pay their dues and were openly protesting against Campau and Milligan. Facing certain defeat in the election for the local's officers in 1935, Campau and Milligan won the election by arranging for members of the International Longshoremen's Association to transfer into 299 and vote for the incumbents.[51]

In January 1936 the Teamsters' international headquarters broke from its traditional laissez-faire policy toward locals, expelled Campau and Milligan, and placed 299 under trusteeship.[52] The trusteeship eliminated elections and installed Bennett as overseer. Implementation of the trusteeship was ostensibly a response to the corruption and financial incompetence of Campau and Milligan, but Tobin may have been motivated by the fear that the FBI's continued investigation and the publicity about the bombings might strain his close relationship with Franklin Roosevelt, for whom he served as chairman of the labor division of the 1932 and 1936 national campaign committees.

The trusteeship under Bennett did help reverse the local's financial fortunes, but 299 remained free of formal democracy and, worse for Tobin, continued for many years to be an embarrassment to the IBT president and the Democratic Party. To the benefit of Bennett, Hoffa, and Squires, the trusteeship stabilized the local and eliminated the rank-and-file's ability to unseat its leadership, although it could not keep the members from leaving the union. The 10 percent wage increase won by the 1934 strike had been a significant victory for the new local, but it did not raise the carhaul drivers' wages above poverty level. Still faced with a membership ready to vote with its feet, the local's new leadership set out to secure itself by delivering the goods.

By the end of the year the membership had reason to stay. In December, with the threat of another strike or more violence from Local 299 looming, the National Automobile Transporters Association (NATA) capitulated to a healthy 30 percent increase in the wage scale of its carhaul drivers.[53] By Depression standards, Teamsters in Local 299 had entered the middle class. At the time of the agreement most of Detroit's carhaul companies were still small and undercapitalized and many operated fewer than ten trucks, making them especially vulnerable to work stoppages and the rapid depreciation caused by well-placed explosives. The NATA may also have been more willing to concede on wages because of the passage in 1935 of the federal Motor Carrier Act (MCA), which limited competition in the traditionally cut-throat interstate trucking industry.

The MCA authorized the Interstate Commerce Commission to issue permits to firms seeking entry into the industry and to set minimum rates, thus curtailing the influx of small "gypsy" firms that under-cut the larger carriers' prices during the rapid expansion of trucking beginning in the late 1920s. In Michigan, the state's Public Utilities Commission granted permits for intra-state routes and strictly controlled the type of freight carried by each line. The industry remained highly competitive, with most firms operating on tight profit margins, but the regulation did at least temporarily help the established companies raise rates and boost revenues, some of which were now passed on to the Teamster drivers.* With Local 299's carhaul members appeased at least temporarily, Bennett, Hoffa, and Squires turned to other industries to build the local's membership. But first they looked for well-placed friends who might help them establish their union on a sure footing amid the unrestrained class warfare that was enveloping Detroit.[54]

Rise of the Rubbish

While Local 299 negotiated with the carhaul companies in December 1936, Detroit was experiencing its first wave of sit-down strikes. At the Kelsey-Hayes Wheel Company on McGraw Avenue and Livernois, in Hoffa's West Side neighborhood, the automobile industry's first sit-down strike in Motor City was galvanizing the local labor movement. Immediately after workers occupied the plant, Teamster leaders provided critical assistance by refusing to move products or equipment into or out of the factory. When Ford officials threatened to send in a squad of "servicemen" to seize brake shoe dies from the hostage supply company, Walter Reuther of the fledgling United Automobile Workers' Local 174, whose headquarters were just blocks from Hoffa's home, called on the burly young Teamster business agent for aid.[55] With Hoffa at the point, a detachment of rugged truck drivers descended on the plant, helping the strikers head off the Ford goons. Unable to end the strike with its own intervention, Ford then forced Kelsey-Hayes to settle with the UAW. The auto workers' successful occupation at the wheel company emboldened the union to use the sit-down tactic a month later in the epochal strike against General Motors in Flint.[56]

In extending aid to Reuther, Hoffa was no doubt motivated by the potential importance of a good relationship with the auto workers union, which occupied the largest industry serviced by Detroit truck-

---

*This state regulation of the trucking industry should not be confused with corporatism, since it did not include labor representatives within the regulatory apparatus. It also did not guarantee that the artificially inflated profits would be passed on to labor in the form of higher wages. Moreover, it should be noted that the regulation produced higher consumer prices for other sections of the working class.

ing firms, for building his own union. In March 1938, he again lent his body to the UAW during the Federal Screw Works strike. The strike, one of the bloodiest in Detroit history, involved the participation of much of Hoffa's neighborhood, which encompassed Federal Screw's plant on Martin and Otis Streets. On March 30, Hoffa was arrested for his part in a melee between the police and an army of UAW members, other union leaders, and neighborhood residents.[57] The Teamster leader was so impressed with the abilities of the UAW's "flying squadrons" of young fighters that he momentarily considered bringing Local 299 into the UAW.[58] Though the unions never merged, Hoffa's assistance in the strikes and his pledge to have Teamster drivers honor the UAW's picket lines cemented an unofficial alliance between the Detroit Teamsters and the UAW leadership that proved to be beneficial for the auto workers union and crucial for the growth of the Teamster locals.[59]

The sit-down actions at Kelsey-Hayes and GM sparked one of the greatest strike waves in American history. In 1937, there were 4,740 work stoppages in the United States, more than double the number during the previous year.[60] Southeastern Michigan was at the epicenter of the labor upheaval, as the UAW established itself as a permanent force with a series of dramatic sit-downs in auto plants. Unions were beneficiaries of the general culture of rebellion and labor solidarity that took hold of Detroit's working class in the winter and spring of 1937, when thousands of workers established new unions or signed on with established ones. The Detroit Teamsters seized the opportunity.

The first local in Joint Council 43 to join in the rush of sit-downs was Isaac Litwak's Laundry and Linen Drivers Local 285. In February, Litwak's Teamsters followed the lead of 800 inside workers, virtually all young Polish women, who spontaneously seized control of twelve laundries to demand union recognition. Local 285's drivers, who picked up and delivered linens, diapers, and factory uniforms for the laundries, stopped working in order to force higher wages and a shorter work week from the employers. During the sit-down, the AFL chartered the inside workers as Laundry Workers Local 129, which remained closely tied to the Teamsters. Litwak refused to settle with the employers until the laundresses' local was given collective bargaining recognition. In April, the two unions negotiated in tandem with the employers and won significant pay raises and a reduction in the mandatory workweek.[61] The close relationship with the female laundry workers was unusual for the Detroit Teamsters, who in the 1930s were almost all men. Trucking and warehousing in the United States have always been mostly white and male, and were almost entirely so in the Midwest in the 1930s. Trucking was particularly exclusionary through the 1930s. The 1940 census reported that only 4.1 percent of trucking and warehousing employees in twelve Midwestern states were female and that 2.3 percent were African-American. Even most southern and eastern European immigrants were barred from the industries by the Teamsters and complicit employers.[62]

In Detroit, local cartage and intercity, "over-the-road" firms were owned almost exclusively by men of British or Irish descent who hired workers of the same ethnicity. Yet this cultural identification did not stop the great strike wave of 1937 from sweeping onto the West Side waterfront, where the city's local and over-the-road trucking companies were clustered. At the time, only firms that transported special commodities, such as automobiles, linens, coal, milk, and bakery products, had been organized by the Detroit Teamsters. Local 299 had yet to make a dent in the city's general freight industry, which was one of the most exploitative in the city. Non-union truck drivers were among the lowest-paid of the city's industrial workers. Drivers normally made less than 50 cents per hour and were expected at times to work up to 80 hours per week.[63] For intercity and especially interstate drivers, crashes caused by falling asleep at the wheel were common.[64]

In March, the drivers and loaders at six trucking companies exploded in a rebellion that spread from dock to dock. The strikers established an impromptu picket line next to several loading docks on Ferdinand Street and were soon set upon by a regiment of mounted police. Fortunately for the workers, a police captain assigned to the strike was also the organizer of a regular blackjack game frequented by many of the truck drivers. Through this business relationship the strikers were able to convince the police to curb the violence and allow the strike to continue. Within days, the walkout had spread to every local cartage and over-the-road company in the city, shutting down Detroit's trucking industry and paralyzing much of the city's transportation system.[65]

Led by Jack Keeshin of the Chicago-based Keeshin Motor Freight Company, who later became one of the leading over-the-road operators in the Midwest, the employers arranged for a meeting with the striking workers at the Fort Shelby Hotel. The strikers formed a motley negotiating committee headed by Rolland McMaster, a physically intimidating twenty-three-year-old driver who rose to a leadership position after punching out one of the Keeshin dispatchers. McMaster had been raised in Onaway, a farming town in the hinterland of northern Michigan. Like most of the truck drivers and dock workers, he had little formal education, having left high school to support his family. Accordingly, meetings of the strike committee did not adhere to parliamentary procedure, but instead usually degenerated into shouting matches.

Aware that the strikers were not only among the lowest-paid workers in Detroit but also notorious for their debauchery, Keeshin had an enormous tub of beer wheeled into the meeting room in the hope of satisfying the strikers with only minor concessions. But sensing that the moment had come for a prize greater than free drinks, the strikers' negotiating committee walked out. These self-organized and militant though naive truck drivers and dock workers were made to order for the Teamsters. Presented with an opportunity to add hundreds of new members with little effort, Victor Tyler, a driver for White Star Freight Lines and an organizer for Local 299, quickly stepped in. He recruited the workers into the local and arranged for continued negotiations with Keeshin and the employers. After several alcohol-free meetings, Local 299 and the operators signed a contract that was the first labor agreement in the Michigan general freight-hauling industry.[66] The contract set minimum wages at 55 to 70 cents per hour for city drivers and dock workers and 3½ cents per mile for over-the-road drivers.[67]

By March of 1937, Locals 299 and 337 had added hundreds of new members in carhauling, local cartage, over-the-road freight hauling, and warehouses. In a virtual instant, these predominantly white, male, Anglo-Saxon, unskilled or low-skilled proletarians filled the ranks of the Detroit Teamsters. Despite the admonitions of Tobin and the craft union stalwarts of the AFL, an industrial union of "rubbish" was being born in the House of Labor.

In July, outstate Teamster locals carried the momentum of what a leading labor newspaper called the "unprecedented rush of truck drivers" in Detroit to the entire Michigan trucking industry.[68] Demanding uniform statewide wages of 55 cents an hour for dock workers, 60 cents for city drivers, and 65 cents for highway drivers—as well as a "closed shop" agreement requiring that only union members would be hired, an automatic dues check-off, and seniority rights—nine Teamster locals across the state, under the leadership of 299's Bennett and James "Red" O'Laughlin, called out more than 20,000 workers.[69] Bennett had selected O'Laughlin from the staff of the van drivers local to help lead the Joint Council's organizing efforts. Like Bennett, O'Laughlin was an ambitious union careerist. He had once been one of Jack Dempsey's sparring partners, and a member of the Industrial Workers of the World (IWW), familiarly known as the "Wobblies." O'Laughlin had, however, absorbed little of the IWW's ideal of a "workers' commonwealth." What he did possess was a Wobbly syndicalist instinct for militant direct action which combined with his pugilistic skills to make him an archetypal Detroit Teamster.[70]

The Michigan locals, including those of Joint Council 43, had vigorously lobbied for a law that substantially reduced license-plate and mileage fees levied against trucking companies by the Michigan Public Utilities Commission. On the eve of the strike, John Reid of the Michigan Federation of Labor announced that the walkout would be an effort to recoup some of the companies' revenues generated by the law. "The boys went out and worked for the bill on the distinct promise that they would get part of its benefits in higher wages," he told the press. "Now it seems the operators don't want to share."[71] While most Detroit firms were exempted because they had already met the wage demands, Teamsters in the city were critical participants in the strike. Pickets from the Joint Council 43 locals patrolled the highways leading into the city and stopped trucks attempting to make deliveries from outstate. Four members of Local 299 were arrested for blocking a truck from entering downtown.[72]

Two days into the strike, Michigan Governor Frank Murphy intervened, forcing both sides to agree to a thirty-day truce while a state board investigated wages and rates in the industry. The board recommended that the operators be allowed to raise their rates so that they could meet the union's demands on wages. In August, the Michigan Public Utilities Commission granted a rate hike sufficient to produce a 12.5 percent increase in revenues.[73] The employers took the rate increase but still refused to meet the union's wage demands. Shortly after the close of the thirty-day truce, the locals began striking several companies at a time. The result was higher wages in most cases, but the union leaders failed to win statewide uniformity as they had originally hoped.[74]

The Limitations of Bricks

At the Kroger's warehouse on Merritt Street, the Strawberry Boys used the energy of 1937 to launch yet another campaign to establish collective bargaining recognition for the union. In March, Hoffa negotiated a one-year contract covering 250 of the warehouse workers that raised wages 10 to 18 percent, outlawed the yellow dog contract, established an arbitration board and a steward system to handle grievances and hirings and firings, mandated overtime pay over 48 hours a week, and guaranteed 40 hours of work per week.[75] Soon after the contract was signed, the Kroger's workers were given a charter by the IBT as Local 337. Perhaps emboldened by the Teamsters' victories over the spring and summer, the new local waged an audacious attack on Kroger's in September, six months before the expiration of the contract. Demanding new raises to one dollar per hour, a closed shop and an automatic dues check-off system, the 250 truck drivers and dock workers in the local walked off the job in violation of the contract's no-strike clause.[76]

Unfortunately for the local, Detroit's culture of solidarity stopped at the gates of the warehouse. The company was able to hire sufficient numbers of replacement drivers and loaders to keep the food moving from the railroad cars to the grocery stores. Desperate and faced with impending defeat, the strikers hurled bricks at trucks entering the warehouse gates and tried to pull drivers through the windows of their cabs. Squads of police were deployed to the scene to escort the trucks to and from the loading docks. After several of the Teamsters were arrested, a young labor lawyer named George Fitzgerald approached Holmes and Hoffa and offered to help the union in its frequent dealings with the police.[77]

Fitzgerald was not only the first lawyer to work for the Detroit Teamsters, he was also the first person with more than a high school education to be affiliated with the union. The son of a streetcar union leader, Fitzgerald worked his way through the University of Detroit law school and then served as an assistant U.S. attorney in the late 1920s. He made his name in Detroit as an assistant Wayne County prosecutor in the early 1930s when he helped destroy the infamous Jewish "Purple Gang" by convicting several of its leaders for a string of murders.[78] A New Deal liberal, Fitzgerald left the prosecutor's office to find work as an attorney and advocate for the labor movement.[79] Over the next twenty-five years, he provided invaluable assistance for Locals 299 and 337 not only as an attorney in their many court battles but also as a liaison with the police and the city government, as the unions' representative in state politics, and as a public spokesman for the often inarticulate Teamsters. Yet despite his many connections with the police department and the district attorney's office, Fitzgerald could not keep the police from intervening in the Kroger's strike. After two weeks of police-escorted scab trucks driving through the picket line, the union finally conceded on every one of its demands and called off the strike. The Kroger's employees would remain without a union contract until 1943.[80]

After the strike, Owen "Bert" Brennan, a veteran of the truck-bombing campaigns, was brought in to head the local, and most of the remaining Strawberry Boys were hired as full-time officers of the Joint Council. Holmes was appointed as the secretary-treasurer of 337. Brennan, who later became Hoffa's chief lieutenant and most notorious crony, had grown up as a street fighter and truck driver in Chicago before moving to Detroit in 1932. After working as a carhaul and general cartage driver, Brennan joined the Teamsters staff in 1934 and was arrested three times for his work as a demolitions expert in the carhaul organizing drive.[81] Despite its initial defeat, Local 337 used the resources of the Joint Council to expand its organizing beyond the Kroger's warehouses. In 1937 and 1938, the local organized and signed contracts with several wholesale grocery and tobacco warehouse companies.[82] Its membership reached 1,000 by the end of 1938, making it one of the largest Detroit locals.

Through bombings, intimidation, and opportunistic organizing, Locals 299 and 337 achieved relative stability by 1938, with a combined membership of more than 3,000 and a leadership that was quickly rising through the ranks of Joint Council 43.[83] Soon Hoffa and the Detroit Teamsters discovered a means to expand their power beyond the provincial confines of southeastern Michigan. But they also encountered challenges to that power from unexpected sources.

Three

The Limits of Brotherhood

The unskilled . . . being poorly paid are the hardest fighters. But they are also the most troublesome, and I fear that this is the element that we will have to cope with if the Socialists behind the industrial union scheme have their way.—M. P. CARRICK, SECRETARY-TREASURER, BROTHERHOOD OF PAINTERS, DECORATORS, AND PAPER-HANGERS, TO SAMUEL GOMPERS, PRESIDENT, AMERICAN FEDERATION OF LABOR, NOVEMBER 9, 1904[1]

By 1938, Carrick's fears had been realized. Legions of unskilled and semiskilled workers, organized according to industry, not craft, had been brought into the labor movement, most notably by the new Congress of Industrial Organizations but also by old-school unions in the American Federation of Labor—among them the International Brotherhood of Teamsters. Jimmy Hoffa, whose sole marketable skill was crate-lifting, was one of the new hard-fighting and "troublesome" recruits. Trained by unionists lacking the gentility so admired by the AFL aristocracy, Hoffa's only lessons before 1938 were that a steady income could be made as a union staffer and that physical force was an effective tool in securing and increasing that income. But from 1938 through 1940, Hoffa received a comprehensive education in industrial relations. By the end of that period he had learned to be wary of the state, to believe that solidarity was useful in many forms, and, perhaps most important, to accept that the law of the jungle extended even into the brotherhood of labor. Oddly enough for a union leader who became famously anti-radical, Hoffa's most important teachers during this time were a small band of socialists in Minneapolis.

Truck Drivers and Utopia

Throughout the twentieth century, socialists of nearly every stripe placed their hopes and plotted their strategies around the working class. This was especially so in the United States during the 1930s, when the labor movement not only expanded rapidly but also began to undertake efforts to enter into and influence the governing institutions of the state. The Communist Party, the remains of the Socialist Party, and a handful of small but vibrant Trotskyist sects all viewed the working-class upsurge that began in 1934 as a historic opportunity. These groups differed, often violently, on many issues, but from 1934 on they shared a strategy of working within established unions to gain influence among workers.[2]

Socialist organizations were leaders in all three of the great general strikes of 1934: the Communist Party in San Francisco, A. J. Muste's American Workers Party in Toledo, and the Trotskyist Communist League of America (CLA) in Minneapolis. These strikes were the first major victories by American radicals since 1919, and on the left they were perceived as harbingers of a revolutionary era. Indeed, after the strikes, Communist Party members and fellow travelers continued to hold leadership positions in what became the International Longshoremen's and Warehousemen's Union (ILWU), and the Socialist Party gained a new lease on life when many of its Detroit members, including the Reuther brothers, helped found the United Automobile Workers. For American Trotskyists, the greatest source of pride was (and still is) the short-lived beachhead established by CLA activists in Minneapolis Teamsters Local 574.

The Trotskyist capture of Local 574 was remarkable not only because the membership of the Minneapolis branch of the CLA was only slightly larger than a baseball team, but also because the IBT since its founding had been the consummate AFL union: politically conservative, exclusionary, and hostile to industrial organization. As Teamster president Dan Tobin moved into the central leadership of the AFL in the 1930s, he publicly assailed the industrial union strategy as a vehicle for unruly immigrants and dangerous radicals. Local Teamster leaders, content with the power afforded them by their control over the trucking "crafts," showed little inclination to expand their jurisdiction beyond the union's traditional domain. To the alarm of

Tobin and the leaders of the IBT, the Minneapolis local became the radical exception in the history of the union. Following the successful 1934 strike, CLA members gained control over Local 574 and transformed the exclusive craft union into an organization that not only disregarded occupational, geographic, and ethnic boundaries between workers but had as its mission nothing less than the complete transformation of society.[3]

The radicalization of Local 574 was the result of a unique confluence of historical circumstances. Chief among these was the peculiar political culture of Minneapolis, which provided relatively fertile ground for the Trotskyists. In the late nineteenth and early twentieth centuries, the city served as a hub for the agricultural and lumber industries of the northern Plains, attracting large numbers of itinerant farmworkers, lumberjacks, miners, and railroad workers. These workers formed the base of the Industrial Workers of the World, which established one of its largest locals in Minneapolis. In the early twentieth century, Local 10 in the hardscrabble Bridge Square district educated thousands of migrant workers in the school of class struggle. Added to these predominantly native-born radicals were the various immigrant groups that settled in Minnesota, in particular the large numbers of Norwegians, Swedes, Finns, Danes, and Germans who brought collectivist proclivities with them from Europe. The Minnesota Socialist Party, one of the largest and most vibrant branches of the national party during its heyday, benefited enormously from this influx of northern European radicals. In 1919, more than half of the state's Socialists were immigrants.[4] Following the demise of the IWW and SP in the 1920s, the unusual demography of the state produced a large and powerful Farmer-Labor Party, whose many electoral successes included winning control of the state house and the governorship in 1930.[5]

Out of these various strands of heartland radicalism came a small but gifted cadre of Trotskyists. These activists rejected both the "Stalinization" of the Communist Party and the "reformism" of the Farmer-Labor Party. They found a home in the Communist League of America, a group founded in 1929 by James P. Cannon, Max Schachtman, and Martin Abern, who had all been expelled from the Communist Party for their criticism of the "degeneration" and "bureaucratization" of the Soviet Union under Joseph Stalin. The CLA leadership was particularly critical of the Communist Party's policy prior to 1934 of forming "Red Unions" outside of the AFL, and instructed its cadres to operate solely within the established labor movement.[6]

In the first years of the Depression, members of the Minneapolis branch of the CLA busied themselves in following the organization's labor strategy. They were led by Vincent Dunne, a former itinerant lumberjack and militant member of the IWW, and Karl Skoglund, a Swedish immigrant who had been a principal figure in the Socialist Party's Scandinavian Federation and a member of the Communist Party before being expelled for Trotskyism. Dunne and Skoglund decided that the Teamsters union, with its strategically powerful position in the transportation system, would be the CLA's point of entry into the Minneapolis labor movement. The pair, along with Vincent's brothers Grant and Miles, took jobs as truck drivers at a city coal yard. By 1933 they had convinced a large segment of the coal workers to organize a union. Among these recruits was Farrell Dobbs, who later became instrumental in the rise of Jimmy Hoffa.

The Teamsters Joint Council in Minneapolis was just as conservative as the IBT's national leadership, but in Local 574 Skoglund and the Dunne brothers saw an opening. Like Local 299 in Detroit, 574 had been chartered with a "general" jurisdiction to take in truck drivers outside the industries covered by the craft locals in the joint council.[7] The Trotskyists recognized the local's ambiguous charter as a possible wedge with which to subvert the structure of the Teamsters. They hoped to use the local in an open-ended organizing drive that would flood the union with new members from all parts of the trucking and related industries and overwhelm Tobin and the joint council's leaders. Luckily for the Trotskyists, Bill Brown, the president of 574, was sympathetic to the idea of industrial organizing and was willing to work with the radicals.

In February 1934, led by Skoglund, Dobbs, and the Dunne brothers and assisted by Local 574, the coal yard workers struck for union recognition. Faced with enormous public pressure to resume coal deliveries in the midst of the frigid Minneapolis winter, the employers were forced to settle with the strikers. The workers gained higher wages, shorter hours, and acknowledgment of Local 574 as their bargaining representative. But for Skoglund, Dobbs, and the Dunne brothers, the strike was a springboard for an effort to realize their broader ambitions. Through it they secured a base of operations within the union.[8] In May, Local 574 was strong enough to call a citywide general strike of members and sympathizers. Under the leadership of the Trotskyists, who managed a headquarters that included a union-run hospital, cafeteria, newspaper, and picket-dispatching center, the strike shut down the city. Despite armed assaults by police and the National Guard, by the end of the summer the employers collapsed, wages were raised, a seniority system was instituted, and Minneapolis was a union town. The success of the strike brought thousands of new members from a variety of occupations into the Teamsters. It also allowed the Trotskyists, now greatly popular with the rank and file, to take control of 574. Communist League members and sympathizers were elected to every one of the local's offices in an election that fall.[9]

In April 1935, Tobin attempted to purge the Trotskyists from the union by revoking the charter of Local 574. He then agreed to reinstate the local, but only under the conditions that its current officers be removed and that it be placed under trusteeship. Tobin also insisted that 574's charter disallow membership for truck drivers who fell under the jurisdictions of other Teamster locals and for all workers who spent less than half their time driving or working on a truck.[10] But the leadership of the local had won substantial support from the rank and file through the dramatic economic gains that had resulted from the 1934 strike. Perhaps more daunting to Tobin, the success of the strike had also persuaded the Minneapolis Central Labor Union to side with the radical leadership of 574. Moreover, most of the employers organized by the local declined to break their contracts, for fear of provoking a new rebellion by the workers. Confronted with the prospect of alienating much of the Minneapolis labor movement, Tobin eventually backed down and granted the local a new charter as 544, with a general jurisdiction that allowed for continued industrial organizing.

Over the Road

Having survived Tobin's attempt to root them out of the union, the Trotskyist Teamsters of Local 544 began to move outward from Minneapolis. They initiated a bold campaign to organize intercity, over-the-road drivers throughout the Midwest. In 1937, along with several sympathetic locals, they established the North Central District Drivers Council (NCDDC) as a central organizing and negotiating committee. Their immediate aim was to bring every worker in trucking and related industries into a single organization and establish uniform wages, hours, and working conditions through centralized collective bargaining. At the center of the campaign was the recruitment of over-the-road drivers, which would force the historically isolated IBT locals to cooperate. Previously, intercity drivers were brought into the union only if their route ended at an organized terminal. They were forced to join the locals controlling the terminal before they were allowed to unload their freight. But as soon as the drivers left the terminal to return home, they effectively lost their membership since they were not covered under the local's contracts. The Trotskyists recognized that centralized organizing and negotiations with employers would be an effective means of bringing over-the-road drivers into the union as full members. Of course, the strategy also conformed with the socialist objective of uniting the entire working class within a single organization. The Trotskyists' ultimate goal was to use the Teamsters to make real the IWW's vision of "One Big Union" as preparation for the final step of seizing control of the means of production and instituting a collective society governed by the working class.

The NCDDC organizers moved quickly. From their base in Minneapolis, they first organized several firms in neighboring St. Paul, then fanned out to smaller cities and towns across Minnesota and into the Dakotas. Along the way, the organizers brought into the union truck drivers from various industries, as well as "inside workers" at groceries, warehouses, and bakeries. In the over-the-road drivers, however, they found a group of workers especially eager for a union.[11] From the birth of the intercity trucking industry in the early 1920s through its rapid growth in the 1930s, over-the-road driving remained one of the most unpleasant professions in industrial America.

Technological advances in manufacturing, the expansion of the highway system, and the decline of the railroads had made trucking impervious to the Depression. The number of motor vehicles used for interstate transportation increased from 1,000 to 70,000 between 1920 and 1938. With improvements in suspension, brakes, lighting, and roads, far fewer skills were necessary to drive a truck over hundreds of miles, thereby dramatically increasing the pool of available labor.[12]

Massive unemployment in manufacturing and agriculture contributed even more desperate workers to the market for truck drivers. As a result, operators who were able to buy more than one truck could hire a driver for rock-bottom wages and make him work an inhuman number of hours. Wages for intercity truck drivers during the Depression sometimes reached as low as five cents per hour. Most drivers worked more than 50 hours per week, and trips of 80 to 120 continuous hours—with short stops on the side of the road for naps—were common. Drivers were forced to work even longer hours when they used sleeper cabs, trucks outfitted with a padded platform behind the seats.[13]

The following excerpt from the testimony of a driver before the Michigan Public Utilities Commission in 1934 provides a precise account of the grueling conditions experienced by over-the-road workers:

> I left Detroit Sunday night, having taken my truck to the terminal at 2 o'clock Sunday afternoon and loaded. I reached Chicago Monday at 7 a.m.; had 5 hours sleep in Chicago; left Chicago Monday 7 p.m. and arrived in Cleveland Tuesday at 2 p.m. I wanted to eat and sleep but could not do both, so I ate. Later in the afternoon, however, I caught an hour's sleep at Cleveland. At 7 p.m. a load of steel came in for Richmond, Indiana. They suggested I take that. I got to Richmond, approximately 200 miles, at 10 a.m. Wednesday; went from there to Indianapolis; reached Indianapolis at 4 p.m. Wednesday, and loaded my truck with some freight which was at the terminal for Chicago. On the way I got so sleepy I parked the truck on the side of the road, slept for a couple of hours, and got in the next morning (Thursday). I found a load waiting for Muskegon, Michigan; drove there with it and found that I had to deliver it myself. I was back in Detroit at 5 a.m. Saturday. This trip took 5 days, from 2 p.m. Sunday to 5 a.m. Saturday. In that time I got not over 14 hours' sleep. The longest at a time was 5 hours Monday at Chicago. The remainder was an hour or so at a time.[14]

When the Minneapolis Teamsters launched their over-the-road organizing campaign, workers like this flocked to the union. By the winter of 1938, the NCDDC had organized large portions of the industry in Minnesota, South Dakota, North Dakota, Iowa, and Wisconsin. The campaign attracted the attention of Teamster locals across the Midwest and Plains states. By March, locals from Nebraska, Missouri, and Illinois were cooperating with the NCDDC. A major turning point came with the recruitment of Chicago Local 710, long a bastion of craft unionism and an esteemed institution within the IBT. The local at the time was dominated by John T. O'Brien and Mike Healy, whose power within the union and the trucking industry provided crucial impetus for the campaign. O'Brien's virtual control of trucking in the transportation hub of the Midwest helped force the many over-the-road operators with routes ending in Chicago to give in to the union. Also, O'Brien was close to the IBT leadership in Indianapolis, and he managed to convince Tobin to allow the NCDDC to expand without interference. Despite Tobin's fear that the new organization would present a challenge to his power, the over-the-road campaign had grown to such proportions that he was forced to give his approval to it. In 1938, with thousands of workers streaming into the union through the apparatus created by the Trotskyists, the socialist objective of a unified working class appeared to be coming to at least partial fruition within the unlikely vessel of the International Brotherhood of Teamsters.[15]

Union Without a Cause

Meanwhile, Jimmy Hoffa and his colleagues in Detroit continued to operate without a master plan. Though their membership had grown dramatically over the four years prior to 1938, the Detroit Teamsters' strategies and ideas about the labor movement had not. The year 1938 began for them much as the years of the union's infancy had unfolded. In January, Local 299 lent its support to a campaign by Isaac Litwak's Local 285 to retain its agreements with several downtown laundries. The campaign was vital for Litwak's local, which had established itself on a sure footing with a string of contracts during the sit-down wave of 1937. Hoffa held a particular personal interest in the laundry industry since he had met his wife, Josephine Poszywak, while helping her and a group of laundry workers organize their shop.[16]

The two locals called a strike of Teamster members at the Crawford Laundry Company on East Jefferson Avenue, where the union was demanding a renewal of a six-month contract it had signed the previous summer. To protect its physical plant and the replacement workers it had recruited, the company hired more than twenty "guards," equipped them with weapons known as "snappers"—rubber hoses filled with metal—and stationed them between the Teamster pickets and the company's storefront. Over two months, fights between pickets and the guards repeatedly broke out in front of the laundry. Hoffa and another union organizer were arrested and fined $10 for assault and battery following one melee. As the strike wore on through February, it appeared that the armed struggle was being won by management. The goon-escorted replacements managed to keep the laundry running, despite the threats and occasional fists directed at them by the Teamsters.[17]

A defeat at Crawford would have come at an inopportune time for the Teamsters, whose contract with the General Linen Supply Company was due to expire March 8. Losing the strike would no doubt send a signal to the General Linen management that the Teamsters could be beaten at their own game, and would encourage other unionized laundries to let their contracts expire. This appears to have been the moment when Local 299's philosophy of industrial relations began to rub off on the laundry drivers local. Shortly before midnight on February 28, an explosion in a sewer vent behind Crawford Laundry rocked the building and knocked bricks off its exterior. The next night, shortly after a meeting between Teamster business agents and General Linen managers at the company's building on Palmer Avenue, a much larger explosion from a black powder bomb destroyed the laundry's loading dock and shattered windows in houses two blocks away. The blast was audible throughout the northeastern section of the city, but it was most clearly heard by Detroit's laundry owners. After the bombings, contract renewal negotiations proceeded more smoothly. Local 285's adoption of 299's tactics helped the union retain its contracts with most of the laundry companies in Detroit.[18]

Successful as the Detroit Teamsters' brand of unionism was on its own terms, it lacked a coherent strategy beyond organizing vulnerable employers through violence and intimidation. Unlike their counterparts in Minneapolis, the Teamsters in Detroit remained free of socialist colonizers who brought to the labor movement strategies that were derived from grander theories of proletarian revolution. Hoffa's union, despite inhabiting a city teeming with socialists and communists of all persuasions, developed entirely independent of radical influences. The reasons for this lay partly in the particular convergence of Detroit's economic structure with the left's strategies.

Trotskyists had virtually no presence in Detroit. The CLA's few members were bunched in New York and Minneapolis, and other Trotskyist sects were too tiny to have much influence anywhere. The larger Socialist and Communist parties devoted most of their resources in Detroit to organizing within the automobile industry. The SP, which despite its precipitous decline in the 1920s still had a significant cadre in Detroit, concentrated its labor work within the United Automobile Workers and especially UAW Local 174, where the Reuthers and other party activists had established themselves in leadership positions during the sit-down strikes of 1936 and 1937.[19] Early in the Depression, the Communist Party, in an effort to end "the isolation of the Party from the decisive masses of the American proletariat," implemented a policy of "concentration" in what it considered to be "the most decisive industries." Party members were instructed to get jobs in mining, steel, textiles, marine shipping, and automobile manufacturing. Perhaps because it was still considered a new industry, motor transport was not targeted by the Communists. The comrades in Detroit focused almost exclusively on the auto plants, in particular Ford's famous River Rouge complex and the Briggs factory.[20]

The Teamsters union in Detroit, though situated in an industry that was central to the nation's economic system and thus a natural target for revolutionaries, was left to its own devices. Free of the intellectuals whom Selig Perlman identified as the progenitors of labor radicalism, the Detroit Teamsters developed as an organic product of the American working class.[21] But they represented a segment of workers that was particularly immune from the strains of socialism that found willing hosts in other unions during the Depression. Nearly all of the Detroit Teamsters were non-intellectuals who ridiculed "long-hairs" and "eggheads," and most were native-born WASPs. The immigrants among them were mostly from Britain or Ireland, not from Southern and Eastern Europe, the wellsprings of radicalism that fed so many of the left organizations. The nature of the trucking industry also fostered a capitalist ethos among Teamsters. The jobs of the union's original constituency of coal, ice, milk, and bakery drivers included selling the commodities as well as delivering them. Moreover, the decentralized, entrepreneurial character of the trucking industry helped to create a culture of petit-bourgeois aspirations especially among Teamster leaders, many of whom identified with the employers. Most of the union officers hoped to accumulate enough cash from their salaries to invest in land, real estate, and their own companies. Perhaps like most union members in the United States, these men were motivated to join the labor movement by a desire for the good life, not for social power. For these reasons, when the interstate organizing campaign came to town, Hoffa and the Detroit Teamsters welcomed the Trotskyists' organizing strategies for building the union but ignored their political implications. Solidarity would be a tool, not a principle.

Industrial School

In March, the Chicago Teamster leaders approached Red O'Laughlin of Local 299 and asked for the Detroit union's help in the over-the-road campaign. O'Laughlin enthusiastically pledged his local's support. Because of Hoffa's experience in "organizing" intercity car-haulers, O'Laughlin brought the young business agent to Chicago to attend a NCDDC conference in March 1938.[22] At the conference a North Central Area Committee (NCAC) was established to direct the organizing campaign. Because of his enthusiasm for the project and 299's success with the carhaulers, O'Laughlin was named to the committee. Farrell Dobbs showed special interest in 299, since the Detroiters were among the first Teamster locals to penetrate over-the-road trucking.[23] According to Hoffa, Dobbs questioned him extensively "about the techniques we had developed for organizing" the carhaul drivers.[24] It appears that those techniques did not greatly influence Dobbs' thinking on the matter, but the Detroit Teamsters' violent tactics were nonetheless fully compatible with the Trotskyists' aims. Dobbs and O'Laughlin assigned Hoffa to direct the organization of all over-the-road drivers in Michigan.

With workers organized in more than one thousand trucking firms over an area stretching from the Ohio River to the foothills of the

Rocky Mountains, Dobbs, who by now had taken command of the operation, decided to begin working towards a single contract that would cover all unionized over-the-road drivers in the eleven-state area.[25] Having organized the workers, the Teamsters now had to organize the employers as well. Trucking was still made up of thousands of small and scattered firms, and unlike other major unionized industries such as auto and steel, none was big enough to be made into a "model" for industry-wide bargaining.

The American Trucking Association (ATA) had been established in 1933 by several of the larger firms to negotiate with the National Recovery Administration a code covering production rates, prices, wages, and working hours. The ATA had little interest in taking over collective bargaining for the industry, preferring to limit its activities to legislative lobbying.[26] When the NCAC formally invited the ATA to begin negotiations for a central states area agreement, the employers' group denied any responsibility for bargaining for its members, and to underscore the point immediately disbanded its Labor Relations Committee.[27] The NCAC then sent a letter to all of the unionized employers in the eleven states threatening a strike if they did not submit to a uniform contract for the entire area.

The first target was Chicago, the linchpin of Midwestern shipping. The Teamsters offered an ultimatum to all trucking firms with lines ending or beginning in the city: negotiate an area contract or face a strike. With thousands of angry, overworked drivers now members of the union, the threat produced the desired effect. A group of several hundred firms quickly formed a negotiating committee, appointed as chairman Jack Keeshin of the (renamed) Keeshin Motor Express Company, and arranged for contract talks with the Teamsters.[28] After two weeks of grueling negotiations at a Chicago hotel, on August 23 the operators' committee and the Teamsters' Area Committee agreed on a contract that established uniform minimum wages, maximum hours, seniority rights, and safety guarantees for 125,000 workers at 1,700 companies in the eleven-state area. For nearly all of the members covered, the agreement provided significant improvements over their existing conditions. Never before had a Teamster contract covered so much territory or so many workers.[29]

Not all employers, however, capitulated so readily to the agreement. In September, militant and well-organized operators in Omaha and Sioux City responded to the signing of the contract by locking out their unionized employees. The NCAC countered by striking terminals in other cities that were owned by the Omaha and Sioux City firms, then expanded the strike to recalcitrant employers in Missouri, South Dakota, and other parts of Iowa. Such an action was only possible because of the new area-wide cooperation among IBT locals. More than 3,000 Teamsters were now engaged in the effort to force the remaining holdouts to sign the contract.

During the strike, Dobbs became ill and returned to Minneapolis, where he was hospitalized for several weeks. Organizers from 299, one of the most active locals in the over-the-road campaign, stepped in. O'Laughlin, whose aggressiveness and dedication to the campaign won him Dobbs' respect, was chosen as the interim spokesman and general organizer for the Area Committee. Hoffa came down from Detroit to help with the strikes in Omaha and Sioux City, and his skills in street combat proved to be particularly useful when the employers began using tear gas, pistols, and trucks as lethal weapons.[30] Local 299 also donated $3,000 to a defense fund for Sioux City Teamsters who had been arrested for kidnapping and carrying concealed weapons.[31]

As the strike moved into November, a few Teamster locals began to express their doubts about the prospects for victory. Tobin, now at the most militant moment in his career, issued a statement to all Midwestern locals pledging the full support of the international for the strike and asserting that the battle against the employers should continue "indefinitely if necessary."[32] The IBT president's change of heart on the issue of organizing highway drivers was likely a result of the considerable increase in the union's membership and dues payments since the Chicago negotiations. Whatever his motivation, Tobin's action convinced several employers that the union was resolved to continue the shutdown at least into the winter. Within a week, the major firms in Des Moines and Sioux Falls, South Dakota, signed the contract, as did several smaller firms throughout the area. Yet the fire-eating operators in Omaha and Sioux City remained steadfast. It soon became apparent that non-union firms in Kansas City were keeping the holdout companies alive by smuggling their freight.

After conducting surveillance work and a careful study of the secret freight routes, Dobbs, O'Laughlin, and Jack Maloney of the Sioux City local agreed that the strike could be won only by expanding it to the smugglers in Kansas City. Securing Tobin's approval, the three leaders flew to Kansas City to deal with the employers there. At a prearranged time, Tobin sent a telegram to Dobbs in Kansas City, pledging the international's financial support for a strike unless the employers agreed to sign the area agreement and stop making shipments for the Omaha and Sioux City operators. Dobbs handed the telegram to the employers, who within hours signed a slightly modified version of the contract and halted the bootleg shipments. The holdouts in Omaha and Sioux City were now completely cut off, their freight frozen by the Teamster cordon that had closed around them. One by one, the employers fell. By February 1939, virtually every trucking firm in Nebraska and Iowa was operating under the area agreement.[33]

The victories in Omaha and Sioux City established an unprecedented area-wide agreement in eleven contiguous states from the Dakotas to Ohio, brought thousands of over-the-road drivers into the Teamsters, and made the IBT one of the most powerful economic institutions in the Midwest. But it also demonstrated the power of the secondary boycott to Hoffa, who used the weapon to great effect in building his and the union's power. He learned that the highly integrated trucking industry was particularly vulnerable to the type of leverage used against the Omaha and Sioux City operators. Routes between cities were often divided into segments assigned to different trucking firms. Thus individual companies were usually dependent on other firms that connected with their terminals. For example, if the route between cities X and Y was divided into two segments, with one controlled by company A and the other by company B, any disruption in business for company A would directly affect company B. Hoffa recognized that if the Teamsters had organized company A, the drivers for that company could refuse to accept freight from company B unless it signed a union contract. This tactic enabled the Teamsters' Midwestern organizing drive to radiate with spectacular speed.[34]

The type of secondary boycott used in the over-the-road campaign inspired an even broader organizing strategy known as "leapfrogging," so-called because it allowed the union to jump from trucking to contiguous industries. Here, non-trucking companies that depended on Teamsters for deliveries and pickups were the target. It was relatively easy to force contracts out of such businesses by refusing service and effectively shutting them down. Warehouses, canneries, laundries, retail stores, bakeries, and breweries fell to this tactic, which Hoffa used to make the Detroit Teamsters and ultimately the entire IBT into a boundless, multi-industry union. But unlike his socialist mentors, Hoffa presupposed no larger, political purpose for the union other than as a vehicle for his own power.

Though Hoffa's use of leapfrogging and other methods of jurisdictional expansion was enormously successful in increasing the union's membership, it also brought the Teamsters into frequent competition with other unions which had either historical claims to the IBT's non-trucking jurisdictions or desires to control them. These often violent rivalries reinforced Hoffa's Hobbesian world-view and did much to determine the character of his career as a labor leader.

Brother Against Brother

Hoffa's first lesson about the limits of working-class solidarity came from within the AFL. The United Brewery Workers Union (UBW) was the first affiliate of the AFL to open its membership to all workers employed in its respective industry regardless of craft. The socialist ideology of the UBW's largely German immigrant membership accounted for the union's commitment to industrial unionism and its avowal to uphold the interests of the entire working class. The union's motto—"Solidarity, man for man from roof to cellar, all for each and each for all"—distinguished it from the other, rigidly exclusionary craft unions in the AFL.[35]

The struggle between the Brewery Workers and the Teamsters, which became the longest jurisdictional conflict in the history of the American labor movement, began in 1899, when the Team Drivers International Union joined the AFL and claimed jurisdiction over the drivers of beer wagons. The federation vacillated on the issue, but in 1915 arranged an agreement between the two unions granting the UBW jurisdiction over brewery drivers and the teamsters union over drivers employed by soft-drink companies.[36] However, between the adoption of the Eighteenth Amendment prohibiting the sale of alcoholic beverages in 1918 and its repeal in 1933, the brewery union became virtually extinct. During that period the Teamsters grew into one of the largest and most powerful unions in the AFL, which convinced the federation's Executive Council to grant Tobin's request to nullify the 1915 agreement and give jurisdiction over beer drivers to the now better-established Teamsters. But once Prohibition was repealed, the UBW, along with the liquor industry, quickly revived, and it proceeded to contest the Executive Council's decision. After various attempted compromises failed, the conflict moved into the courts and onto the streets.[37]

In 1938, the long-standing struggle between the Teamsters and the Brewery Workers reached Detroit, as the two unions battled for control over the city's beer drivers. The local dispute started when the Teamsters began recruiting disgruntled members of Brewery Workers Local 38, which had transferred lower-paid beer distributor drivers into a separate local. The transfer made the distributor drivers ineligible for the higher wages guaranteed by Local 38's citywide closed-shop contract for drivers employed by Detroit's seven breweries. It also made them easy pickings for the Teamsters. O'Laughlin, Hoffa, and Bert Brennan of Local 337 led a recruitment campaign that brought hundreds of the disaffected distributor drivers, as well as regular brewery drivers now suspicious of the UBW's intentions, into the newly created Teamsters Local 271. Never beholden to legalisms, the Teamsters ignored the clause in the brewery contract asserting that "none but good standing members" of the UBW "shall be employed" by the breweries, and informed the employers that the agreement covered its members in Local 271 as well. Unimpressed by this argument, the breweries, with the encouragement of the Brewery Workers, began firing the defectors. Detroit's beer war was on.[38]

In January, the Teamsters called a strike against the breweries and began using their favorite tactics of militant direct action against the employers, the Brewery Workers, and drivers who refused to switch to the IBT. Pickets made up of Local 271 members and led by 299's officers were deployed to each of the seven breweries, where they stopped trucks, pulled drivers wearing UBW buttons through the cab windows into the snow, and pounded them. Several drivers began replacing their Brewery Worker buttons with Teamster buttons as they left the plant gates. After the police were brought in to protect the UBW drivers, the Teamsters blocked the trucks by filling the streets around the breweries with automobiles. When some trucks managed to squeeze through, cars full of Teamsters chased them through the city. One

Pfeiffer Brewing Company truck was forced to take shelter in the police headquarters garage when fifteen Teamster cars tried to force it off the road. Helpers on Tivoli and Stroh's Brewing Company trucks were kidnapped and beaten with blackjacks after going into bars to make deliveries.[39]

The conflict came to a head when Brennan announced that the Teamsters would call a citywide general trucking strike unless the breweries recognized Local 271 under the terms of the Brewery Workers' contract.[40] Brennan was likely emboldened by the success a month earlier of Local 299, which was able to win the first industry-wide contract for Detroit cartage drivers and helpers by threatening a similar strike that would have paralyzed the city's commercial districts just before Christmas.[41] O'Laughlin, Brennan, and Hoffa, who were by now acting as spokesmen for the entire Detroit Joint Council, had perhaps found a lesson in the 1934 Minneapolis strike that with a sufficient number of trucking lines organized, the Teamsters held the power to shut down an entire city or at least threaten to do so. In both the cartage and the brewery cases the government intervened to stop the Detroit Teamsters from carrying out their threat. In the first instance the employers capitulated under pressure from the city mayor. But in the case of the breweries, the state government in Lansing acted against the Teamsters.

At the time of the beer war the state of Michigan exerted considerable and unusual control over the Detroit brewing industry's labor force. In an effort to curb what it saw as an influx of "muscle men" into the beer business, the Michigan Liquor Control Commission began regulating the employment of beer drivers in 1936. The commission required all beer drivers who also acted as salesmen, as most did, to pay an annual fee and register with the state. The rule was challenged by Local 38 but was upheld by the Michigan Supreme Court in 1937.[42] The commission used this power in an attempt to end the Teamsters' strike against the breweries in 1939 and to quash Brennan's threat of a general trucking strike. Commission chairman Orrin DeMass announced that any beer driver interfering with deliveries would have his license "forever revoked."[43] This cooled the Teamsters to the idea of calling a general strike and turned their attention to the more familiar battleground of the streets. But the Brewery Workers proved to be formidable opponents even on the Teamsters' terrain.

At the end of January, the police reported that "a bus load of 40 hoodlums," apparently hired by the Brewery Workers, had arrived in Detroit. A few hours after the bus reached the city, two shots were fired at Brennan as he was driving home from the Local 271 headquarters. The bullets shattered one of the car's windows but missed the Teamster leader. The previous day, an anonymous call came into the headquarters warning that Frank Ford, who had defected from the Brewery Workers and taken the presidency of 271, was "on the spot." Bodyguards were assigned to Ford and Brennan, but Brewery Worker goons continued to shadow them.[44]

With the jurisdictional struggle filling the pages of the city's newspapers, Frank Martel of the Detroit and Wayne County Federation of Labor (WCFL) stepped in to end the embarrassment caused by the two affiliates of the federation. He convinced the Brewery Workers and Teamsters to allow him to arbitrate the dispute. Soon thereafter, Martel ruled that Local 271 had no rights under the contract between Local 38 and the breweries, and that all members of the Teamsters local should re-affiliate with the Brewery Workers within 48 hours or lose their jobs permanently.[45]

Immediately after Martel announced his decision, Brennan and Local 299 trustee Ray Bennett flew to Miami to urge AFL President William Green, who was attending a meeting of the federation's Executive Council, to overturn the ruling.[46] The Detroit Teamsters even suggested publicly that the IBT would withdraw from the federation if Green did not revoke the charter of the Brewery Workers.[47] Martel then fired off a letter to Green justifying his ruling on the grounds that the battle between the two unions was "bringing extreme discredit upon the labor movement as represented by the American Federation of Labor unions in this city," and that the Teamsters' threat of a citywide strike placed them among the "irresponsible" elements in the labor movement.[48]

The Teamsters filed suit in federal court requesting an injunction restraining the breweries and Local 38 from putting Martel's decision into effect, but Judge Arthur J. Tuttle refused to intervene, stating that the AFL's internal machinery for handling conflicts was more appropriate than recourse to external coercion. Despite his refusal to enter the dispute, the judge did offer criticisms of both Martel and the Teamsters. "I do not believe Martel can Hitlerize these men but I do not see how they can keep any rights under the labor contract with the breweries except as members of Local 38," he added. "To me it is like a man joining a club. If he does not like the waiters or the other members do not like him he cannot go to court about it. All he can do is get out."[49]

Following Tuttle's ruling, the Teamsters and the Brewery Workers filed a series of suits seeking injunctions against each other. During a hearing, the citizenry of Detroit got its first glimpse of Hoffa's personality, which was a pure expression of the world of strife in which he operated. Local newspapers reported the accusation made by the attorney for the Brewery Workers that Hoffa had intimidated a witness by swearing at him and calling him "vile names" as he left the courtroom. The accusation was no doubt true, since Hoffa was well known for both his penchant for personal assault and his ability to use the word "fucking" as a modifier for virtually every noun in a sentence.[50] This type of behavior became the hallmark of Hoffa's public image as uncouth, malicious, and willing to use any means against his adversaries. It also proved ineffective against the Brewery Workers. Despite Hoffa's threats, the witness testified and the judge ruled against the Teamsters.[51]

Rebuffed by the courts, the Teamsters brought their case to the leadership of the labor movement. Tobin, who had been elected to the AFL Executive Council in 1933, demonstrated his growing power within the federation by persuading the board to reverse Martel's arbitration decision and reaffirm its prior ruling granting jurisdiction over beer drivers to the Teamsters.[52] Two weeks later the executive board of the Detroit and Wayne County Federation of Labor met to decide on the dispute. During the meeting Martel was flayed by the Teamsters, who had waged a harassment campaign against the county federation president since the arbitration decision. Choosing to avoid conflict with its parent organization and the Teamsters, who were by now the largest union in the WCFL, the board voted to abide by the AFL's ruling and rescind Martel's decision. Thereupon Martel, who had held the presidency of the county federation since 1919, announced his resignation. "I do not see where I can continue as president in view of the attacks made upon myself in this controversy," he told the gathering, referring to the Teamsters' harassment. Another executive board member, Dwight Erskine, also resigned, bemoaning the controversy that had pushed even the notorious UAW factional strife "off the front pages." The Teamsters leapt at the opportunity. They immediately began organizing among their allies in the federation to replace Martel with someone friendly to the IBT. Rumors circulated in the press that O'Laughlin was planning to campaign to replace Martel, which prompted the latter to announce that he would seek reelection. "I felt it was time we found out just who was running the federation," Martel said.[53]

The election campaign allowed the much shrewder Martel to discredit the Teamsters in the press. "O'Laughlin and the rest of the Teamsters think a trade union consists solely of a lot of muscle men," Martel told the *Detroit News*. "They have picked a lot of tough boys off the streets and made organizers of them." As opposed to this picture of thuggery and chaos, the veteran labor leader offered himself as an exemplar of solidity and responsibility. "We had better find out now whether a bunch of newcomers in the labor movement are going to muscle in or if the people who have been in the labor movement for years are going to continue to have their say," he said. "We always have kept this organization free of intimidation and rough stuff and it will stay that way as long as I have anything to say about it."

Against Martel's statesmanlike indictment, the Teamsters demonstrated their limited skills in public relations. O'Laughlin offered no defense of his union and could retort only that Martel was a "guy who was afraid to admit he was wrong." Martel won the battle in the press, and the friends he had gained over twenty years as head of the county federation also won him reelection. With support from much of the powerful Building Trades Council, he was renamed president by acclamation at a meeting of the WCFL in March. Though this contest ended in defeat for the Detroit Teamsters, it was only the first of many wars they would wage with fellow unionists who believed the labor movement should be responsible for protecting social order.[54]

Relations of Exchange

The indifference of the courts and the nullification of Martel's decision left the conflict between the Brewery Workers and the Detroit Teamsters formally unresolved. Unable to win the war by appealing to higher authorities, the Teamsters wisely began to concentrate on implementing a more informal strategy. Hoffa and his colleagues devoted considerable energy and financial resources to developing a network of allies that extended from local saloons to the Michigan statehouse. This network provided substantial leverage to the union during its formative years in Detroit, but because it included a number of street criminals, including remnants of the Jewish Purple Gang and the still vital East Side Sicilian mob, it also supplied the union's future enemies with ample moral ammunition.

In a sense, the Detroit Teamsters used their own brand of solidarity against the Brewery Workers. Knowing that the breweries depended on sales to local bars, the Teamsters liberally distributed favors and bribes to the owners and employees of Detroit's saloons, especially the 1,000 members of Bartenders Local 562 of the Hotel and Restaurant Employees International Alliance and Bartenders International League (AFL). Detroit's bars provided a hospitable environment for the Teamsters' illegal advances. The repeal of Prohibition forced many Midwestern bootleggers to convert their operations into legitimate breweries and distilleries. To help ensure the continued flow of profits, they bribed bar owners to buy only their liquor and muscled their way into unions whose members were employed in the liquor industry. Former East Side and Purple Gang rumrunners, now legitimately employed in bars, helped create a culture concordant with the Teamster ethos. In addition to supporting the truckers' union against Martel, on March 5, the Detroit bartenders local announced that 400 of its members would accept only beer delivered by Teamsters. Many bar owners, who were either friendly with the Teamsters or fearful of reprisals, also agreed to refuse deliveries from Brewery Worker members.[55]

Herman Kierdorf, a former bar owner who was especially friendly with the Teamsters, was the kind of thuggish petty criminal typical of the milieu inhabited by the union. In the early 1930s he had been arrested for the kidnapping of Canadian brewing magnate John Labatt and later served a year in Leavenworth Penitentiary for extortion and impersonating a federal officer. After leaving prison he opened the Marquette Garden, a bar on Woodward Avenue and Six Mile Road, and became involved in the local labor movement. In 1937 he was recruited by Martel to join the staff of the UAW as a director of organizing in various non-automotive fields. When local newspapers began publicizing Kierdorf's police record, UAW vice president George Addes fired him, claiming that "it is a very definite policy of the UAW to keep such people out of its ranks." Less concerned about their public image, the Teamsters soon thereafter hired Kierdorf as a business agent. In his new job he made headlines again after he and Brennan were arrested for the bombing of a non-union trucking firm.[56]

Higher up the social ladder, the beer war caused the Detroit Teamsters to adopt a political strategy that resembled more closely the attitudes of the early AFL than of their contemporary counterparts in the labor movement. When AFL president Samuel Gompers wrote in the May 1906 issue of *The American Federationist* that organized labor should "stand by our friends and administer a stinging rebuke to men or parties who are either indifferent, negligent or hostile," he articulated the federation's long-standing policy of independence from political parties. This doctrine, known as "voluntarism," grew out of a distrust of the state, which Gompers and others believed to be the tool of capital and therefore unreliable as a vehicle for labor's interests. "What the law gives or what the state gives, the state can take away," he cautioned an affiliated union that had petitioned the government for reforms. "But what you get through your own exertions you can hold as long as you maintain your strength."[57]

The voluntarist strategy, which was distilled into the slogan "Reward your friends and punish your enemies," remained the declared policy of the AFL through the 1930s but gradually eroded as a practice. The decline of the union movement that began after World War I and accelerated in the first years of the Great Depression caused many of the federation's affiliates to look to the state for assistance. With Roosevelt in office, several union leaders, most notably Tobin, effectively abandoned voluntarism and pledged their loyalty to the Democratic Party. The CIO continued this trend, becoming a de facto auxiliary of the Democrats. Although the AFL remained officially neutral in national elections, by the end of the 1930s many of its leaders were making clear their support for the Democratic Party and its policies of government intervention in the economy.[58]

The Detroit Teamsters drew a different lesson from their experiences with the state. Having eschewed the model of government-regulated industrial relations embodied in the Wagner Act, they experienced the realization of Gompers' warnings during the war with the Brewery Workers.[59] The intervention of the Michigan Liquor Control Commission in behalf of the employers and a rival union led the Detroit Teamsters to adopt Gompers' strategy but with a distinctive twist. Their slogan might have been "Reward your friends and bribe your enemies." Hoffa and Brennan arranged for a relationship of mutual aid with Commissioner DeMass. By taking care of the tax payments on DeMass' lake-front house in Oakland County, the Teamsters purchased a laissez-faire approach by the Liquor Commission in jurisdictional conflicts as well as DeMass' assistance in granting beer-driver licenses to IBT members and saloon licenses to friends of the union. DeMass, a leading member of the Wayne County Republican Party, later served as an unofficial political advisor to Hoffa and Brennan.[60] Over the next decade, new exigencies pushed Hoffa to broaden his involvement with the state, although he continued to view it with a cynical eye.

The Teamsters' network of allies helped the union keep its foothold in several breweries, but the Brewery Workers doggedly protected its jurisdictional claims. The war between the two unions settled into an uneasy truce within the local brewing industry but later spread to new fields of contestation.

The Best Friends in Detroit

During a strike by Locals 299 and 337 against the Crowley-Milner department store, the Detroit Teamsters were persuaded to pursue another, distinctively non-ideological alliance with a branch of government that posed a direct threat to the very existence of the union. Running from September 1939 to April 1940, the strike affected only sixty-three truck drivers and helpers but was remarkable for its violence. Replacement workers armed with blackjacks, knives, jack handles, and tear gas put up a fierce defense against the attacks of the Teamsters, but the intervention of the police gave the management its greatest advantage.[61] Teamster pickets, in particular leaders of the union familiar to the police, were arrested repeatedly during the Crowley-Milner strike on charges of "molesting" the replacement workers. Hoffa claimed that while picketing in front of the department store he was detained at least fourteen times during one twenty-four-hour period. The scabs received further protection from ex-policemen hired by the company to serve as armed escorts.[62] Having suffered at the hands of the police on many occasions, most notably during the war with the Brewery Workers and in the disastrous strike against Kroger's in 1937, the Teamsters put into action a strategy to protect themselves from the repressive apparatus of the city government.

Shortly after the Crowley-Milner strike, the Teamsters began a systematic infiltration of the Detroit Police Department through both furtive and highly public means. Beginning at the bottom, the Teamsters initiated a policy of great friendliness toward members of the department, including the provision of jobs, gifts, loans, and favors. Members of the union even served as hearse drivers at police funerals.[63] As with the saloon owners and bartenders, the Teamsters found a culture in the department that was receptive to such offers. A grand jury investigation in 1939 and 1940 revealed a vast system of bribery in the department and led to the indictment of the mayor, county prosecutor, police superintendent, and nearly two hundred officers.[64] The Teamsters made a number of valuable acquisitions in this underground market, most importantly the friendship of several members of the Wayne County Prosecuting Attorney's staff and of Albert DeLamielleure, a detective in charge of monitoring the union. In exchange for helping to keep the police at bay, DeLamielleure received favors, including legal representation by Teamster attorney George Fitzgerald and later a job with the union after he was forced from the department by a grand jury disclosure that he held an illegal interest in a bar. Hoffa, who had been charged fifteen times with various crimes between 1937 and 1939, maintained a virtually spotless police record over the next seven years.[65]

The relationships Fitzgerald developed during the four years he served as Assistant Prosecuting Attorney of Wayne County helped him establish friendly relations between the Teamsters and the police and Prosecutor's office.[66] But he gained special status within the police department when he represented several of the defendants in bribery trials.[67] Apparently undaunted by potential charges of hypocrisy, Fitzgerald then used the graft scandal to blast his opponents during his Teamster-financed campaign for Prosecuting Attorney in 1940.[68] Though Fitzgerald lost the election, during his career with the Teamsters he was still able in many cases to exert enough influence to keep the cops from siding with employers and rival unions against his clients.[69]

While improving their relations with the prosecutors and police department, the Detroit Teamsters also began to use new methods to deal with employers. After three years of trying unsuccessfully to organize the local wastepaper recycling and wholesale business, in 1940 Hoffa and Brennan conspired with a group of Jewish hoodlums (possibly former Purple Gang members or fellow travelers) to establish four wastepaper companies under Teamster contracts and then force out the non-union competitors. A federal grand jury investigation showed that among other acts of intimidation, business agents from Locals 299 and 337 threatened to picket paper mills that purchased from firms outside the cartel and almost certainly were responsible for the bombing of the home of one of the non-union employers. Hoffa, Brennan, and their businessmen associates pleaded no contest to charges of violating the Sherman Act and were each fined $1,000.[70]

The Teamsters would have successfully monopolized the local wastepaper industry were it not for the intervention of Thurman Arnold, the zealous chief of the U.S. Justice Department's antitrust division. In his crusade against anticompetitive practices, Arnold included prosecution of labor unions that "used coercion" for the purpose of restraining trade. He was particularly irritated by the Teamsters, and saw the wastepaper case as part of a national conspiracy by the union. In a letter encouraging the editor of *Fortune* to run an exposé of the Detroit Teamsters, Arnold wrote, "We are rapidly drifting into a situation where the entire trucking transportation of the United States is going to be controlled by a few big companies, which in turn are controlled by the Teamsters' Union."[71] This was the first of many such charges made against Hoffa's Teamsters, who were later often portrayed by federal officials and journalists as a threat to the nation's economy.

Though his naïveté was evident in hatching the plot during the height of the federal antitrust effort, Hoffa took away two important lessons from the episode.[72] First, his suspicion of the state was confirmed, since the federal attack against his union was carried out by an administration ostensibly supportive of the labor movement. Second, he learned that capitalists were not necessarily his enemies. Indeed, over the next year Hoffa found that his most implacable foes were not employers but fellow members of the brotherhood of labor.

Four

The Wages of War

It will never be fully proven what a real man is, the head of a house or family, until his house and family are attacked. Then he will show the stuff of which he is made. That's the case with the Teamsters.—DAN TOBIN, *OFFICIAL MAGAZINE, I.B.T., C., S. AND H. OF A., OCTOBER 1941*

From 1935 to 1941, the membership of the Teamsters increased from 146,035 to 544,247, making it the fastest-growing affiliate of the AFL during that period. This was a remarkable transformation in a union that had previously been one of the weakest in the United States, prompting labor historian Walter Galenson to claim that "the period of the nineteen-thirties was characterized fully as much by the rise of the Teamsters as it was by the establishment of the CIO." Writing nineteen years later in *The Journal of American History*, Christopher Tomlins acknowledged the rapid expansion of the Teamsters and other AFL unions in the 1930s but argued against Galenson and others whose narratives suggested that the growth of the AFL was spurred by competition from the newly created Congress of Industrial Organizations. Tomlins maintained that the expansion of the AFL unions in the 1930s was instead the result of their adaptation to structural changes in their respective industries. He asserted that the simultaneous growth of the Teamsters, other AFL building trades unions, and the CIO was simply coincidental and that, indeed, "neither the teamsters nor the construction unions faced any competition from the CIO." Had he lived long enough and were he inclined to peruse historical journals, Jimmy Hoffa would have been amazed to read this.[1]

In fact, competition from CIO unions was a principal determinant of the IBT's ascendancy from a tiny craft union to the largest and most powerful labor organization in the United States. While it could be argued that the great midwestern over-the-road organizing campaign of 1938 was largely driven by the ideological motivations of the Trotskyist Teamsters from Minneapolis, most of the IBT's expansion, especially its growth in non-trucking industries, was compelled by competition from rival unions, in particular those affiliated with the CIO.[2]

Because of its location in an industry that was contiguous and interdependent with virtually every other sector of the economy, the Teamsters faced more jurisdictional competition than any union in the United States.[3] Dan Tobin well understood this unique problem. In 1936 he published in the IBT's official magazine a series of editorials on jurisdictional conflicts with other unions. Tobin complained that in his thirty years as Teamster president he had been "engaged continuously" in jurisdictional disputes:

> This is mainly due to the composition of our organization, as we touch every craft and every industry. Our members are on the job before the foundation stone of a building is laid and remain until its completion; we haul the raw material into a newspaper office and we deliver the finished product. As a result we are in a more conspicuous position with other trades than any other International Union.

Tobin noted with particular alarm the CIO's commitment to organize workers according to industry rather than craft:

> Although the American Federation of Labor has voted down such attempts, there is some friendliness, more than before, towards industrial trade unionism. If such a proceeding takes place it will in time totally destroy our organization, because every trade or calling can admit to membership the chauffeurs or truck drivers touching or hauling material manufactured or worked on by their particular trade.[4]

Tobin indeed had much to fear. Because of the centrality of trucking, a union exerting control over the industry's workers could expand rapidly and with relative ease, making it especially attractive for ambitious rival union leaders. During the central states over-the-road organizing drive in 1938, the Teamsters learned that they could quickly organize warehouses and other industries dependent on trucking by simply refusing to unload freight at companies whose workers were not IBT members. A non-union firm would be cut off from its supplies until it signed an agreement recognizing the Teamsters as the collective bargaining agent for its employees. This particular type of secondary boycott enabled the Teamsters to move past the confines of their traditional jurisdiction without engaging in lengthy and expensive organizing drives among the workers themselves. However, the IBT soon learned from rivals in the CIO that "leapfrogging" could just as easily be used in reverse against them.[5]

The House Divided

Leaders of the CIO were well aware of the strategic power of the trucking union. From the time of its formation through the years of World War II, the CIO and its member unions waged a series of attempts to surround and supplant the Teamsters, forcing the trucking union to fight back with counterassaults on CIO terrain. In the fall of 1936, West Coast locals of the International Longshoremen's Association, which were preparing to bolt to the CIO, began organizing the previously non-union warehouse industry in San Francisco and Oakland. The Longshoremen's "March Inland" was driven by the ILA's Bay Area leadership, whose socialist instincts caused them to view unorganized industries as stepping-stones on the way to a single, monolithic union. Louis Goldblatt, one of the lead organizers of the March Inland and a Communist, announced, "We are beginning to organize for something bigger than the ILA itself—the organization of the transportation [and] distribution workers. Once such a union is formed . . . we will become really invincible."[6]

The stodgy and provincial Bay Area Teamsters took no notice of the ILA organizing campaign until more than 3,000 local warehousemen were members of the longshore union. When ILA job actions began paralyzing some of their largest trucking employers, the local Teamsters finally realized that an expansionist organization was on the verge of holding a vise around their industry. Fearing that the ILA was likely to use that leverage to invade trucking, the Teamsters launched a vigorous counterattack. At the request of the Bay Area locals, Dan Tobin appealed to the AFL Executive Council to extend IBT jurisdiction to warehouse workers, explaining that Teamster drivers were "caught in a trap in the loading and delivery of merchandise between the Longshoremen on the wharf—in many instances controlled by radicals—and warehousemen at the other end."[7] Knowing that the West Coast longshoremen would soon receive a charter from the CIO, the AFL leadership quickly gave the Teamsters the jurisdictional extension as well as encouragement to take the fight to their competitors.

In September 1937, the Bay Area Teamsters brought all their resources to bear against the new International Longshoremen's and Warehousemen's Union, CIO (ILWU). Hoping to strangle their rival's primary industry, the Teamsters refused to haul cargo from the docks in San Francisco and Oakland. Picket lines of thousands of IBT men faced assaults by "flying wedges" of longshoremen. To break the Teamster blockade, the waterfront employers brought trains directly to the docks. Eventually the IBT called off their pickets, allowing the ILWU to maintain its presence both on the docks and in the warehouses. However, the Longshoremen's March Inland had the unintended consequence of producing a Teamsters' March Inland. Following the war on the docks, the Teamsters turned to a new tactic against their opponents—organizing. In 1938 the IBT established several warehouse locals in the Bay Area, while Teamster organizers mounted successful drives among warehouse workers from Los Angeles to Seattle. By 1939 the formerly exclusive trucking union had 68 warehouse locals in eleven states and a new warehouse division in its Western Conference, contributing substantially to the union's rapid rise in membership.[8]

Tobin rightly assumed that the CIO's attack on the West Coast was merely an opening salvo in a national war against the Teamsters. In his editorials he warned the officers of the union that their source of livelihood would be lost if they did not fight with unrelenting militancy against their competitors:

Unless you determine to put forth every ounce of energy and strategy within you to protect your union in this instance, you are not doing your duty to this organization. . . . If you are one of those who want to evade a struggle . . . you are taking the position that will not only in time destroy you but will destroy your union, because we are living in the age of change, not a healthy change for us. . . . Every man added to our membership in your locality is a strengthening of your union. . . . The local unions must do this work. . . . In doing this you are doing your duty as a man and you are fulfilling the obligation to preserve the life and perpetuate the existence of the International Union.[9]

No local Teamster official took this to heart more than Jimmy Hoffa. In 1939, the job that had originally served as a means to survive the Depression allowed Hoffa and his wife to buy a two-story house on Robson Avenue in a modest but solid white middle-class section of the West Side. When Hoffa found that he was situated at the center of the Teamsters' war with the CIO, in a city with the highest concentration of CIO power, he had ample motivation to protect his job and the union that provided it.[10]

"We Must Protect Our Jurisdiction"

Emboldened by the ILWU's March Inland and the UAW's spectacular victories over General Motors and Chrysler, CIO organizers descended on Detroit in the spring and summer of 1937, bringing union cards and promises of better contracts to workers in various industries, including those already under contract with AFL unions or in close proximity to AFL jurisdictions. The CIO laid siege to traditional AFL fields such as retail stores, groceries, the city transit system, cigar factories, and barbershops, but also to dairies, bakeries, and construction companies, whose drivers had been represented by the Teamsters since the turn of the century. In the Detroit dairy industry, which had been organized by Teamsters Local 155 for decades, the confrontation was particularly unpleasant. The Teamster milk drivers' union was one of the oldest and best-established of the IBT locals in Detroit, but because Hoffa's Local 299 had the most aggressive, most ambitious, and toughest organizers, it served as the frontline defense against the CIO. In June 1937, a street fight broke out between IBT members and organizers from the CIO's newly formed United Dairy Workers (UDW), which, because of its ideological commitment to industrial organization, claimed jurisdiction over milk drivers as well as the dairies' "inside" workers. Brawlers from 299 sent three of the raiders to the hospital. A week after the melee, a bomb destroyed the car owned by "Red" O'Laughlin, president of Local 299, and a stick of dynamite was found on the front porch of Patrick Brady, one of the Teamsters' strong-arm organizers.[11]

Though their tactics resembled those of their relatively primitive and thoroughly non-intellectual opponents, the UDW's drive against the Teamsters was guided by a sophisticated ideology. The Dairy Workers' Detroit local was founded by John W. Gibson, who while directing the organizing campaign in the city's dairies also held top positions in the Michigan CIO Council. Gibson was a classic CIO corporatist. Throughout his career, first as a union leader and later in various government offices, he worked toward the vision, propounded most famously by CIO leaders Sidney Hillman, Philip Murray, and Walter Reuther, of an economy managed coequally by labor, capital, and government. This vision extended from the shop floor, where corporatists advocated worker participation in the management of production, to every branch of the government, which would include labor representatives working as partners with businessmen and politicians. The primary purpose of the labor movement, in the words of Hillman, was to provide workers with "power to establish themselves as a full-fledged part of organized society." To accomplish this, labor would, according to Hillman advisor J. B. S. Hardman, "assume responsibilities for production and ascend to active participation in the control of industry." The replacement of the many craft unions with organizations established along industrial lines was a prerequisite for the corporatist plan, since a centralization of labor organizations would be necessary for the smooth running of the tripartite state. For the fulfillment of the corporatist vision it was also necessary to eliminate socially irresponsible unionists like Jimmy Hoffa who had no interest in managing production or society at large. It was therefore perhaps inevitable that Gibson would devote a great deal of his energy, both as a union leader in Detroit and later as an assistant secretary of labor in the Truman administration, to attempting to replace Hoffa with more responsible labor statesmen.[12]

Despite its failure to dislodge the Teamsters with fists and dynamite in the summer of 1937, Gibson's local continued its campaign to bring the CIO's "industrial democracy" to the Detroit dairies. The persistence of the UDW forced the Teamsters to adopt a defensive strategy that altered the composition of their union and greatly expanded its size. Following intensive organizing drives at two non-union dairies in the summer of 1939, the UDW claimed that a majority of the workers at the plants had signed membership cards. When the employers refused to negotiate with the new union, the UDW announced it would call strikes for recognition rights. Both dairies immediately signed contracts with Teamsters Local 155, heading off the CIO. The closed-shop contracts covered inside workers, who for the first time were brought into the IBT. The UDW threw up pickets around the dairies in protest, but were met by armed detachments of Teamsters. Several UDW members were beaten. After one such fray, Hoffa offered a justification for his union's actions to the press. "The Teamsters Union has no quarrel with the CIO or the UAW," he told the *Detroit News*. "We only want to protect our members where we have contracts. We are absolutely in sympathy with the CIO and the UAW, but when a plant under contract with us is threatened we must protect our jurisdiction."[13]

Hoffa's statement was partly disingenuous. The Teamsters' agreements with the dairies, which the UDW called "sweetheart contracts," were indeed an attempt to protect the IBT's jurisdiction, but they were also, as the UDW claimed, an obvious marriage of convenience for the IBT and the employers. The Teamsters learned that companies besieged by CIO unions seeking control over management practices were easily persuaded to sign with the Teamsters, who had no interest in supervising production. Yet despite the fact that the dairy contracts were signed with little or no mandate from the workers they covered, the continuing threat posed by the UDW compelled Hoffa and the Teamsters to respond in ways that were beneficial to their new members. Teamster leaders found that as long as they delivered the "bread and butter"—higher wages, shorter hours, and better working conditions—their members were likewise satisfied with leaving managerial responsibility to the employers. Knowing this, the UDW and other unions in competition with the Teamsters increasingly pitched their appeals to workers in strict economic terms and muted their calls for "industrial democracy."

Despite losing the two dairies to the Teamsters, the UDW intensified its organizing crusade, winning several contracts at other plants and continuing its recruiting efforts at the dairies under the "sweetheart" pacts. The Teamsters were forced to provide for their members. In 1941, when the contracts at the two dairies were renewed, the Teamsters won sufficient economic gains to keep the workers from bolting to the CIO union and even secured a closed shop in one of the dairies' retail chains for a Detroit local of the Retail Clerks International Protective Association (RCIPA), which Hoffa was converting into a satellite of the IBT. So long as competition between the two unions existed, Detroit's dairy workers could be sure of getting good representation for their dues.[14]

While the milk war raged, the Detroit Teamsters learned that far greater trouble for them was brewing inside the CIO. Ironically, this trouble came from Hoffa's closest counterpart in the labor movement, CIO president John L. Lewis. Like Hoffa, Lewis was a product of the midwestern coal mining country, and like Hoffa he took from his early environment a creed that combined possessive individualism with a belief in collective action as a means for economic advancement, not as a good in itself. "Self-assertion, pretentiousness, fondness for worldly goods, and social climbing characterized much of Lewis's personal behavior," according to Lewis biographers Melvyn Dubofsky and Warren Van Tine. "Paradoxically, however, without the collective strength and solidarity of common folk, Lewis could never have satisfied his more personal, selfish ambitions." Having rejected the faith in subordinating personal freedom and desire to social organization that guided Hillman, Reuther, and Murray, Lewis and Hoffa also shared an abiding distrust of the state and a belief that the power of the labor movement could be derived only from the strength and size of its organizations. Lewis's suspicion that the government could turn against labor at any moment was confirmed during the Little Steel strike of 1937, when the ostensibly pro-labor Roosevelt refused to protect the strikers after several had been killed by police in the "Memorial Day Massacre" in Chicago. Roosevelt's betrayal spurred Lewis to redouble the CIO's efforts to "organize the unorganized" and create a vast and united labor movement, which he believed to be the only sure path to power for himself and the movement. This strategy, however, led the CIO chief into a fateful conflict with Hoffa and the Teamsters.[15]

When unity negotiations with the AFL broke down, Lewis set himself the task of eliminating the greatest obstacle in the way of his attaining control over a monolithic organization of workers. For two years Lewis struck at smaller crafts like dairy that were on the edges of the AFL, but in 1939 he decided to invade the very core of the older federation's constituency. On July 31, 1939, Lewis announced the formation of the United Construction Workers Organizing Committee (UCWOC), a spear pointed directly at the building trades unions, the largest and most powerful members of the AFL. The UCWOC claimed as part of its jurisdiction the thousands of Teamster drivers who delivered materials to construction sites and hauled away the debris. To encourage public support for his initiative, Lewis crafted a manifesto that spoke as much to employers and the federal government as it did to construction workers. New Deal liberals, who dominated the National Labor Relations Board and would potentially decide on jurisdictional issues, were promised an end to corrupt and racist unions, while employers were offered a cooperative and efficient partner in place of the restrictive, obstructionist unions of old. The *CIO News* presented the UCWOC as an aid, not a hindrance, to capital:

> The contractor using CIO labor does not worry about having to bargain with 20 separate craft unions. One single union speaks for every worker on the job. Since there are no jurisdictions he does not have to worry about jurisdictional strikes. There are no regulations against the use of new materials. Hourly rates are calculated on a reasonable basis.

The construction workers themselves were offered something far more attractive than racial harmony and friendly relations with the boss—Lewis set dues that were 25 percent lower than those charged by the AFL unions. As an additional enticement, the UCWOC would charge no initiation fees, which in the Teamsters were typically $25, a hefty sum for a construction worker or truck driver in 1939. While Lewis's rhetoric spoke of unionism as part of a progressive communitarian movement, his policies revealed his cold-blooded understanding—which Hoffa soon would share—that the labor movement was also a market in which union members and potential union members acted as consumers in search of effective representation at a low price.[16]

Lewis made the attack on the building trades his pet project. To ensure that the new organization adhered to his objectives, he appointed his brother Dennie as its director. Lewis instructed CIO affiliates to support the UCWOC in its organizing drives, used the *CIO News* as its propaganda organ, and poured money into the new union. In the first two years of its existence, the UCWOC received substantial subsidies and scores of organizers from the UMW and at least $313,000 in CIO funds, the most given to any CIO affiliate other than the Steelworkers. The Teamsters, the building trades, and the rest of the AFL had reason to take the threat of the UCWOC seriously. Soon Jimmy Hoffa learned just how serious was the threat when he found himself standing on the front line in a war for his union's survival.[17]

Invasion

In his classic *History of Western Philosophy*, Bertrand Russell argued that Darwin's theory of evolution was misappropriated by those who applied it to modern social relations. "There was a great difference between the competition admired by orthodox economists and the struggle for existence which Darwin proclaimed as the motive force of evolution," Russell wrote. " 'Free competition,' in orthodox economics, is a very artificial conception, hedged in by legal restrictions. You may undersell a competitor, but you must not murder him. . . . Darwinian competition was not of this limited sort; there were no rules against hitting below the belt. The framework of law does not exist among animals, nor is war excluded as a competitive method."[18] Russell's argument notwithstanding, Jimmy Hoffa's social environment was entirely Darwinian. This was especially so in the period prior to the United States' entry into World War II, when thoroughgoing state regulation of industrial relations had not yet reached the milieu in which Hoffa operated. And despite Russell's disdain for their view of unrestrained competition as being beneficial to human beings, the social Darwinists were proved right at least in Hoffa's world. Though unrestrained competition between unions created difficult and often deadly circumstances for Hoffa and his opponents in labor's official-dom, it proved to be immensely profitable for workers and the labor movement as a whole.

From 1939 through the fall of 1941, the Detroit Teamster locals experienced as much unmitigated struggle for survival as any animal observed by Darwin. Employers continued to put up violent resistance to the Teamsters' organizing efforts. The Kroger Company, which had expelled the union in 1937 with the aid of the police, augmented its own defenses to keep the Teamsters at bay. In February 1939, three of Hoffa's lieutenants were dispatched to the Kroger warehouse, only to find that the company had become less dependent on the police for protection. Martin Haggerty, a young organizer who later became a top officer in Local 337, was shot by a company security guard, and Steve Stasko and Sam Calhoun, who also went on to become leaders in Detroit Teamster locals, received serious beatings when they arrived at the warehouse. The guard responsible for this mayhem had fought in local boxing matches under the name "Dynamite Jackson" before being hired by Kroger. A year later, employers' violence against the union hit even closer to home for Hoffa: In February 1940 his brother Billy, an organizer for 337, was shot in the stomach while picketing a grocery warehouse.[19]

But while Billy Hoffa and the Teamsters survived the attacks from employers, the union faced a far more deadly threat from its enemies inside the labor movement. By the winter of 1940, John L. Lewis had decided that the CIO's offensive against the AFL would center on Detroit. Lewis hoped that the UAW, which was by then the largest CIO affiliate and the dominant union in the Motor City, would serve as a base of support for the raids. In January, Gus Scholle, president of the Michigan CIO Council, announced that the building trades and the retail and wholesale industry would be the "concentration points" in an organizing campaign in the state. Tucker Smith and James Boyne were named to head the two drives. Boyne, who was put in charge of the new Detroit Local 98 of the United Construction Workers Organizing Committee, was a CIO apparatchik who had worked as an organizer in various midwestern industrial areas. The appointment of Boyne was little more than a formality, since all important UCWOC decisions would be made by Lewis and enacted by his brother Dennie. Tucker Smith, on the other hand, was no ordinary union staffer, and his appointment as head of the Detroit branch of the newly established United Retail, Wholesale, and Department Store Employees (URWDSE) indicated both the politics behind much of the CIO's expansion and the seriousness of its intention to overthrow the AFL. Smith was the chairman of the Michigan Socialist Party, which by then had shed its revolutionary politics for a reformist, social democratic orientation, and a close friend of the Reuther brothers. His politics fit well with those of the URWDSE, which had grown out of a department store organizing committee formed by Sidney Hillman.

Hillman biographer Steven Fraser described the CIO's campaign to organize in the retail trades as one of Hillman's attempts to "call mass movements into being by bureaucratic-administrative fiat." Hillman was just as keen as Lewis to create an immense and monolithic labor movement, though his intentions for it were far different. Whereas Lewis saw no ultimate objective for his organizing, to Hillman the labor movement served as a vehicle for his ambition to create a scientifically managed society. Much of this inspiration came from his involvement with the Bund in Lithuania and later from the socialist politics of New York's Lower East Side. Not coincidentally, Hillman's selection to head the URWDSE, Samuel Wolchok, was also a product of the socialist Lower East Side. In addition to their cultural background, Wolchok and Hillman shared a conversion from revolutionary socialism to a belief in non-revolutionary social engineering. As part of their plan to create a far-reaching and centrally coordinated labor organization that would share power in a tripartite state, they hoped to extend the CIO into the strategically critical warehousing and retail industries, vital components of the economy's distribution system. Unfortunately for the Teamsters, those industries were symbiotically connected to both ends of the IBT's principal jurisdiction.[20]

With the agents of Lewis's personal ambition attacking construction trucking and the Hillmanite social engineers moving on warehousing and retail, the Detroit Teamsters found themselves surrounded by rivals. The designs of the Retail Workers were especially ominous. The URWDSE threatened to control the warehouses where Teamster drivers picked up freight and the retail stores where they made deliveries. From either end, boycotts against Teamster trucks could quickly force trucking firms to sign URWDSE contracts, thereby making the entire transportation system a CIO domain. These possibilities did not escape Hoffa's attention. When the URWDSE came to town, Hoffa knew that an expansionist Teamster organizing campaign was necessary so that, as he later recalled, "we would not wake up some morning and find out that the clerks, being CIO, would be in a position to refuse delivery by an A. F. of L. driver." He also knew that the CIO's move into dairy, warehousing, construction, and retail was merely "a spearhead" with which to begin an attack on the Teamsters' hold on general trucking.[21]

The Detroit Teamsters responded to the CIO challenge with unprecedented militancy. In the summer of 1940 they struck virtually every trucking firm in the city. The expiration on July 1 of the citywide cartage contract, covering 1,800 workers at 237 firms, presented Hoffa with an opportunity to safeguard the largest portion of Local 299's membership against potential predators. Hoffa and his negotiating team forced a strike by holding to their demand for enormous 25 percent wage increases. Disregarding both a state law requiring a thirty-day notice before calling a work stoppage against public utilities and a Circuit Court injunction against the strike, Hoffa pulled the 1,800 drivers and helpers from their jobs and held them out for three weeks, shutting down all freight shipments into and out of the city. Much of Detroit's economy remained paralyzed, despite several appeals by businessmen for the Mayor to intervene. The Teamsters finally won a 10 percent increase, which was well under their original, pretentious demand but still comparable to the best contracts won by large CIO unions, including the Steelworkers and the UAW, allowing Hoffa to claim victory. More significantly for Hoffa and his fellow officers in 299, the contract they won guaranteed sole recognition of their union for two years.[22]

Shortly after the settlement of the cartage strike, Teamsters Building Materials Drivers Local 247, with whom Hoffa worked closely, likewise responded to the CIO threat with a burst of militancy. The local had been under siege by the UCWOC since the announcement of the CIO's drive on the Detroit building trades in January. Organizers for UCWOC not only had lower dues to offer Teamster members, but were also able to point to Local 247's substandard contract with the city's forty building materials firms, which provided only 60 cents an hour for yard workers and truck helpers and 75 cents for drivers, significantly less than the prevailing wages in other midwestern cities. When negotiations over the renewal of the contract began in August, the Teamsters were well aware of their rivals. In addition to large wage increases, Local 247 president Bill Roe demanded from the employers a "preferential shop," an agreement that members of the Teamsters be given preference in hiring. When the owners balked at the Teamsters' demands, Roe called a strike of 1,000 workers that lasted for three weeks. The walkout ended in a one-year contract that included pay raises short of the union's original demands, but that also granted the IBT its preferential shop.[23]

While the Detroit Teamsters fought to secure their base against the CIO in the traditional IBT jurisdictions of local cartage and construction trucking, they were forced to expand their organizing in another field to fend off both an ancient rival and their newest competitors. In 1940 the Teamsters moved into the previously unorganized Detroit soft-drink industry, which in other cities had been a field of contestation between the IBT and the United Brewery Workers. Teamsters Local 337, now headed jointly by its president, Bert Brennan, and unofficially by Hoffa, signed contracts covering both drivers and inside workers with the Coca-Cola bottling plant and the Dossin Food Products Company, which bottled and distributed Pepsi-Cola in Detroit. It was common for Teamster locals to organize soft-drink drivers but highly unusual to include in their contracts workers employed inside the bottling plants. The Teamsters' contracts with Coca-Cola and Dossin were attacks against their old foes the Brewery Workers, who had always claimed jurisdiction over soft-drink bottlers and production workers, but the move inside the plants was also a defensive gambit on a larger front. AFL president William Green acknowledged that Local 337 "felt itself under obligation to organize the inside workers rather than permit them to become organized into the CIO."[24]

At the time of the Detroit Teamsters' drive on the soft-drink industry, the UBW was seeking a federal injunction granting it de facto independence from the AFL, while the CIO openly courted the Detroit local of the brewery union. This intensified the battle over the

Detroit soft-drink employees and probably hastened the Teamsters' move to sign up the inside workers. Since Tobin held a seat and considerable influence on the AFL Executive Council, he was able in many jurisdictional conflicts between the two unions to win rulings that were favorable to the IBT, as he did during the Detroit beer war in 1938. The Detroit Brewery Workers' imminent defection to the CIO made the conflict into a fight to the finish—no longer could the dispute be resolved within the AFL, where the politically stronger Teamsters were more likely to be favored by the federation.[25]

In December, when the Brewery Workers assembled hundreds of men, some borrowed from the UAW and other CIO unions, armed them with baseball bats and sent them to blockade the Dossin and Coca-Cola plants, the entire staff of the Detroit Teamsters Joint Council mobilized for war. With scores of drivers staying home to avoid the wrath of the UBW pickets, Hoffa and Brennan organized a replacement force of Teamster officers and stewards from every local in the Joint Council to drive the trucks and keep the plants open. Predictably, the violence that erupted when the trucks came into or left the plants was spectacular. The cab of every truck driven by the Teamsters was filled with weapons of various sorts: chains, bats, and "poker sticks"—heavy hickory poles used to move cattle at stockyards. For months, melees involving hundreds of men filled downtown Gratiot Avenue where both plants were located. In the summer of 1941 the federal government finally stepped in, ordering NLRB-monitored elections at both plants to determine which union was preferred by the workers. Coca-Cola went to the UBW in a close vote, but the Teamsters held on to the Dossin workers. Perhaps the most significant outcome, however, was that bottlers and other production workers at Dossin were now members of the IBT. The Detroit Teamsters were now committed to organizing outside their traditional ranks to preclude the forays of rival unions.[26]

Five

The Price of Peace

The national defense program requires the greatest possible unity of the American people in order that Hitlerism can be wiped from the face of the earth.—DETROIT AND WAYNE COUNTY INDUSTRIAL UNION COUNCIL, OCTOBER 21, 1941[1]

Jimmy Hoffa's world in the climactic year of 1941 was shaped by the twin impulses that defined the CIO. The first CIO impulse—to expand the industrial union movement—produced a challenge to Hoffa's power that forced the young Teamster leader and his colleagues to transform themselves not only into a potent military force but, more important, into an effective vehicle for the interests of the working class. At the end of the year, however, the CIO's second impulse—to participate in the management of society—trumped the desire to expand and created for the Teamsters an unrivaled position in the trucking industry.

By the winter of 1941, participants on both sides of the war between the Teamsters and the CIO knew that the attitude of the United Automobile Workers would be a critical determinant of the outcome. The full support of the drive against the IBT by the auto union, which had become one of the largest and most powerful institutions in Detroit, would almost certainly doom the Teamsters. In February, the internal political dynamics of the CIO appeared to settle the matter decisively against Hoffa's union. R. J. Thomas, president of the UAW, endorsed the CIO's campaign to organize construction workers and instructed all UAW locals to assist the efforts of Lewis's UCWOC by "[calling] to the attention of A. F. of L. workers the fact they should join a CIO union." Further, UAW locals were directed to demand contract clauses mandating that the employers hire only CIO contractors for construction work. This coup for the Lewis forces was the end result of a long trail of patronage. In 1939 Thomas was selected to be UAW president by Philip Murray, who had been John L. Lewis's right-hand man in the United Mine Workers for twenty years. In the first months of his presidency, Murray was still loyal to his mentor despite their disagreement over labor's involvement with the state generally and with Roosevelt's war mobilization in particular.[2] Until their relationship soured later, Murray was willing to lend his support to Lewis's organizing initiatives and therefore instructed Thomas to throw the weight of his union behind the UCWOC. Hoffa and the Detroit Teamsters were no doubt unaware of the politics behind Thomas's announcement, but they knew well that their vitally important unofficial non-aggression pact with the UAW, which had been maintained since the founding of the auto union, was in jeopardy.[3]

Shortly after Thomas's announcement, another shot was fired across the Teamsters' bow. At the annual conference of the United Retail Workers in Chicago, URWDSE president Samuel Wolchok announced the beginning of a nationwide warehouse organizing drive concentrating in New York, Boston, Chicago, and Detroit. Tucker Smith was appointed to a special committee to oversee the warehouse drive. In the Retail Workers' newspaper, Smith was quoted as saying that "the unscrupulous methods of AFL Teamsters in signing backdoor contracts" at warehouses in Detroit that were already organized by the URWDSE "was the main deterrent to organization." The CIO union had been organizing warehouse workers in Detroit for more than a year, often in conflict with the Teamsters, but the full commitment of the international union's resources to the drive made the URWDSE an even more potent opponent for the Teamsters. Over the next several months the URWDSE scored several victories at warehouses in Detroit, many in competition with the Teamsters. The most damaging blow came at the annex of the C. F. Smith grocery chain (Hoffa's employer when he was twelve years old), whose 335 employees made it one of the largest warehouses in Detroit. In a March 13 recognition election overseen by a federal arbitrator, the URWDSE defeated the Teamsters in a humiliating shutout, 197 to zero (121 workers voted for "no union").[4]

Ten days after losing C. F. Smith to the URWDSE, the Teamsters fought against another incursion by their opponents. On March 24, Hoffa and Brennan directed a blockade of the Detroit Union Produce Terminal, a central depot that distributed perishable foods to every grocery store and wholesaler in the city, and which was then negotiating a contract with the URWDSE. At 4 a.m., 200 trucks driven by Teamster members and owned by companies under Teamster contracts filled the streets around the produce terminal, shutting off most of the city's fresh food supply. Later that day Hoffa was quoted in the *Detroit News* as rejecting an appeal to allow some food to be moved to a tuberculosis sanitarium. On March 25, Hoffa and Brennan issued an ultimatum through the press declaring that unless the 400 employees of the terminal joined Teamsters Local 337, "the blockade will stay in effect until the last brick falls out of the terminal." This convinced enough of the workers, who had previously voted 41 to 40 against joining the union, to accede to the Teamsters' demands. The company then signed a closed-shop contract with the IBT, granting Hoffa and Brennan considerable power over the Detroit grocery industry. To extend their hold over the city's food distribution industry, the Teamsters also blockaded the Eastern and Western produce markets, where they won similar contracts, and took control of the workers at the city's egg and poultry wholesalers from the much smaller Amalgamated Meat Cutters and Butcher Workers. Every carton of produce, eggs, or poultry sold by any grocer, from mom-and-pop stores to Kroger, would have to first pass through the hands of a Teamster who could refuse delivery until the retailer signed a union contract. For several more years, the Teamsters used that leverage in their campaign to keep the CIO out of the grocery business.[5]

The results at the produce terminal, however, did not stop the CIO's metastatic expansion into IBT domains. While the Teamsters were surrounding the grocery depot, newly formed bakery locals of the URWDSE met in Detroit to establish the Michigan CIO Bakery and Confectionery Workers Council and to map out "a coordinated drive for the state." The announcement of the drive did not mention that Teamsters Local 51, one of the oldest locals in the Detroit Joint Council, had organized bakery drivers since the early 1930s. Meanwhile, the Retail Workers were also moving into drugstores, threatening to break the grip of the Retail Clerks' Independent Protective Association (RCIPA), which in Detroit had become in fact the Teamsters' dependent protective association. In April, the URWDSE and the RCIPA both began organizing workers at Cunningham drugstores, whose 99 outlets made it the largest chain in Eastern Michigan. Hoffa initially used the RCIPA as a bulwark against the URWDSE, but later converted it into a vehicle for a counterattack against the CIO union.[6]

As threatening as the encroachments of the Retail Workers were, even worse news for the Teamsters came in April, when the UAW announced it would join the fight against the IBT. Thomas, whose selection to head the UAW was largely engineered by Hillman, pledged the support of his union's 200,000 members to the Retail Workers' organizing drive in Michigan. "The two CIO unions will work as a unit to complete the organization of retail, wholesale and warehouse employees in every city and town of the state," Thomas declared.

> There have been reports that the AFL Teamsters union is attempting to organize in the jurisdiction of the CIO's retail and wholesale union. Some claims have been made that there is a "deal" between the UAW-CIO and the teamsters to further such organization work. I want to make it plain that the UAW-CIO is solidly behind the United Retail, Wholesale and Warehouse Employees Union, will give it all possible support in its organizing campaigns and will not agree to any deal which would hand over retail, wholesale and warehouse workers to any other union.[7]

To the Teamsters and the rest of the Wayne County Federation of Labor (WCFL), this was outright treachery. In a front-page editorial, the *Detroit Labor News*, the newspaper of the WCFL, bitterly remarked that the Teamsters' many boycotts of General Motors and Chrysler during UAW strikes, which gave crucial support to the fledgling auto union in its initial organizing drives, "did not prevent" Thomas from assisting the CIO pirates. Far more important to the Teamsters than their sense of being betrayed, it appeared that their opposition now included the awesome might of the auto workers union.[8]

Soon after the UAW's announcement, the Teamsters' war with the CIO grew deadly. As federal defense spending pumped resources into the previously depleted Detroit construction industry, the Teamsters and other AFL building trades unions fought with the UCWOC over a share of the largesse, creating a vicious battlefield on the city's streets. While claiming to be defending the UCWOC against AFL raids, Dennie Lewis clearly suggested that his union was intended to replace, not complement, the older construction unions. "We cannot sit back while the AFL building trades pile up a war chest of millions through picking the pockets of helpless workers who ask only a chance to work on defense projects," he announced in late February. "The time has come when we must strike against the racketeer who preys on national defense."

Following Lewis's declaration, UCWOC organizers fanned out to various construction companies in the Detroit area. The Detroit Teamsters responded once again with unrestrained militancy. On April 21, Teamsters Local 247, with the aid of Hoffa's Local 299, struck the Detroit Lumber Company after its owners refused to grant recognition to the union. Two weeks later, with the company still holding firm, the Teamsters expanded the strike to include all of the union's lumber drivers in the Detroit area, claiming that other firms were assisting the struck company by secretly filling its orders. Shortly thereafter the Detroit Building Trades Council, the local federation of AFL construction unions, shut down operations at all commercial and non-defense sites in support of the Teamsters. With the employers remaining steadfast, and violent confrontations between scabs and strikers breaking out at lumberyards and construction sites across the city, on May 10 the Teamsters further escalated the conflict with a threat to call a general strike of all trucking in Detroit.[9]

Much of the violence was taking place outside the P. J. Currier Lumber Company, one of the largest building materials suppliers in southeast Michigan. Both the building trades and UAW Local 3 had tried without success to organize the Currier employees since the company's founding in 1937. In the fall of 1940, P. J. Currier sought to take advantage of the round-the-clock construction of airplane and tank factories in the Detroit area by expanding his operations into prefabricated housing for defense workers. Currier's business took off, reaching a payroll of 1,000 employees by 1941, and so did the unions' drives to organize it. For the Teamsters and the building trades, the Currier firm was an especially important target because it was the only construction company in Detroit with its own supply-and-delivery system, including trucks, which meant that it was fully autonomous and virtually invulnerable to secondary boycotts. During the strike, Currier hired scores of "guards," many of them African-American, outfitted them with helmets and clubs, and assigned them to accompany his trucks into and out of the company gates at Van Dyke Avenue and Davison Street on the East Side. Teamster pickets attacked the trucks and the guards at the gates, then sent convoys of cars loaded with men to intercept the trucks that got through. Several Currier trucks were overturned, and injuries mounted on both sides as the strike continued to escalate.[10]

On May 12, a Teamster picket named Arthur G. Queasbarth died after he was struck on the head by a brick thrown by a Currier guard outside the company gates. More than 7,000 people attended the funeral, held during a rainstorm in a modest mortuary on Mack Avenue. The surge of solidarity generated by Queasbarth's martyrdom and the public scorn directed at Currier brought victory to the Teamsters in what the *Detroit Labor News* called "the greatest strike the AFL unions have called in Detroit in many years." Two days after Queasbarth's funeral, the Detroit Retail Lumber Dealers' Association signed a contract with Local 247 granting increased wages and improved working conditions to the 4,000 workers at several companies covered under the agreement. It also gave the Teamsters a union shop, which secured almost the entire Detroit building materials delivery industry against the UCWOC. The only exception was the Currier Company, which refused to sign the agreement and was soon offered a new way to hold off the Teamsters by the CIO.

Shortly after the announcement of the contract with the lumber association, the Michigan State Convention of the CIO passed a resolution condemning the "graft-ridden" building trades unions, endorsing UCWOC, and adopting the slogan "CIO factories to work in and CIO-built homes to live in." Negotiations between Currier and representatives from the industrial union organization soon commenced.

Meanwhile, John L. Lewis was setting his sights even higher, threatening to take from the Teamsters the very heart of their union.[11]

Purge

Following the 1938 central states organizing campaign, Tobin and the Trotskyist leaders of Local 544 in Minneapolis maintained an uneasy coexistence. The IBT president and close ally of Franklin Roosevelt was embarrassed by the presence of unabashed antiwar radicals in the midst of his union, but he was reluctant to move against them, knowing that the Trotskyists' organizing success had extended their power base deep into the Minneapolis labor hierarchy. All that changed in the spring of 1941, when Tobin decided to prove his loyalty to Roosevelt and the war preparedness program by purging the Trotskyists. After a series of meetings devoted to the question of the "communistic, alien" officers of Local 544, in June the IBT General Executive Board declared that all officers and members of the union were barred from membership in "subversive, revolutionary" organizations and ordered 544 to be placed under Tobin's trusteeship. But before an emissary from the international reached Minneapolis to inform the local of the board's decision, the leaders of 544 called a general meeting of the local at which the membership voted to break with the IBT and ask for a CIO charter.[12]

The Lewis brothers, who did not mind having anti-Roosevelt, antiwar unionists in their organization, leapt at the opportunity to take a large portion of the Teamsters' membership without spending a dollar on an organizing drive. Dennie Lewis immediately wired the leadership of the newly renamed Local 544-CIO with both a warm welcome and an open declaration of war against the Teamsters. "Will be happy to charter a local union of truck drivers and helpers in the Minneapolis area," proclaimed Lewis. "We visualize this move on the part of truck drivers in Minneapolis into our organization as the first step towards the complete organization of truck drivers in the United States in the CIO." Just three days later, at a CIO conference in Chicago, Dennie Lewis announced the formation of the Motor Transport and Allied Workers Industrial Union as a subsidiary of the UCWOC, and the launching of "a streamlined CIO organizing campaign among the motor transport and allied workers of the entire Midwest area" to bring them "into a modern, progressive industrial union."[13]

While Local 544 was severing its ties with the Teamsters, reports arrived at the IBT headquarters that the general trucking industry in Detroit would be the next target for the Lewis crew and that Dennie Lewis was asking for assistance from key leaders in the UAW. These developments reverberated throughout the Teamsters' hierarchy. Tobin shot off a letter to R. J. Thomas that contained a less-than-subtle threat. "Of course we must, we are bound and obligated, as you know, to protect the jurisdiction of our International Organization in Detroit or any other place," Tobin warned the auto workers president. "I am writing you now so that in your official capacity you may give thought and consideration to whether it is not better to try to continue the harmonious relations which have existed for many years past between our respective organizations . . . or to open up other avenues of encroachment which will lead only to bitterness and conflict." In Detroit, Hoffa and his colleagues, all of them grade-school or high-school dropouts, didn't know or care about the Lewis brothers' ideas about "modern, progressive" unions. What they did know was that a competitor was coming to town to take away their members. When Tobin asked for their assistance in a counteroffensive, they gladly obliged.[14]

At Tobin's request, Hoffa and a squad of his locals' best fighters headed for Minneapolis, where they joined hundreds of IBT men from across the Midwest in an invasion of the CIO stronghold. Over the next two weeks, Hoffa and the Detroit Teamsters distinguished themselves in what the *Minneapolis Times* described as a mission of forceful diplomacy:

Scores of cars, carrying an estimated 200 AFL men cruised the warehouse district and the larger plants, putting the pressure on, when necessary, to sign up drivers and helpers. . . . One big caravan in the mop-up consisted of several cars with Michigan license plates. The Michigan cars bore nearly a score of labor huskies who were very determined and very tough when they moved into the various plants of the wholesale district. In each instance these huskies simply accosted 544 men, persuaded them to accept the new 544-AFL buttons and sign up with the new AFL setup.[15]

Hoffa's men often did more than "persuade" the defectors to rejoin the Teamsters. The Detroit crew, the largest contingent in the invasion force, literally knocked hundreds of truck drivers and warehousemen out of the CIO and back into the IBT by beating them until they agreed to sign Teamster membership cards. The newspaper of 544-CIO called such tactics the work of "the bottom muck of the IBT."[16]

In addition to sending in the military, Tobin employed several other coercive measures against the Trotskyists and their CIO allies in Minneapolis. The Teamster president declared a national boycott on trucks driven by CIO members, and through the services of a powerful law firm procured a court order that forced the CIO to return Local 544's office, funds, and property to the IBT. Tobin also asked for assistance from his friend in the White House by warning of the dangers posed by the Trotskyists, "who believe in the policies of foreign, radical governments" and who "must be in some way prevented from pursuing this dangerous course."

Roosevelt was eager to quell both disruptive jurisdictional conflicts and antiwar sentiment in the labor movement. Late in June, while Tobin's heavies were wreaking havoc against the Trotskyist-CIO alliance, agents from the FBI raided Socialist Workers Party headquarters in Minneapolis and St. Paul. Less than a month later, Farrell Dobbs, the three Dunne brothers, and five other 544-CIO officials were indicted for violation of the recently passed Smith Act, which made it a crime to advocate the violent overthrow of the government. After a month-long trial that began in October, several 544-CIO leaders, including Vince Dunne and Farrell Dobbs, were convicted and given sentences ranging from twelve to eighteen months in prison. Grant Dunne had committed suicide shortly before the trial began and two other leaders of 544-CIO, Kelly Postal and Karl Skoglund, received prison terms for convictions on other charges.[17]

Much has been made of the violence directed against the Trotskyist-CIO alliance and the government's intervention on behalf of the IBT. Partisans and academics alike have concluded that these acts of heavy-handed coercion were the decisive elements in the Minneapolis purge, and indeed they were important in determining the outcome. But another determinant of the conflict has been ignored by the chroniclers of this important episode, a dynamic that provided an important lesson in the education of Jimmy Hoffa.[18] On June 24, nearly ten days after the federal indictment was handed down and two weeks after the arrival of Tobin's ground forces, Joe Casey, who was directing IBT activities in Minneapolis, telephoned Tom Flynn, Tobin's chief assistant, to explain that such measures were not sufficient for the Teamsters to recapture Local 544:

> Now here is a thing that I would like you to get over to Tobin. The idea is this: And if I am to work this thing, I want this thoroughly understood—that this thing, as far as the rank and file is concerned, is not at all stabilized. Here is the kick-back we are getting now—that these fellows are like a pendulum on a clock which swings back and forth—C.I.O.—A.F.L.—C.I.O.—A.F.L., depending entirely on who was the last group that talked to them. They say that the boys have two buttons—C.I.O. in one pocket and A.F.L. in the other, and they don't wear any button, but when an A.F.L. [organizer] comes up, they start putting on the A.F.L. button. . . . Now if you can see my point, my contention is that this thing is not at all won. We have not got an organization here in the strict sense of the word. It is true that some dues have been coming in, but as far as the bulk of the membership, represented by over five thousand people, I don't want anybody to get the impression, because it is not true that we have them solidly with us.

Casey understood from the behavior of the rank and file that force could win them over only temporarily. Once the fists stopped flying and the Trotskyists were removed from the scene, the contest boiled down to its essence, as far as the workers were concerned. "They swing back and forth," he explained to Flynn, "and it is just a job that will take about two or three weeks to get over, and what we have to do is get two or three good contracts behind us, and that is what we are working on." Behind the pronouncements by both sides that the struggle was an ideological contest, Casey recognized that it was now simply a market competition in which the union that produced the best contracts would win. Tobin followed Casey's advice.[19]

In mid-July, the IBT president ordered Teamster organizers in Minneapolis to redirect their intimidation tactics toward employers. Within one week of Tobin's directive, Local 544-AFL unleashed a torrent of demands for large wage increases. When most of the firms refused to accede to the union's wishes, strike notices went out to four department stores, sixteen wholesale grocers, twenty grocery markets, fifteen wholesale paper houses, and seven bedding and furniture manufacturers. The city's trucking employers, who were feeling the heat from both the Teamsters and the CIO, offered Local 544-AFL an increase of five cents per hour, hoping to head off what they considered to be the more aggressive of the two competing unions. The Teamsters refused what they called a "sweetheart" offer, demanded wage increases of 10 to 12 cents per hour, and threatened a general trucking strike to get the raises.

With thousands of workers on the verge of reaping a bonanza from inter-union competition, the state stepped in to save the employers and restore industrial order. Minnesota Governor Harold Stassen invoked the "public interest" clause in the state's Labor Relations Act and imposed a thirty-day strike ban and mandatory arbitration. The state labor conciliator, Alfred P. Blair, then proposed terms for an agreement between the Teamsters and the trucking firms, ignoring the CIO. The proposal granted only six-cent raises, but because Blair indicated that he would keep the CIO out of the picture, Casey quickly consented. In September, Blair granted Local 544-AFL exclusive representation rights for all truck drivers and helpers, effectively eliminating competition between unions in the Minneapolis trucking industry. Blair correctly argued that his ruling would "promote and preserve industrial peace and safeguard the continued flow of commerce." What he did not mention was that by barring the CIO from competing for workers in trucking, the Teamsters would have little incentive to be accountable to those workers and would be happy to settle for meager raises. A similar chain of events soon occurred in Detroit, where Hoffa applied the lessons he had learned from Joe Casey in Minneapolis.[20]

Counterattack

When Hoffa returned to Detroit in late June, Dennie Lewis's forces had not yet arrived, but other CIO unions were closing in from every direction. The IBT's old nemesis on the West Coast, the International Longshoremen's and Warehousemen's Union, had begun expanding into the longshore industry in midwestern port cities and assisting its sister organization, the National Maritime Union (NMU), in organizing seamen on the Great Lakes. The IBT was naturally concerned when ILWU and NMU organizers appeared on the docks in Detroit, since many of the Teamsters' employers did business with the shipping lines arrayed along the Detroit River and would be susceptible to secondary boycotts were the CIO to organize the longshore workers and sailors. On June 20, while Hoffa was still in Minneapolis, Bert Brennan and Local 299 military captain Rolland McMaster led a squad of men in a frontal assault against a picket line of ILWU and NMU members at the Nicholson Terminal and Dock Company in Ecorse, a port town adjacent to Detroit. After the pickets were dispelled, Brennan and McMaster cornered one of the NMU men and beat him with a baseball bat. The next day the man died of a heart attack, which the NMU national office claimed was a result of the beating. A month later, McMaster and two other Teamsters were charged with assault for an attack that put two organizers from the bakery division of the URWDSE in the hospital. When word came from the Teamsters' friends in the police department that McMaster would be charged with murder for the assault on the NMU picket if he didn't leave town, George Fitzgerald, the union's lawyer, convinced the burly Teamster to enlist in the Army. McMaster served four years overseas, where he was put to good use as a military policeman.[21]

Further inland, the CIO's Retail Workers union continued its vigorous organizing. By the end of June, the URWDSE had reeled off a string of impressive contracts with clothing and department stores, warehouses, and bakeries in the city and had persuaded hundreds of Teamsters and other AFL members to switch affiliation. In an act of desperation, twenty Teamsters ambushed and stomped URWDSE regional director Tucker Smith, putting him in the hospital with a concussion. Taking a page from the Teamsters' experiences in Minneapolis, Hoffa then chose a more effective response to the Retail Workers.

In August, he negotiated "peace terms" with the URWDSE which included an agreement that the Retail Workers would not launch organizing drives in plants where the Teamsters or other AFL unions had existing contracts and the Teamsters would not sign contracts covering plants where the Retail Workers were organizing. By barring violence and sweetheart contracts, the two unions essentially agreed to reduce the conflict to a simple market competition for unorganized workers. This was bad news for Detroit's employers.[22]

Shortly after making the peace agreement with the URWDSE, Hoffa and Brennan launched a massive organizing campaign in concert with their front union, the RCIPA, in department stores and warehouses across the city. By November, the Teamsters and the RCIPA scored several contract victories and recruited seven other local unions into their newly established Department Store Organizing Committee. Their CIO rival responded to the challenge with even greater militancy, signing generous contracts at several department stores and warehouses within weeks. Best of all for the workers, the competition between the two unions forced the terms of contracts onto the front pages of Detroit's labor newspapers. Throughout the late summer and fall, the *Michigan CIO News*, the Retail Workers' newspaper, and the Michigan Federation of Labor's *Detroit Labor News* not only carried headlines trumpeting their most recent victories and denigrating their rivals' efforts, but often published the entire texts of the opposition's contracts. The language used by the unions indicated the principal interests of the workers for whom they competed. Gone were the CIO's pledges to bring "patriotic responsibility" and "American democracy" to the workplace, as were the Teamsters' accusations that their rivals were "radicals" bearing "foreign ideas." Now both sides limited their appeals to strict economic terms: "AFL Clerks to Make Comparison of CIO Pacts," "Detroit Bakery Wins 10 to 17 Cents Higher Wages Than AFL," "Neisner Contract with CIO Called 'Disgrace' by AFL," "Clerks Call Sears CIO Strike a 'Boner'."[23]

The rivalry between the unions guaranteed that workers would get militant, accountable representation for their dues. Though both sides continued to accuse each other of signing sweetheart deals with employers, in such a fierce contest for members neither union could hope to agree to an inferior contract and hold on to the workers after it expired. Finally, the competition forced both unions to grow exponentially. By the end of 1941 the URWDSE, the Teamsters, and the RCIPA had organized virtually every retail store, warehouse, bakery, and dairy in the Detroit area. In 1942 the membership of Teamsters Local 337, which handled the retail and warehousing industries for the Detroit Joint Council, stood at 3,500, an increase of 250 percent in less than four years. Even Tobin, writing in the October 1941 issue of the union's magazine, acknowledged that the tremendous expansion of the IBT "was due to the fact that the CIO decided to spend their money in an endeavor to raid the International Brotherhood of Teamsters . . . especially in Detroit."[24]

Showdown

By the summer of 1941, Hoffa had gained a reputation as the leading CIO-fighter in the Wayne County Federation of Labor (WCFL). In August, when a CIO union was attempting to organize Detroit Street Railway (DSR) workers, which had been under contract with an AFL affiliate, the WCFL asked the Teamsters to help physically repel the poachers. But instead of contributing his men to bust heads, Hoffa stepped in to help broker a deal with the mayor that allowed the AFL to maintain control over the streetcar workers. At a rally following the recognition of the AFL union, Hoffa indulged in the obligatory red-baiting of the CIO. The rival municipal employees union "and their communist pals are not going to take over the city government," he declared to a hall of 2,000 streetcar workers. "The Teamsters District Council will do everything in its power to protect legitimate trade unions in the AFL from CIO raids. This CIO gang is the greatest spreader of false propaganda and the greatest operators of mimeo-graph machines that you ever saw. They promise you their shirt and all they want is your vote but they won't give you any representation with your boss." Behind the rhetoric there was a more practical result of Hoffa's intervention in the streetcar jurisdictional struggle—he had headed off one avenue for the CIO while saving his forces for the more important battle ahead.[25]

The climactic showdown with John L. Lewis's troops came in September. By that time, the UCWOC had largely abandoned the cause in Minneapolis and began concentrating on Detroit. The Lewis brothers brought in C. Russell Turner, an official from the Washington office of the CIO, to direct the drive against the Detroit Teamsters. At a press conference on September 5 in the newly established UCWOC headquarters in downtown Detroit, Turner announced that the Motor City would be the spearhead of a national organizing campaign among truck drivers, both non-union and Teamster members. Turner claimed that he had already begun negotiating with automobile transport firms in southeast Michigan, the core of Hoffa's Local 299.[26] Standing with Turner at the press conference were R. J. Thomas of the UAW and Joseph Pagano, treasurer of the Detroit and Wayne County CIO Council, who condemned the Teamsters and pledged their organizations' support for the UCWOC drive. Thomas attacked the "arbitrary conduct of the AFL Teamster big-shots" while Pagano promised that his organization would "guarantee protection and offer the benefits of the CIO to any teamsters or driver[s] in [the trucking] industry against gangsterism or hoodlumism." A few days later, Turner made clear the scope of the CIO's intentions at a meeting of Local 544-CIO in Minneapolis. "You started something in Minneapolis which has the AFL racketeers trembling in their boots," Turner declared. "Another blow like that—and the organization of the Michigan teamsters will be such a blow—will mean the crumbling of the AFL Teamsters Union as a national organization." The Detroit Teamsters were targeted by the UCWOC not only for their size and importance within the IBT, Turner told the meeting, but also because they "became drunk with power" and had prevented the growth of smaller CIO unions such as the Dairy Workers and Retail Workers.[27]

Frank Martel, president of the Wayne County Federation of Labor and no friend of the Teamsters, issued a rebuttal to the CIO which was less an endorsement of the IBT than a warning of the Teamsters' ability to defend themselves. "Fools rush in where angels fear to tread," said Martel, who knew well the Detroit Teamsters' hardball tactics. "Of all the places that the CIO could choose to attack the AFL, I am sure that they will get all the entertainment they are looking for from the Teamsters." Indeed, the UCWOC "organizers," many of whom were actually petty criminals brought in by bus from Minneapolis, were given an energetic welcome soon after they arrived in Detroit. Upon getting word that the invasion had begun, Hoffa and his men armed themselves to the teeth and cruised the streets on the lookout for CIO poachers. When they saw one talking to a Teamster carhaul driver, they attacked with breathtaking ferocity. Baseball bats, blackjacks, and knives were the favorite weapons, but for the first time the Teamsters also used guns. The UCWOC's musclemen did not back down. Over several days, Detroit's downtown streets were frequently filled with car chases, shoot-outs, and sprawling fistfights.[28]

Several journalistic and scholarly accounts of the dramatic battle with the UCWOC accept a claim, made shortly after Hoffa's disappearance in 1975, that the CIO raid led the Teamster leader to establish an alliance with Santo Perrone, head of the notorious Sicilian criminal organization on Detroit's East Side, and that the manpower provided by Perrone's henchmen decided the outcome of the battle. The claim was first made by the journalist Dan Moldea in a series of articles written about Hoffa's disappearance for *Playboy* magazine (published as a book in 1978) that also suggested Hoffa's involvement in Central Intelligence Agency plots to assassinate Fidel Castro and in the assassination of John F. Kennedy. Moldea's evidence tying Hoffa to Perrone in 1941 consists of a purported statement made by Dave Johnson—an organizer for Local 299 who became president of the local shortly before Hoffa's disappearance—that because the CIO presented an unexpected physical challenge, "Jimmy went to see Santo Perrone," and a similar quote from an unnamed "close Hoffa associate." From this, Moldea builds his thesis that the "tragedy" of Hoffa's subsequent career and ultimate demise was determined in the fall of 1941 by a fateful "pact with the underworld." Hoffa's alleged employment of criminals against the CIO "became the major factor in his rapid plunge from union reformer to labor racketeer."[29]

Moldea's claim provides a convenient historical narrative to accompany his more legitimate assumption that Hoffa's apparent assassination in 1975 was carried out by Mafia members, yet the available evidence suggests that it is false. Johnson did not join the staff of Local 299 until after 1941, and his recollection contradicts that of Rolland McMaster, who was a leading participant in the street fights with the CIO. Both McMaster and Joe Franco, one of Hoffa's chief lieutenants, admit that the Teamsters initiated relations with Perrone, but not until the late 1940s, several years after the UCWOC invasion. It is also significant that of the twelve men from the Teamsters' forces who were reported in the press to have been arrested or sent to the hospital after altercations with CIO men in 1941, only two, Tom Briglia and Joe Galbo, had Italian surnames, and both were longtime officers of Teamster locals.[30] The only participant in the battles who possessed an Italian surname, a criminal record, and no prior union experience was Joseph Delia, who was arrested for possession of a machine gun while fighting on behalf of the UCWOC against the Teamsters. These facts perhaps explain why neither of the congressional committees that later investigated Hoffa's ties to criminals mentioned any connection with Perrone or the East Side gang.[31]

Dennie Lewis and other CIO leaders in Detroit did complain to the press that the Teamsters were using "thugs and racketeers" to intimidate drivers into staying with the IBT, but the CIO accused the Teamsters of "importing" the goon squads from "out of town," not from the East Side. It is possible that men were brought in to assist the Detroit Teamsters, but most likely they would have been Teamsters from other cities, as had been the case in Minneapolis. By September, Tobin had made the defense of the Detroit jurisdictions the union's chief priority and offered to send in reinforcements from as far away as the West Coast. In response to a *Detroit News* reporter's question as to whether they had brought in outside help, an anonymous Detroit Teamster official provided a remarkably candid answer. "We don't have to yet," he said. "We have enough boys of our own to handle the present situation. Naturally, if this gets to open warfare we will have to bring in some outsiders to present our case just as we helped out in Minneapolis."[32]

Though it is doubtful that Hoffa allied his Detroit locals with criminal organizations, it is certainly true that he employed a number of independent criminals as organizers and enforcers. James Cassily, one of the lead organizers for the Detroit Joint Council in the 1940s, had a twenty-year career as a burglar before joining the Teamsters. Harry Ames, who worked for several Detroit unions after serving a lengthy prison sentence for blowing up a theater in Indiana to help the owner collect insurance payments, was hired by Hoffa after he defected from the UCWOC. Perhaps the most notorious Teamster organizer, however, was Tom Burke, a street tough recruited from Chicago by Brennan. Burke took pride in his ability to handle a pistol and often posed for official union photographs with his right hand inside the pocket of his overcoat. He was also known as the most efficient organizer on the staff. Several owners of Detroit trucking firms signed contracts with the union after only a few seconds of Burke holding a gun to their head.[33]

Unlikely Allies

The image of clandestine dealings with Mafia godfathers makes for dramatic (and cinematic) history, but it obscures a more important story about the benefits of rival unionism and the contrary effects of corporatism. Typically, Hoffa's first response to the CIO challengers was to bash in their heads, which he and several other Teamsters did in a bloody invasion of the UCWOC headquarters. This slowed the Lewis forces for a moment, but some carhaul drivers continued to defect to the CIO. After a week of the baseball-bat approach, Hoffa was forced yet again to confront the fact that the allegiance of his members could be secured only by giving them what they wanted. On September 10, Hoffa issued a statement to his members via the *Detroit News*. "We have been organized six years in the car-hauling field and never had any trouble, which is proof our members are satisfied," Hoffa claimed. Yet in the same statement he announced that new wage scales were being negotiated with carhaul firms, implicitly acknowledging that the CIO posed a real threat to his union. A few days later Hoffa threatened to strike the carhaul firms if his demands weren't met, then upped the ante, vowing in a conference with the mayor to close down the city "tighter than a drum." As in the competitions with the Dairy Workers and the Retail Workers, the Teamsters were forced by their rivals to be accountable to their members' economic desires.[34]

The Lewis brothers and Russell Turner now hoped for the active assistance of the mighty UAW, which by refusing to hand over new cars from the assembly lines could exert enormous pressure on carhaul firms to sign with the CIO. Were this to happen, the only hope for Hoffa and the Teamsters would be to mobilize the rank and file by proving their ability to win first-rate contracts from the employers. Given the statements made by R. J. Thomas through the summer of 1941, it seemed likely the pressure would soon be on the Teamsters.[35] Unfortunately for the carhaul drivers of Detroit, the same logic of corporatism that created the beneficial competition between unions would soon save Hoffa and the Teamster leaders from having to work for their members.

Like Hillman and Murray, Walter Reuther, the rising star in the UAW, welcomed the Roosevelt administration's war mobilization efforts as an opportunity to advance the idea of a managed economy. At the time of the UCWOC raid on the Teamsters, Reuther was aggressively promoting his plan to convert Detroit into a mammoth military production complex. His "500 planes a day" program would be overseen by "industrial councils" made up of representatives from labor, corporations, and the government. To enact such a plan—and make it politically palatable for Roosevelt—Reuther knew that the fractious and increasingly aggressive labor movement would have to be shaped into a disciplined and unified workforce. So when Dennie Lewis and representatives from the Dairy Workers and Retail Workers asked the UAW Executive Board at its quarterly meeting in Chicago to assist the UCWOC raid on the Teamsters, Reuther stood in the way of his militant brothers in the industrial union movement. Countering calls by some of his colleagues on the board to join the attack on the Teamsters, Reuther argued that such all-out warfare between the workers who delivered the parts and materials to airplane factories and the workers inside those factories could virtually cripple the center of the nation's defense industry. Reuther also feared that helping the UCWOC would further the ascendancy of John L. Lewis, the "irresponsible" opponent of Roosevelt and the war.[36]

Once word hit the streets that the UAW might not come to the aid of the UCWOC, the Teamsters cooled their strike threats and stood pat, hoping to be let off the hook by the socially responsible leaders sitting in Chicago. On September 19, their prayers were answered. Cajoled by Reuther through five days of meetings on the issue, the UAW Executive Board passed a resolution extending only moral support to the Teamsters' rivals. Opening with an admonishment to the UCWOC raiders that "the organization of the unorganized workers is the main task of the CIO," the resolution offered only a condemnation of the Teamsters' strong-arm tactics and an endorsement of the CIO unions' right to protect themselves "in the pursuit of their legitimate union activities." Dennie Lewis soon abandoned the UCWOC campaign in carhauling, and Hoffa's promises to raise wages in the industry were not heard again. The Detroit Teamsters had achieved their first monopoly—carhaul drivers had nowhere else to go.[37]

Meanwhile, Reuther's corporatist counterpart in Washington, Sidney Hillman, was putting an end to the UCWOC's incursions into another Teamster field. On September 12, the UCWOC announced that it had signed a contract with the Currier Lumber Company, the lone holdout after the Teamsters' lumber strike in May, making Currier the first major lumber company in Detroit to sign with the CIO. The five-year agreement, signed by Currier only one hour after the company received it, granted the UCWOC exclusive bargaining rights and an automatic dues check-off system for the 1,000 employees of the company but did not alter the wage scales. According to the apoplectic *Detroit Labor News*, this was a "stinking sweetheart agreement" made by the "prostitute" CIO and the "fink lumber yard" that chained the Currier employees to the CIO solely to keep out the Teamsters and was therefore nothing less than "a repeal of the emancipation proclamation." Such protests did not stop the Federal Works Administration (FWA) a week later from accepting Currier's bid for the construction of 300 houses for defense workers. The Detroit Teamsters and the Wayne County Building Trades Council immediately threatened a general strike that would cause the "paralyzing of defense and other construction in the Detroit area," including the enormous Willow Run airplane plant near Ypsilanti, if the FWA awarded the contract to Currier. Hillman, then associate director of the Office of Production Management (OPM), promptly instructed the FWA to reverse its decision and issued an order granting AFL unions a monopoly over all defense building contracts.[38]

Hillman, one of the principal architects of the CIO, was forced to explain his actions to the militants in the industrial union movement as well as to government officials wary of granting monopoly power to any labor organization. In his testimony to the Special Committee to Investigate the National Defense Program and in correspondence with associates, Hillman alluded to the Teamsters' strike in May and the ferocity of inter-union competition in Detroit as evidence that the IBT and the Building Trades were serious about their threat to shut down the heart of the defense industry. "My task is to make sure, as far as possible, that production proceeds without interruptions that might arise from unsound labor practices," Hillman told the committee. Despite widespread criticism leveled at Hillman and the OPM, the policy barring the CIO from defense construction stood.[39]

Word went out from Hillman and Murray in Washington to CIO affiliates in Michigan that the Lewis brothers and UCWOC were *personae non gratae*. On October 21, the Wayne County CIO Council condemned the raid on the Teamsters, arguing that the effort to defeat fascism in Europe required a unified labor force. At the national CIO Convention, held the week of November 17 in Detroit, the hopes of the Lewis brothers to win grassroots support for the UCWOC drive were dashed as patriotic fervor swept over the delegates. The UAW, Steel Workers, and Amalgamated Clothing Workers campaigned against the UCWOC, as did the hundreds of communist and fellow-traveler delegates who had been staunch defenders of Roosevelt's war policies since the German invasion of the Soviet Union in June. Dennie Lewis, organizers for the UCWOC, and Mineworkers delegates stalked the floor, haranguing their opponents and shouting "To hell with Murray." Fistfights broke out, including one between Dennie Lewis and Michigan CIO Council president Gus Scholle. After a resolution supporting the UCWOC died in a subcommittee, the Lewis group finally accepted defeat.[40]

Reuther, Hillman, and Murray had placed their desires to be responsible social managers over even the interest of building the CIO, and in so doing dealt devastating blows to John L. Lewis's project of organizing the transportation industry. Ironically, the winners in this strange episode were none other than Jimmy Hoffa and his band of outlaws, who now held unchallenged control over carhauling and construction trucking. Without abandoning their hostility toward the government and labor statesmen such as the leaders of the CIO, Hoffa and the Detroit Teamsters were quickly learning that in certain circumstances even the most socially responsible interventions could work in their favor.

Despite their abandonment by the CIO, the Lewis brothers refused to quit. In a final attempt to gain a foothold in trucking, they concentrated their diminished but still considerable resources on intercity ("over-the-road") drivers in Michigan and neighboring states. This placed new pressure on Hoffa, who had become one of the lead negotiators for the Teamsters' Central States Drivers Council (CSDC). The

CSDC was then bargaining with a committee representing 6,000 inter-city trucking firms in twelve midwestern states over the renewal of an agreement that would expire in November. Knowing that a weak contract would throw open the door to the UCWOC, the drivers council, led by Hoffa, demanded substantial wage increases in a contract that had already moved truckers from the lowest level of industrial workers into the middle class. When the employers refused to back down, Teamster locals in Michigan and the rest of the midwestern states prepared their members for a strike. Hoffa announced that if the employers refused to accept the union's revision of the wage scale, "no freight will move over the highways." Fearing that such a walkout would cripple defense production, Tobin, who was still Franklin Roosevelt's closest friend in the labor movement, called off the strike and submitted the dispute to the National Defense Mediation Board (NDMB).[41]

The IBT president, who was keenly aware that wage increases were necessary to avoid losing the heart of the union's membership to the CIO, was no doubt banking on his pull with the Roosevelt administration and the recently altered composition of the NDMB to win a favorable settlement from the mediation board. Four days before Tobin submitted the dispute to the board, both of its CIO members, including Thomas Kennedy of the United Mine Workers, who served as John L. Lewis's mouthpiece, resigned to protest the board's decision against the UMW in the "captive mines" strike.[42] George Meany and Robert Watt, both AFL stalwarts, remained as the sole labor representatives, while the chairman, William H. Davis, an arch-corporatist and Hillman appointee, was no friend of Lewis. In December, Tobin's wishes were met, as the NDMB awarded over-the-road drivers a 13 percent wage increase, which was less than Hoffa's negotiating team had demanded but more than enough to keep the drivers from switching unions. The decision effectively destroyed the UCWOC. Soon afterward Lewis's union closed its headquarters in Detroit, and in the summer of 1942 it left the CIO to join the catch-all District 50 of the United Mine Workers.

Interventions by the state and its agents in the labor movement effectively banished the CIO from the trucking industry, leaving the Teamsters with a monopoly that remained unchallenged to the present day. Though ostensible champions of industrial democracy, Hillman,

Reuther, and Murray helped eliminate a vital source of democracy for truck drivers in the Midwest—the ability to choose their bargaining representative. The same corporatists who spurred Hoffa to be militant in 1940 and 1941 ultimately cleared his path to becoming an imperious "labor boss."[43]

Six

A New Man of Power

Trade-union organization has become an exercise in power accumulation, and logically enough, all problems of labor organization must be subordinated to the aim of organization, the accumulation of power. Any method that points toward a possible increase in the power of the organization is the right method, even if the most sophisticated and difficult. Any procedure by which the central aim and the chief reason for the existence of the union is likely to be advanced will command approval. Power of, by, and for the union, is the issue and the acid test of every trade-union organizing campaign.—J. B. S. HARDMAN, "PROBLEMS OF LABOR ORGANIZATION"[1]

The Detroit Teamsters began the war years with the opening of a lavish new downtown headquarters, situated four blocks from Briggs Stadium on Trumbull Avenue. The air-conditioned offices, mahogany walls, and leather furniture in what the *Detroit News* called "the swankiest labor temple in the Midwest" announced that Joint Council 43 had arrived.[2] By 1942, less than a decade after its origin as a struggling, rough-and-tumble outfit, the Detroit Teamster organization had become a force in the Motor City rivaled only by the United Automobile Workers. The combined membership of its affiliated locals had grown from a few hundred truck drivers to more than 20,000 workers in scores of occupations.

Working behind a maple desk in a well-appointed second-floor office, Jimmy Hoffa held tenuous control over this nascent empire. By 1942 Hoffa had taken over the de facto leadership of the joint council and directed the daily operations of its two largest affiliates, his own

Local 299 and Local 337, whose president, Bert Brennan, worked as Hoffa's junior partner. His power over general trucking in Detroit had been left virtually unchallenged after Walter Reuther, Sidney Hillman, and the federal government destroyed his sole rival in the field, the UCWOC, in the fall of 1941. Moreover, as the newly appointed negotiating chairman of the Central States Drivers Council (CSDC), Hoffa's monopoly control extended over thousands of truck drivers across the Midwest. However, the core of his power in Detroit continued to be threatened from all sides by CIO unions working in a myriad of industries that were interdependent with trucking. Despite the constraints placed on organizing by its patriotic leaders, the CIO continued its march into Detroit's retail stores, warehouses, groceries, bottling plants, dairies, and bakeries. Still fearing that if left unchecked the CIO would surround and conquer the Teamsters' primary industry, Hoffa used Local 337 as a protective bulwark around his domain in trucking. Local 337 countered every thrust by the CIO in the ancillary industries, allowing Hoffa to continue the centralization of the trucking divisions under his command.[3]

"Keep the Wheels Rolling"

Complicating Hoffa's designs to hold off the CIO was Dan Tobin's relationship with Franklin Roosevelt. Tobin's devotion to the President and the war effort was unsurpassed in the labor movement. Beginning immediately after the bombing of Pearl Harbor and continuing through the war, Tobin made it clear that his union would sacrifice everything short of its existence for an American victory. Thousands of Teamster members were immediately recruited by the union's national office to drive Army supply trucks in Asia, and in January 1942 Tobin authorized an interest-free loan of $8 million from the IBT treasury to the federal government. Most important for Hoffa and the Detroit Teamsters, Tobin worked assiduously to discipline the union's members and rigidly enforced the no-strike pledge he had taken along with most of the nation's labor leaders. In addition to warnings sent to every local that disregarding the ban on strikes would result in immediate expulsion, Tobin issued orders for all Teamster truck drivers to disregard picket lines of other unions, even fellow AFL unions asking for assistance. "We are pledged to keep the wheels rolling," he sternly declared in the IBT magazine. "Members who refuse to obey orders should be suspended or expelled." This prohibition of strikes and especially of the secondary boycott, the favorite weapon of the Detroit Teamsters to force employers to sign recognition contracts or to insert friendly unions into industries being organized by the CIO, created considerable tension between Trumbull Avenue and the IBT headquarters in Indianapolis.[4]

While national CIO leaders joined Tobin in calling for a strict adherence to the no-strike pledge, as far as Hoffa could tell, the CIO organizers in Detroit were not aware of it. Still guided by their mission to create one big union, after Pearl Harbor the socialists and liberal corporatists in the Detroit branch of the United Retail, Wholesale, and Department Store Employees seemed only to increase the ambition and militancy of their drives in the city's retail, warehouse, and food industries. Three Montgomery Ward department stores, all 438 stores of the C. F. Smith grocery chain, and several Kresge variety stores signed contracts with the CIO union in the first few months of 1942. Another longtime rival of the Detroit Teamsters, the United Dairy Workers, merged with the URWDSE and continued its coordinated organizing drive in the dairies, bakeries, and ice cream plants of the city. Though no one in the CIO publicly expressed a desire to compete with the Teamsters in trucking, Hoffa and his comrades had no reason to believe that men such as Tucker Smith, head of the Michigan Socialist Party branch and state director for the Retail Workers, and John Gibson, leader of the Dairy Workers and chairman of the Michigan CIO's political action committee, would be content with leaving a large, hostile, and "reactionary" union in command of a strategically vital industry. With warehousing under its control on one end of the trucking lines and retail stores on the other, the ambitious, expansionistic local leaders of the CIO could destroy the Teamsters with a simple order to boycott trucks driven by IBT members.[5]

In the spring of 1942 Hoffa attempted to fortify his position by outflanking his rivals in the field. In 1941 the Teamsters had forced the city's produce, egg, and poultry wholesale distributors to sign closed-shop contracts, making every CIO grocer susceptible to secondary boycotts. To complete their monopoly over the city's food distribution industry, in January 1942 Hoffa, Bert Brennan, and Local 337 moved into meat. They first took possession of the tiny Local 428 of the Amalgamated Meat Cutters and Butcher Workers, then began organizing among yard employees at the Detroit stockyards, whose three companies supplied 80 percent of the city's beef and pork.[6] Exhibiting both their anxiety to check the advance of the CIO and their ability to close down a business with only minimal organizing, the Teamsters called a strike to demand a closed-shop contract after recruiting only six of the 71 yard workers. The new Teamsters in the butcher shops put down their knives while the union's truck drivers announced their refusal to pick up any meat from the stockyards. Though the truck boycott alone completely shut down the yard, the six Teamster yard workers maintained a picket line, which was less a blockade than a feeble pretense that the strike was their initiative. More than 800 head of cattle that had been destined for the grocery stores milled about the yards, saved for the moment by the strike, while the city's newspapers blared headlines warning of an impending meat shortage. But when the employers stood firm and the union's actions failed to generate an uprising among the 65 other yard workers, Hoffa and Brennan made plans to dramatically escalate the strike. They convinced the rest of the Joint Council leadership to authorize the extension of the strike to the city's entire food supply industry, which would have pulled 550 members from their jobs. Meanwhile, Thurman Arnold, head of the Justice Department's antitrust division, who held a special loathing for the union and had indicted Hoffa and Brennan in 1940 for an attempt to monopolize the Detroit wastepaper business, began investigating whether the union's manipulation of the city's food supply was another "restraint of trade" in violation of the Sherman Act.[7]

Of course, none of this comported with the way Dan Tobin wanted his union to behave during the war. Brazenly breaking the no-strike pledge, cutting off a city's food supply, and provoking the wrath of the government were not what the IBT president had in mind when he promised full cooperation with the war effort. Tobin's top assistant, Tom Flynn, fired off a letter to the Detroit leaders ordering them to scuttle the general food strike, then began plans to depose Hoffa. Yet rather than expel Hoffa, who had demonstrated loyalty to Tobin in the Minneapolis purge, Flynn convinced the IBT president to lift the trusteeship over Local 299, which had remained in effect since 1936, and order elections for the local's officers. Hoping an election would produce more responsible leadership, in May, Flynn ordered Ray Bennett, the local's nominal overseer, to "turn the organization back to the membership."[8]

Bennett, who usually followed Hoffa's lead, responded with a lengthy letter to the international office warning of the dangers of democracy. "If there were to be an election, the organization would absolutely get out of control," Bennett wrote. He explained that nearly every local in the Joint Council was beset by CIO unions, none more so than Local 299. Hoffa and his business agents were "continuously harassed by the United Construction Workers CIO, and it is the opinion of the writer that if a notice was placed for election . . . it would be a wide open opportunity for some of our disgruntled members to get to work and cause us no end of trouble with this particular branch of the CIO." Bennett went on to suggest the existence of a CIO conspiracy to infiltrate the Teamsters and destroy them from within:

> . . . while a Receiver is over them, some of our trouble makers are just a little afraid to come out in the front because the ones we have found and we were able to prove that they did have connections, or memberships, in the CIO, were removed. But there are others that we have had suspicions about, and we feel very certain that they are carrying membership cards in both our organizations and also the United Construction Workers CIO, which we have not been able to get sufficient evidence to warrant their expulsions from the membership. But if we had an election, that particular type would soon have themselves out in front.[9]

Since Bennett's central claim is almost certainly false, it is difficult to discern the veracity of any part of this remarkable letter. At the time the letter was written, the United Construction Workers, which according to Bennett was on the verge of subverting Local 299, was a virtual nonentity and had abandoned organizing in the trucking industries under the local's jurisdictions. By 1942 the UCWOC had lost virtually all of its institutional support from the CIO and had radically scaled back its operations. In the spring it moved its Detroit local out of the CIO headquarters in the Hoffman Building and was devoting most of its remaining organizing resources to recruiting production workers at a few bottling plants and construction companies. Bennett's estimation of the UCWOC's potential therefore appears inflated at best. Yet the menace posed by other CIO unions, in the field if not within the Teamsters union itself, was real indeed, and so the letter may have been an effort to preclude any CIO attempt to "bore from within." Whatever the motivation behind Bennett's letter, Flynn was not persuaded by it—the order to hold elections remained in force.[10]

Acid Test

Fortunately for Bennett and Hoffa, Tobin soon learned that the Detroit local of the United Brewery Workers union had been granted a charter by the Michigan CIO Council and was renewing its drive on the soft-drink industry in competition with Local 337. After a series of angry inquiries from Tobin and Flynn, Allan Haywood, the CIO's national director of organization, acknowledged the extent of the Detroit CIO's activities in or near Teamster jurisdictions. Tobin learned that in addition to the Brewery Workers, the Retail Workers, and the Dairy Workers, the Detroit Teamsters were competing with the Packinghouse Workers Organizing Committee and even Sidney Hillman's Amalgamated Clothing Workers. It became clear to Tobin that Hoffa, who was directing all of the fights against these rivals, was operating in a hornet's nest of CIO unions. The election in Local 299 was cancelled and the trusteeship renewed.[11] In the July issue of the *International Teamster*, Tobin offered a rationale for reversing his decision that relied on Bennett's dramatic scenario:

> The International Union does not like to be placing trustees over local unions, and as soon as we find that local unions are able to handle their own affairs we are only too happy to relinquish the trusteeship. It costs the International Union real money to place a trustee or receiver over a local union. The law of the International Unions, however, compels us to place trustees over local unions that are not properly handled by the officers or by the members.
>
> Especially do we have to place trustees over unions in districts that are surrounded by the C.I.O., because we have found

from experience that the local officers in C.I.O districts have sometimes been bribed, sitting around a barroom, to sell their loyalty to some of the C.I.O. officials who are also hanging around endeavoring to win those weak fellows away from the International. . . .

Out of one thousand local unions we may have twenty-five unions, many of them small, over which we have some receivers at present. In some instances, while the locals might be able to take care of themselves now, the surroundings in the district are so bad that we dare not take any chances.[12]

Ironically, Tobin's argument was essentially the same as that made by two of the principal intellectual leaders of the CIO, J. B. S. Hardman and Arthur Goldberg. In an essay written in the 1920s, Hardman, one of Sidney Hillman's closest advisors during the founding of the CIO, maintained that trade unions existed in a perpetual state of war and therefore had no choice but to behave as an army in which the democratic rights of the members had to be curtailed in order to ensure the survival of the organization. Though the warfare to which Hardman referred was that between unions and employers and not between rival unions, his argument is strikingly similar to Tobin's:

. . . it is dangerous to lay everything open to the members and through them before the employers. And how can one prevent demagoguery, or any kind of political opposition from taking advantage of easy opportunities to make it hot for the administration? Democracy is lovely, but not innocent.[13]

This justification for the restriction of democracy was taken up thirty years later by Goldberg, who as general counsel for the AFL-CIO had recommended the expulsion of the Hoffa-led Teamsters from the federation for unethical practices:

If there is analogy to political government, the analogy is to a political government which may simultaneously face uncertainty as to its continued existence: i.e., a revolution, and which is periodically at war. The constraints which by common consent we accept temporarily in the political arena when such conditions exist may perhaps explain and justify the existence of similar, although permanent, restraints in the practice of union democracy.[14]

When used by Tobin in 1942, this argument, made by three labor leaders who upheld social responsibility as a cardinal principle of trade unionism, allowed the most famously irresponsible trade union leader in the United States to preserve and extend his rule.

Soon after Tobin's order to continue the trusteeship over 299, Bennett appointed a new set of officers for the local, naming Frank Fitzsimmons as president and Hoffa as secretary-treasurer. Fitzsimmons was a former over-the-road driver who, like Hoffa, had found that the economic prospects for a Teamster officer were greater than for an ordinary member. He had risen quickly from shop steward to business agent to president of the local, but there was no doubt that his new title was merely a formality. Hoffa ran the local and by the end of 1942 was busy extending his control to truck drivers outside Detroit.[15]

Before he ran afoul of the international office for his unstatesmanlike conduct, Hoffa had asked Flynn to instruct Michigan locals to turn over their negotiations to him so that he could institute a uniform statewide contract in place of the variety of cartage agreements that were bargained locally. Flynn complied, and once the controversy over the trusteeship of Local 299 was resolved, Hoffa moved ahead swiftly to centralize the state's cartage locals under his control. In December he asked the international to order intransigent locals to submit to his leadership. "We feel that we have more at stake than the smaller local unions outstate," he explained. The question of competition, this time between his locals and others in the IBT, was once again paramount. "What we are concerned about [is that] other local unions within the state of Michigan, doing the same type of work [as] our Detroit locals, are going to make applications [to the National War Labor Board] for wage increases that are very liable and likely to upset all applications for raises filled by our locals within the state of Michigan."[16]

Locals in Flint, Grand Rapids, Jackson, and Kalamazoo rebelled when the terms of the statewide contract were shown to be inferior to their own city contracts. Bennett, who was sent in by Tobin to quell the uprisings, reported back to the IBT headquarters about a meeting of the Kalamazoo local at which the officers of the local "reminded the membership of all the so-called rotten deals that they have received" and attempted to pass a motion to ignore the statewide contract in favor of their own. At this and other meetings across the state, Bennett informed the rebels that their unions would be put under trusteeship and their officers expelled unless they followed Hoffa's instructions. "A few of the more reasonable members soon grasped the meaning of this, and a motion was put on the floor that the question of the city contract be tabled." Thanks to the heavy-handed intervention by Bennett and the international, Hoffa was soon able to consolidate his control over Michigan. Apparently, Tobin and Flynn had been convinced by Hoffa's argument that the centralization of negotiations with employers or the National War Labor Board (NWLB) would eliminate the downward pressure on wages from weaker or more submissive locals.[17]

Hoffa was correct that centralization would raise the floor for wages in trucking, thereby greatly improving the economic conditions of the poorest members of the union and protecting the wages of "middle class" locals such as Local 299, but centralization also eliminated the *upward* pressure on wages from more ambitious locals such as those in Flint, Grand Rapids, Jackson, and Kalamazoo. His plan guaranteed for the members both a decent living and a cap on their desires. This creation of a vast middle class provided just the right conditions to sustain Hoffa's absolute authority over the Michigan Teamsters. Hoffa's plan not only placed unchecked institutional power in his hands but also secured the loyalty of the thousands of members whose wages were raised by the imposition of the statewide contract. Those locals that were not content with the standard wage provisions and sought to raise the bar were greatly outnumbered by those that received wage increases and suffered swift and severe disciplinary actions by the international. By the end of the year, Hoffa formalized his ascendancy over the outstate locals by establishing and appointing himself chairman of the Michigan Conference of Teamsters. He also began publishing the *Michigan Teamster*, a newspaper distributed throughout the state that trumpeted the accomplishments of the Detroit locals and in particular the leadership of Hoffa.

As further insurance that his support among the state's Teamsters would remain constant, Hoffa used his growing influence in the Detroit and Michigan AFL organizations to help pacify his members.

After his election to the board of directors of the Wayne County Federation of Labor in the spring of 1942, Hoffa was able to secure the appointment of Solomon Sniderman as one of the four AFL representatives on the Michigan branch of the National War Labor Board. Sniderman, a business agent for Local 337, was one of the more unusual figures on the Detroit Teamsters staff. A former professor at Wayne State University and a leftist, Sniderman in the late 1930s took a job with the local despite the Teamsters' disdain for intellectuals and radicals and the unabashed anti-Semitism of Bert Brennan. The Local 337 president, who once attributed difficulties he was having negotiating with a soft-drink bottling company to its being a "Jewish owned concern," was nonetheless willing to hire Jews who could provide skills useful to the union. In addition to Sniderman, the local's business agents included Herman Kierdorf, a demolitions expert, and Morris Coleman, whose fearlessness and street-fighting skills were demonstrated when he was one of a handful of Teamsters who took on several hundred members of the Railway Clerks union in 1941.

Considered an "egghead" and a "sissy" by his colleagues, Sniderman nonetheless won their respect during the battles with rival unions in 1941, when he was twice nearly killed by bat-wielding goons (once while fighting with Coleman against a phalanx of Railway Clerks). More important, Sniderman was articulate and comfortable with legal terms and probably the only Detroit Teamster other than Hoffa capable of being an effective agent for the union on the War Labor Board. For the next two years Sniderman proved his value to the Teamsters time and again as one of the most aggressive labor representatives on the board. He helped to slow the CIO's advances and worked diligently to keep a lid on discontent among the state's Teamster rank and file by pushing wages for cartage drivers as high as the limits imposed by the national board would allow.[18]

Hoffa's efforts to subdue unruly unions were also aided by the structure of the trucking industry itself. Trucking employers and Teamster leaders were almost entirely immune from the unauthorized "wildcat" strikes that disrupted military production and precipitated crises in other major unions during the war. Trucking never experienced the fundamental wartime conversion that transformed such industries as automobile, rubber, steel, and shipbuilding into satellites of the military. In the converted industries, speedups, increased production standards, and new disciplinary measures created sufficient resentment to cause workers to break the no-strike pledge against the orders of their unions' leaders. While the Trucking Commission of the National War Labor Board did allow most employers to force drivers to work longer hours, it could not make the truckers get to their destinations any faster nor could it assign supervisors to sit in every cab and monitor the work habits of the drivers.[19] The relative autonomy of the truck drivers' work environment shielded them from the major causes of the wartime wildcat strikes and helped make them amenable to Tobin's policy and Hoffa's control. The rank and file in the heart of the union remained relatively peaceful during the war years, but Teamster locals not willing to submit to Hoffa's authority presented other challenges to the rising leader.[20]

Roadblock

As he moved outside the confines of Michigan, Hoffa confronted fellow Teamsters who were unwilling to accept the limitations on their aspirations that he sought to impose under his central authority. He found the most ambitious and successful—and therefore the most problematic—Teamster locals right down the road in Ohio, where drivers in Cleveland, Toledo, and Akron enjoyed the highest wages in the Midwest. The Ohio locals were able to win such high wages partly because they had refused to sign the agreements negotiated by the Central States Drivers Council (CSDC), preferring instead to bargain with their state's employers on their own. As the CSDC Executive Board began meeting in the early months of 1943 to consider its strategies for the upcoming bargaining sessions with employers, Hoffa worked to eliminate any source of inspiration for the members under his purview. He urged Tobin to force the recalcitrant Ohio locals to abide by the provisions of the CSDC contract. In February, Tobin called Ed Murphy and Harry Card, the leaders of the Ohio drivers council, to meet with Hoffa and CSDC director Dexter Lewis in Indianapolis. At that meeting Tobin instructed the Ohio men that they would join the CSDC negotiations for a new contract and be bound by its terms, even if it reduced their members' wages. But when Murphy and Card returned to Ohio and announced Tobin's order to the state council members, a revolt ensued. The members of the Ohio Highway Drivers Council sent a new, less submissive emissary, Rudy Minkin, to the next meeting of the CSDC Executive Board, held April 21 in the Sherman Hotel in Chicago.

Despite the openly hostile presence of Hoffa, Minkin began the meeting by informing the gathered leaders of the CSDC that the Ohio council would not and could not sign the central states agreement until the state's locals were guaranteed that their wages and conditions would not be adversely affected by it. After Dexter Lewis admitted that "only the War Labor Board or the result of negotiations can possibly answer that question," Minkin remained steadfast, refusing to authorize Ohio's participation in the central states agreement without ratification from the state's locals. Several members of the CSDC were sympathetic to the Ohio council's desire to keep their high wages. "As far as this Committee over here is concerned, we have no intention of taking anything away from anybody," said Joe Scislowski, one of the founders of the CSDC who had worked closely with Farrell Dobbs on the first area contract in 1938. "In fact, if they can better their contract over and above the contract that we are going to negotiate this coming fall, more power to them." Several members of the board then urged Lewis to attend a meeting of the Ohio locals to address their concerns and politely request their compliance with Tobin's order. Hoffa would have none of this. "I did not see anybody come in and speak to my Union and ask me whether I wanted to become a part of this or not, or whether I was going to receive a condition," he said, exhibiting his tendency to bully those standing in his way. "I do not know of anybody sitting at this table who had anybody come down and say to them, 'Will you please come in the Area?' They told me to get in the Area.... They said, 'Get in there.' " When this failed to sway Minkin, Hoffa threatened to block Ohio drivers from coming into Michigan until they agreed to the area contract. Perhaps fearing Hoffa's wrath more than the anger of their own members, the Ohio council eventually announced their intention to join the other midwestern states in negotiating and signing a new central states agreement.[21]

With Ohio brought into line, Hoffa, Lewis and the rest of the CSDC Executive Board now faced the challenge of confronting the employers. With the UCWOC raid on trucking still fresh in his mind and the rest of the CIO showing no intention of slowing its incursions into Teamster jurisdictions, negotiating committee chairman Hoffa put forward a set of eleven demands that included a 25-cent raise and time-and-a-half pay for hours worked in excess of 40 in one week or eight in one day. The latter demand was especially important to truckers, since there was no overtime provision in the Central States Area agreement imposed by the NDMB in 1942 and the average workweek for over-the-road drivers remained at 60 hours, virtually unchanged since the Depression. As the November expiration date neared, the employers, fully aware of Tobin's ban on strikes and knowing that a deadlock would place the dispute in the hands of the increasingly conservative NWLB for arbitration, unanimously rejected Hoffa's demands.[22] To make matters worse, operators from Ohio refused to negotiate with the other central states employers.[23] They were soon followed by firms in North Dakota, South Dakota, Nebraska, Kansas, Minnesota, Iowa, Missouri, and parts of Wisconsin, who formed their own negotiating group, the Midwest Operators Association. In November, one week before the expiration date of the old contract, the case was forwarded to the NWLB. The board ruled in favor of the Teamsters for a uniform contract covering all twelve states but granted only a seven-cent raise and rejected every other union demand.[24]

Fearful that the members would rise up against the union and the government, Hoffa and the CSDC Executive Board were surprised to find that they had more difficulty persuading the employers to accept the award than the drivers, who still faced 60-hour weeks with no overtime pay. Trouble started in Nebraska, Iowa, and the Dakotas, which had been bastions of employer opposition to the Teamsters since the first central states over-the-road organizing drive in 1937 and 1938. Operators in those states simply refused to raise their wages, and were soon followed by employers in Missouri, Kansas, and parts of Minnesota. By July, 103 firms were continuing to ignore the NWLB order. In August, after six months of holding the rising anger of the membership in check and with the tacit approval of the Army and the Roosevelt Administration, Tobin finally authorized a strike of the holdout firms. The Teamsters had warned the federal government that a walkout was imminent and made arrangements with the Army to continue moving war materials. When the strike began, however, several operators locked their garages and refused to let any trucks move, provoking the chief of the highway branch of the Army Transportation Corps to announce that the shutdown was "turning into an operators' strike." As expected, Roosevelt moved in, signing an executive order expropriating the struck companies and directing the Office of Defense Transportation to begin operating the lines under the terms of the NWLB wage award. The last of the firms to agree to pay back wages and abide by the NWLB directive was not released until November 1945.[25]

Wars at Home

Through the war years, Hoffa busily shuttled between Chicago, for CSDC meetings and negotiations, Washington, to appear before the War Labor Board, and Detroit, where he was kept busy protecting his home locals from a swarm of CIO competitors. The peace agreement announced in December 1942 by national leaders of the CIO and AFL had little effect on Detroit. Of greatest concern to Hoffa's locals was the conglomerate of the CIO Retail Workers and Dairy Workers, which continued its drive to organize every worker in Michigan's retailing, warehousing, and food industries. Michigan URWDSE director Tucker Smith and Detroit Dairy Workers leader John Gibson, who was elected president of the Michigan CIO Council in July 1943, were on one level as different from Hoffa as union leaders could be. The socialist Smith and social-democrat Gibson were motivated by an ideology of worker communitarianism while Hoffa was driven by nothing more than the self-interest of an economic rationalist. Yet all three were equally intent on creating a monopoly over the labor market. For the CIO men, such a monopoly was necessary to establish a unified worker organization in preparation for entry into the state; for Hoffa, it was necessary for the protection of his livelihood, power, and by the 1940s his very identity. These two unstoppable forces, the CIO organizations under Smith and Gibson and the Teamsters under Hoffa, collided continuously during the war years and after, each hoping to destroy the other through organizing, street fights, boycotts, and sweetheart deals, and finally through the accumulation of political power.[26]

By 1942 the Detroit local of the Retail Clerks Independent Protective Association had dropped all pretense that it was an independent union and moved into the IBT headquarters, where it not only fielded a team in the Teamster bowling league but also followed Hoffa's directions to head off CIO rivals. The relatively weak RCIPA operated as a front for the Teamsters in their war against the Retail Workers and Dairy Workers. Hoffa, Brennan, and other Teamster officials provided leadership, money, muscle, and economic leverage in contested shops in the Detroit area. Yet even the Detroit Teamsters, who by 1943 boasted a combined membership of close to 30,000, faced an uphill struggle against the locals of the Retail Workers and Dairy Workers, which were highly organized and received substantial financial assistance from the URWDSE national office. In February 1943, Bennett requested from Tobin a continuation of the $1,300 monthly allowance that had been granted to the Detroit Joint Council in 1941 for its campaigns against the CIO. Bennett reported that the "situation is no better and the joint council is unable to carry on the fight alone." It is unclear whether the request was granted, but there is no doubt Bennett's anxiety was well founded.[27]

In department stores, the URWDSE and Teamster-backed RCIPA were locked in a tight battle for control of clerks and warehousemen. In 1943, organizing by both sides was especially vigorous at the Detroit retail outlets and warehouses of the Sears, Roebuck chain. The CIO accused the Sears management of colluding with the Teamsters and allowing "two well-known AFL business agents [to sell] men's furnishings in Sears' largest store," and of leaving the agents "free to spend their time cruising about the stores electioneering." Despite the charges, the RCIPA registered victories in NLRB elections in two stores while their CIO rival took another store and the two warehouses. At the J. L. Hudson store, a fixture on Woodward Avenue in downtown Detroit, the CIO continued its organizing virtually without competition; but at the warehouse for the People's Outfitting Company, one of Detroit's largest department stores, the Teamsters at least managed to distract their opponents. After securing the services of a member of the Retail Workers local at the warehouse, the Teamsters attempted to install undercover agents as officers of the Detroit Joint Board of the URWDSE. When that failed, the Teamsters tried to capture the People's Outfitting shop by claiming representation rights over the employees. Rebuffed by the state labor board, Hoffa ordered a freeze on all shipments to the company and directed scores of his organizers to blockade the warehouse with trucks. With the help of

Sniderman, Hoffa managed to convince the regional War Labor Board to withhold a ruling on representation rights at the warehouse. But after one hundred Retail Worker members marched on the board's Detroit office, an election was ordered to determine the bargaining agent for the shop. Since the RCIPA and Teamsters had devoted far less time to recruiting than to other, more expedient means of organizing, they were overwhelmingly defeated and were forced to concede control over the warehouse to the CIO.[28]

The fight between the two rivals was especially intense in, of all places, the milk business. In the early 1940s, the Dairy Workers, under the direction of Gibson and Roy Scoggins, had moved steadily through the dairies and milk retail depots of southeastern Michigan. By 1942 the CIO union claimed to have signed up 86 percent of the area's milk drivers and plant workers, which had formerly been under the unchallenged domain of Teamsters Local 155. In September of that year, Hoffa, who had just won a reprieve from Tobin for militant measures against the CIO, issued a 48-hour ultimatum to all of Detroit's hotels, restaurants, and supermarkets that unless they transferred their milk business from CIO-organized dairies to those with Teamster contracts they would be cut off from all truck deliveries. Not to be outdone, the Dairy Workers followed Hoffa's ultimatum with one of their own. Scoggins wired the War Production Board and Secretary of Labor Frances Perkins with a threat to "cut off all milk deliveries in Michigan" if the federal government allowed the Teamsters to continue their coercion. Neither of the threats materialized, however, after a last-minute conference between Hoffa and Detroit CIO leaders granted the Teamsters jurisdiction over a retail shop in exchange for calling off the trucking boycott.[29]

The truce in the milk war lasted only a few months, until the spring of 1943, when, in an effort to circumvent his opponents further up the supply chain, Hoffa announced the launching of a recruitment campaign among Michigan dairy farmers. If established, a Teamster-farmer organization could have boycotted the CIO out of urban milk distribution companies. Hoffa had attempted to move the Teamsters into farming the previous summer while under effective probation from the international office. Flynn, who at the time was irritated with Hoffa's threat to cut off Detroit's food supply, had instructed Bennett to "go over this matter with Jimmy, as you are well aware of the fact that the Teamsters International Union does not want any part in the organizing of farmers." After the continued march of the CIO through Detroit, however, by the spring of 1943 Flynn seemed to have forgotten his earlier feelings about a Teamsters agricultural division.[30]

Undaunted by the prospect of Teamster dairy farmers encircling them, the Dairy Workers established a Michigan Dairy Division within the URWDSE and adopted a "far-reaching organizational program for the mobilization of dairy, bakery, cereal and food workers under the banner of the URWDSE." A principal target of the Dairy Workers' "mobilization" was the Johnson Milk Company in Hamtramck, which had signed with the Teamsters in 1938 to escape a CIO organizing drive. To keep the workers from bolting to the CIO, the Teamsters and the company renewed the agreement in 1941 with substantial wage increases, a reduced work week, and paid vacations, and then handed the shop to the RCIPA. When that contract expired in April 1943, the Dairy Workers revived their recruitment efforts among the 600 Johnson employees. By August, whether through a show of organizational strength or through a sweetheart understanding, they convinced the company to abandon its negotiations with the RCIPA and sign with the CIO.[31]

After the announcement that Johnson had rejected the Teamster front union in favor of the Dairy Workers, both labor organizations prepared for war. Weighing in with the brass-knuckled Teamster brawlers was a crew of off-duty police officers and sheriff's deputies armed with pistols. The Teamsters had gained the assistance of the ringers through years of favors to the Detroit and Hamtramck police departments and the presence of several ex-Teamster officers in the Wayne County Sheriff's Department.[32] With the armed men at the point, 25 Teamsters charged into the plant and rousted the workers from their machines and into the street. The invaders then threw up a picket line and refused to let the company resume operations until it re-signed with the RCIPA. The next morning, hundreds of Dairy Worker members from across Detroit were trucked in by the CIO to break through the Teamster picket line. As the two sides tore into each other, the Teamster "guards" wounded three of the CIO men with gunshots. The melee resulted in serious but, remarkably, nonfatal injuries to five Teamster combatants, three of the off-duty police, four on-duty police, and five CIO members. Ultimately the dispute went to the Teamsters' favorite government agency, the Michigan War Labor Board. Sniderman managed to persuade the board to find Johnson guilty of "unethical dealing and disregard of its contractual relation" with the RCIPA, which was ruled in force despite the company's agreement with the CIO.[33]

In 1943 the competition between the Teamsters and Dairy Workers extended into the smaller cities across central and northern Michigan. In Port Huron, where the CIO union had not concentrated its organizers, the Teamsters tried to take advantage of what appeared to be an easy opportunity to forestall their opponents' organizing drive. Led by Morris Coleman and James Cassily, teams of Teamster organizers shuttled to Port Huron to persuade the milk drivers there to join the IBT. Rebuffed after making their initial entreaties, the Teamsters adopted a less friendly approach. Recalcitrant milk drivers were followed on their deliveries and threatened with bodily harm. The drivers then refused to work until the union men left town. In interviews with the local newspaper, the drivers perhaps demonstrated why the CIO had focused its efforts elsewhere. "We're satisfied with our wages," the spokesman for the drivers told the *Port Huron Times-Herald.* "As for working hours—if we were limited to a certain working schedule the people would not be served." Another driver spoke proudly of working until 11 p.m. during a snowstorm. "If we'd been in the union, we couldn't have done it." Detroit Teamster officers often referred to these kinds of workers as having a "slave mentality." Such backward proletarians, in the Teamsters' view, had to be forced to organize.

After the War Production Board declared their strike illegal, the Port Huron milk drivers returned to work but continued to resist the shouted threats of the union men from Detroit. Even the *Michigan Teamster*'s "Message to the Port Huron Milk Salesmen," arguing that unionization was necessary for the survival of their businesses, failed to sway the drivers. Seeing that the "slaves" would not give in to mere words, Hoffa sent in an all-star team to unleash his favorite weapon, the secondary boycott. Along with Coleman and Cassily, four of Hoffa's chief lieutenants, Tom Briglia, Al Squires, Bobby Holmes, and Martin Haggerty, fanned out to groceries, drugstores, and restaurants and informed the owners that their businesses would not receive any other food shipments as long as they accepted deliveries by non-Teamster milk drivers.

The Port Huron campaign failed to produce many new members, but it did bring national attention to the Detroit Teamsters. Clare Hoffman, a congressman from rural Michigan whose hatred for labor unions and Franklin Roosevelt was surpassed by none of his fellow Republicans, seized on the Teamsters' exploits in Port Huron as a means of bashing the objects of his loathing. From March through May, Hoffman filled the *Congressional Record* with his speeches lambasting the "ex-convicts from Detroit, traveling in Buick automobiles" fueled by rationed gas supplied by the Office of Price Administration (OPA). Most of the Detroit Teamster officers had in fact received draft deferments and gas allotments of up to 3,000 miles per month because of their work in an essential industry. So not only were the Teamsters "willing to deprive the babies of Port Huron of their milk," but they were aided in their nefarious activities by a federal administration that was their "political ally." After listing both the extensive criminal records and OPA mileage allowances of the Detroit Teamsters, Hoffman declared the harassment of the milk drivers and the secondary boycott to be a threat to the liberty of the nation, "the sort of thing that Adolf Hitler has tried to force upon free men and women all over the world."

> The people of the United States know that while this administration talks about freedom from want and freedom from fear and a free press and free speech, it does not mean a word of what it preaches.
>
> While thousands of American boys are sacrificing their lives, while the whole country is going without and doing its utmost, the planners and the new dealers are undermining the very foundation of our Government, are standing back of crooked political labor politicians and racketeers, who are compelling honest, patriotic Americans to pay tribute for the privilege of working to support the men they have sent to the front.

In addition to these rhetorical salvos, Hoffman used the Port Huron case for more practical purposes. His speeches against the Teamsters coincided with the House's consideration of a bill introduced by Democrat Samuel Hobbs of Alabama to amend the Antiracketeering Act of 1934 so as to cover extortion and violence carried on by trade unions. Passed by the House on April 9, the Hobbs Bill became law in 1946 and was widely considered to be primarily aimed at the Teamsters. It was later used against Jimmy Hoffa.[34]

Reluctant Citizens

During the war years the attitude of Hoffa and the Detroit Teamsters toward the state took a subtle turn. Previously they had shunned involvement in government, but with a large treasury and the ability to influence and mobilize thousands of members, the Teamsters began to assert themselves in the realm of electoral politics. Here, too, the competition with the CIO was a principal motivator.

The 1943 mayoral election marked the first concerted effort by the UAW and the Detroit CIO locals to run a liberal candidate, Frank Fitzgerald, against the incumbent, Edward Jeffries, who had shifted dramatically to the right during the war. Jeffries used the increasingly polarized racial politics of the city to build his support among whites, accusing "un-American" UAW leaders and blacks of attempting to "take over the city" and force "the mingling of Negroes and whites in the same neighborhoods." Jeffries's red-baiting and racist appeals to whites were too much even for the Wayne County Federation of Labor, which endorsed Fitzgerald almost unanimously. Only two of the unions affiliated with the WCFL backed Jeffries: the Fire Fighters, whose president had been promoted to captain by Jeffries, and the Teamsters. To Hoffa and Brennan, the prospect of the mayor's office becoming the tool of their rivals far outweighed the liberal cries for racial unity. In fact, the question of whom to support in the mayoral campaign was really no question at all for the Teamster leaders. Their main trucking local, 299, was entirely segregated owing to the universal wishes of the white members, and their feelings for African Americans were not improved by the riots in June, in which a member of Local 155 was killed by black rioters while driving his milk truck. The choice for mayor was clear. "We do not think it is in labor's best interest, nor in the interest of good government, for a Mayor to owe his election to any particular group or clique," Brennan wrote in announcing the Teamsters' endorsement of Jeffries.

> Maybe he should have appointed exclusively, certain union leaders, or representatives of racial groups to head up the activities of City departments or commissions, but we don't think so and Jeffries didn't either. Some of the people he picked to advise on their specialties are now saying that he does not take their advice on all subjects.
> Well, after all, it was Jeffries who was elected as Mayor and not certain union leaders who would like to keep the City Hall in their vest pocket. . . . How much more do these certain labor leaders want?

In addition to its endorsement, the union gave $2,100 to the Jeffries campaign and free advertisements on the Teamsters' radio program. After Jeffries's landslide victory, the Teamsters claimed partial credit for it and reaffirmed their belief "in good City Government controlled by no group or individual."[35]

Finally taking notice that his public image would have to be improved were he to continue to wield political influence, Hoffa made efforts during the war to project a sense of patriotic responsibility. He squelched several strikes, including the threatened citywide walkout of Teamster garbage workers and a strike of the employees of the Detroit Street Railway. After the drivers at a grocery trucking company walked off the job in a rejection of his statewide cartage contract, Hoffa called the strikers to a meeting and "strongly advised" them to return to work, urging them to "remember there is a war going on and that food is necessary." The strike was called off, but probably not because of concerns for national security.[36] Despite his longstanding distrust of the federal government, Hoffa did his best to put up a patriotic front in order to please Tobin. At the request of the War Manpower Commission, which was gravely concerned about the "critical" labor shortage in the Detroit trucking industry, he opened a training school for truck drivers that graduated fewer than one hundred workers but nonetheless provided the *Michigan Teamster* with plenty of photos showing union volunteers contributing to the war effort.[37]

Especially useful to the Detroit Teamsters' public relations campaign during the war was Isaac Litwak's Laundry and Linen Drivers Local 285. As a Russian Jewish immigrant, Litwak had stronger feelings about the war than most of his colleagues in Joint Council 43. Local 285 served as headquarters for the sale of war bonds for all the locals in the joint council and received commendations from the military for its contributions to the war effort. In 1943 the Joint Council purchased enough bonds for a new Air Force bomber with "Detroit Teamsters" inscribed on its nose. The purchase of the bomber, however, was not sufficient to convince the state of the Teamsters' patriotism. At the end of the war, local and federal government agencies tested Hoffa's commitment to community and nation. The results would define him and his union for decades to come.[38]

Seven

The Making of a "Labor Boss"

Human life in common is only made possible when a majority comes together which is stronger than any separate individual and which remains united against all separate individuals. The power of this community is then set up as "right" in opposition to the power of the individual, which is condemned as "brute force." This replacement of the power of the individual by the power of a community constitutes the decisive step of civilization. The essence of it lies in the fact that the members of the community restrict themselves in their possibilities of satisfaction, whereas the individual knew no such restrictions.—SIGMUND FREUD, CIVILIZATION AND ITS DISCONTENTS[1]

The end of the war forced the coming out of the Detroit Teamsters. Jimmy Hoffa and his colleagues had always been belligerent, ill-mannered, and thoroughly illiberal, but few outside the union knew it until government authorities preparing for a new postwar order deemed those characteristics to be unacceptable in a labor union. The resulting clash of cultures thrust the men on Trumbull Avenue squarely into public view and created for them a social identity that would prove highly useful to their enemies in the decades to come.

The Brotherhood

While they usually chafed at regulations imposed by war labor boards, the Detroit Teamsters actually welcomed, of all things, orders by the War Manpower Commission (WMC) to allow women to fill the jobs

118

of union members serving in the armed forces. Of course, this generosity was not an act of feminism or patriotism. Hoffa's men maintained that female truck drivers could not permanently supplant the all-male regular membership "because of the high degree of skill necessary to handle this type of equipment," and, much to the Teamsters' delight, the presence of women gave them an opportunity to affirm their manhood. The hypermasculine culture of the union permitted the members to assert their sexuality without restraint. The *Michigan Teamster* frequently included salacious references to the secretaries at union headquarters and during the war encouraged the members to "make a motion to have our office girls wear bathing suits." The presence of female truck drivers not only provided the Teamster men with additional objects for their sexual predations, it also allowed them to distinguish themselves from the new members, to whom they regularly referred as "the Fairer Sex." In their language, their behavior, and even in their politics, the Detroit Teamsters consciously projected themselves as the manliest of men.[2]

The manliness of truck drivers first gained public notice in 1940 with the release of *They Drive by Night*, a Warner Bros. film starring George Raft (who was later compared to Hoffa by a writer for *Time* magazine) and Humphrey Bogart as Joe and Paul Fabrini, two brothers struggling to survive the dangerous roads, miserable working conditions, and cutthroat economy of the trucking industry. The film depicts truck drivers as brawling, tough-talking men who risk their lives on the highways and spend their free time at roadside cafes ogling women and swapping stories of their sexual conquests. Joe Fabrini tells a waitress, played by Ann Sheridan, that she has a "classy chassis" and that he likes the way she "fills out" her clothes. Later he wins a fistfight with another trucker and boasts that he and his brother are "tougher than any truck ever come off an assembly line."[3]

Indeed, the social environment and work culture of real truck drivers, and especially the Detroit Teamsters, produced the same combination of licentiousness and glorification of physical courage depicted by Hollywood. The remote supervision and autonomous work setting of trucking afforded drivers a protected space that was free of the limitations normally imposed on the behavior of other workers. Unlike manufacturing workers under the eye of a foreman or retail clerks obliged to be polite to customers, truck drivers could shout profanities or make lewd remarks to women from high up in the safety of their cabs, with no fear of punishment. Additionally, the constant and ferocious violence the Detroit Teamsters faced from employers, rival unions, and police during the union's formative years in the 1930s and 1940s placed a premium on one's toughness and ability to fight. A member of the bakery drivers local who was hospitalized as a result of a violent strike in 1944 was ridiculed as physically inadequate. "Wonder if the strike was a bit too much for his little delicate body!" crowed the *Michigan Teamster.* For these men, manhood was the product of a savage world; respectability and decorum could be expected of citizens, but not of warriors. After a Christian clergyman publicly criticized General George Patton, the paragon of violent manhood, for using too much profanity in a speech broadcast over the radio, the union's newspaper asked, "doesn't he know fighting words from a real fighting man and leader?"[4]

Hoffa was the General Patton of the Detroit Teamsters. He exalted bravery and despised frailty, and presented himself as the toughest, strongest, and most ruthless fighter in the union. He was proud of his muscular, five-foot, five-inch, 180-pound body and advertised the fact that he began each day with a strenuous program of physical exercise. In his relatively few moments away from union work, Hoffa enjoyed nothing more than a weekend of hunting in the woods around his second home in northern Michigan. To keep his son Jim from going "soft," he trained the boy to lift weights and took him on rugged hunting expeditions. Hoffa once proudly declared his potential to be "the meanest bastard that God ever created," and his manner of speech helped project the image he desired for himself. Local 299 organizer Joe Franco recalled a typical Hoffa instruction to one of his business agents:

> You cocksucker, you. I don't give a fuck, just do the fucking job, get it done and get the goddamn thing done with. I don't want to hear your bullshit on the fucking phone. You want to talk to me, get your goddamn ass over here. Get that goddamn contract straightened away. I don't want to hear nothing.

Teamster business agents may not always have appreciated this style of personnel management, but many in the union's rank and file respected Hoffa for what they considered to be his honest, "no bull-shit" approach. "He handled everything, I guess you would say, rough," remembered an over-the-road driver and member of Local 299. "You might not like the names he called you, but we trusted him."[5]

White Power, Workers' Power

Though the Detroit Teamsters were happy to oblige the War Manpower Commission's orders to include women in the membership, when it came to African Americans, Hoffa was less willing to take responsibility for alleviating the nation's growing shortage of workers. Trouble first began in the fall of 1942, when a black truck driver named Festus Hairston applied for a job with the White Star Trucking Company, an over-the-road firm under contract with Hoffa's Local 299. The owner of the company told Hairston that he would have to join the local before he could be hired, since the union held a closed-shop contract with White Star. Hairston, who had been a building materials driver and a member of Local 247, arranged with a friend who was one of Local 299's secretaries to transfer his membership. But when he returned to White Star with his Local 299 card, he was told that he would have to get approval from the union to drive long hauls. Hairston went to the Teamsters hall, where Hoffa informed him that he would not be permitted to take the White Star job because the membership of the local would not allow black drivers on over-the-road jobs.[6]

Hoffa was unaware that the man pleading for a job was no ordinary black truck driver. In fact, Hairston was an agent of the Detroit civil rights movement. A graduate of Ohio State University, Hairston worked in partnership with C. LeBron Simmons, a member of the all-black garbage truck drivers Local 663, which was an affiliate of Teamsters Joint Council 43. And Simmons was certainly no ordinary garbageman. He was also an attorney, a founder of the anti-discrimination Citizens Committee for Jobs in War Industry, a member of the Communist Party, and the president of the Detroit branch of the National Negro Congress, which in the 1940s was the civil rights front organization of the CP. Immediately after the confrontation with Hoffa, Hairston and Simmons launched a campaign to

121

desegregate the Teamsters. They arranged for articles on the union's Jim Crow policy to be published in local black newspapers, filed suit in federal court seeking an injunction to restrain the Teamsters from interfering with black drivers' right to work, and in December 1942 submitted a complaint to the newly opened Detroit branch of the President's Fair Employment Practice Committee (FEPC).[7]

When the federal anti-discrimination agency began investigating Hairston's complaint in the winter of 1943, it found that while a sizable portion of the membership of the Detroit Teamsters was black, some of the locals were nearly all white, many remained strictly segregated, and all relegated nonwhite members to the lowest-paying jobs. During the war, nearly one-third of the members of the locals in Joint Council 43 were African-American, many of them concentrated in Local 337, where black warehousemen, dock workers, and bottling plant workers made up close to half the membership. However, as Hoffa admitted to FEPC investigators, black Teamsters were barred from several job categories by informal but strictly enforced union policies. He explained that retail and wholesale employers under contract with Local 337 did not allow black delivery drivers because of the objections of customers. In Local 299, Hoffa claimed that over-the-road drivers, who constituted a major portion of the local's membership and were the highest-paid truck drivers in the union, refused to allow black members since long-distance hauls required two drivers to share a cab, meals, and a sleeping compartment. The FEPC investigators soon found that this "understanding" about highway jobs was shared by all the Teamster locals in the twelve states covered by the Central States Drivers Council (CSDC).[8]

Though all the locals affiliated with the Central States Drivers Council were shown to discriminate against black drivers, the most blatant offender was the home local of the CSDC's own negotiating chairman. A report by the Detroit branch of the FEPC stated that "of all the groups amenable to Executive Order 9346 [which granted the agency specific investigative powers], Teamsters Local 299, through its officers, has shown the greatest disregard and contempt for the non-discrimination order than any other." Hoffa and Dexter Lewis of the CSDC were called to a meeting with Hairston and representatives of the WMC and the FEPC in February 1943. At the meeting, the Teamster leaders predicted widespread strikes if blacks were allowed to work as highway drivers. Hoffa remained "belligerent and defiant" toward the federal agents and threatened that Hairston would be barred from all trucking jobs in Detroit if he continued to press his case against the union.[9]

In August, another black truck driver came forward, charging that Local 299 would not allow him to haul war materials over the highways for his employer, the Mannion Express Company. George Johnson claimed that the company was desperate to give him the better-paying highway routes but was so intimidated by the union that he was occasionally assigned to make trips to Saginaw at night, "when there was less danger of being caught by Local 299." Johnson was subsequently fired from the company, which the employer claimed was demanded by the union. By the end of the year several other black truckers, perhaps emboldened by Hairston and Simmons's efforts and the FEPC investigation, submitted complaints to the agency. As in Johnson's case, nearly all the employers interviewed by the FEPC claimed they were willing to assign black drivers to highway jobs, and all without exception insisted that the Teamsters did not allow them to do so. Several managers testified that when they did hire black drivers for over-the-road jobs, either the white drivers refused to work with them or officials from Local 299 appeared at the loading docks and threatened to pull their men off the trucks if the black drivers were not discharged.[10]

In another conference with the FEPC in August 1944, Hoffa protested that civil rights organizations had been satisfied with the Teamsters' efforts on behalf of black workers and were "going along with them." In fact, the Detroit branch of the NAACP had actually assisted the union's organizing efforts in black neighborhoods and had encouraged black truck drivers to join the Teamsters. But when asked in 1944 whether he was aware of the union's policy barring black drivers from certain jobs, Detroit NAACP director Gloster Current claimed he had "little knowledge of the inner workings of the various locals of the Teamsters union." Leaders of the local branch of the National Urban League also denied knowledge of the Teamsters' color line. Hoffa and the Teamsters had been able to hide the discrimination behind the union's record of providing decent, if not the highest-paying, jobs to thousands of black workers.[11]

Also helping to shield the Detroit Teamsters from criticism was the public activism of Clifford Moore, president of the all-black Local 663, who was a leading voice for civil rights within the Wayne County AFL. During the war, Moore submitted resolutions at the Michigan Federation of Labor convention endorsing the FEPC, condemning the poll tax, and calling for the integration of the armed forces. In 1942 he headed a delegation of Detroit unionists who traveled to Washington, D.C., to pressure the federal government to maintain its commitment to house blacks at the Sojourner Truth housing project despite militant white opposition. Moore criticized the national CIO leadership for its reluctance to enter the Sojourner Truth controversy, and presented the AFL as the true labor champion of black civil rights. Nonetheless, Moore's apparently sincere efforts were belied not only by the fact that he represented the lowest-paid Teamsters in Detroit but also by the number of complaints submitted to the FEPC by black truck drivers, which by the end of 1944 had swelled to more than fifty.[12]

When the Teamsters' discrimination and Hoffa's attitude toward the FEPC became increasingly public, official black Detroit finally took notice. In January 1945, Hoffa admitted to the agency's charges in the *Detroit Free Press*. "There is no secret about our position," he said. "This union is clean as a whistle. The members have voted that Negroes can't be drivers." With characteristic candor, Hoffa also acknowledged that the pay differential between highway work and jobs assigned to blacks was 20 cents per hour. He then insisted that he would "work this thing out in my own way" but offered no promises of a quick remedy. "It takes time to work a thing like that out," he told the newspaper. To conclude the interview, Hoffa neatly summed up not only his attitude toward the FEPC investigation but also his views on state intervention in industrial relations and the social responsibility of labor leaders: "I'm getting tired of having war agencies and newspapers trying to tell me how to run this union." A few days later, the Detroit NAACP issued a public protest against Hoffa's "defiance." In a telegram sent to the chairman of the FEPC and published in the Detroit newspapers, Gloster Current declared "it is evident that the union does not intend to comply unless drastic action is taken."[13]

While local FEPC officials were attempting to persuade Hoffa to consent to the President's anti-discrimination order, members of the national FEPC were working to force compliance through the IBT headquarters in Indianapolis. In May, Boris Shishkin, the AFL representative on the national FEPC, cajoled AFL president William Green into putting pressure on Dan Tobin. Green urged the IBT chief to act "before a public hearing by the Committee in Detroit may embarrass the Union and the A. F. of L." Tobin stonewalled for more than a year, claiming that the Teamsters did not discriminate against any truck drivers and refusing to make a commitment that he would intervene in Detroit. Finally, at a conference with FEPC members in Washington in August 1944, Tobin expressed his indignation at the "innuendoes" that the Teamsters barred blacks from working as highway drivers and claimed that he had no knowledge of the situation in Local 299. However, despite his protestations of ignorance, Tobin also declared that the complaints were "highly exaggerated" and instigated by a "Negro agitator," and that the trucking employers in Detroit were using the issue to weaken the union and embarrass him, a known supporter of the Roosevelt administration. To the bemusement of the FEPC officials, Tobin then let slip that the members of Local 299 were "backward" and that their objection to sharing a cab with a black driver was "frivolous." In almost the same breath, however, he acknowledged that he "would not want to sleep with a Negro" either.[14]

Faced with Tobin's intransigence and Hoffa's outright hostility, by 1945 the FEPC was running out of options. Executive Order 9346 gave the agency the right to conduct hearings, make findings of fact, issue employment policy directives to war agencies and industries, and recommend to the chairman of the War Manpower Commission measures to be used in eliminating discrimination, but withheld the enforcement powers of subpoena and criminal prosecution. The committee could hold a hearing on discrimination in Local 299 but could not force Hoffa or any other Teamster officials to testify. Some members cautioned that such a hearing would accomplish little and might embarrass the agency. Yet as the war was drawing to a close with no sign of Hoffa's compliance, a sense of desperation began to creep into the Detroit office. "To postpone or cancel plans for public hearing against this union will have an adverse effect on the Detroit community's reaction to the program of the FEPC," warned William T. McKnight, the agency's Midwest region director, in a memorandum to the national office. "For more than two years the people of Detroit have expected the Committee to hold hearings in Detroit. . . . There has been more newspaper publicity in Detroit concerning the exclusion of Negroes from membership in this local union than all other groups combined." McKnight also argued that Hoffa's Teamsters could be used as an example to bolster the agency's credibility with the powerful automobile companies:

> Because of the almost constant warfare that has gone on between management and labor in this area, with management being held up to the public as almost the sole opponent to the acceptance of the non-discrimination principle in employment, a hearing against a labor union would go a long way to establish in the minds of the public generally and management particularly that the Committee intends to fight discrimination wherever found. There is strong likelihood that respect for, if not support of, the Committee's program would be obtained from additional elements in the community if the hearings are held as contemplated.[15]

After McKnight succeeded in convincing his superiors in Washington to allow a hearing in Detroit, a notice went out to the Teamsters requesting their presence. Hoffa phoned the lawyers representing the FEPC and asked if the agency could subpoena him or invoke criminal penalties. When he received answers in the negative to both queries, the Teamster leader informed the lawyers that he did not intend "to be at the goddamn meeting." Nonetheless, the hearing was held on June 2. Present were several of the complainants, attorneys representing three of the eleven trucking companies that were also charged with discrimination, and members of the Detroit FEPC and the U.S. Employment Service, which had stopped referring drivers to the companies under contract with 299.[16]

The FEPC attorney began the hearing by describing the union's racist policies and Hoffa's open contempt for the agency, then charged the Teamsters with "creating and maintaining a pattern of discrimination in a segment of the trucking industry which has circumscribed the job opportunities of qualified Negroes, and has seriously impaired their effectiveness in contributing to the nation's war effort." Though the thrust of the hearing was directed at the Teamsters, the employers were criticized for demonstrating "a weakness which one does not normally associate with American management." The FEPC attorney acknowledged that the union possessed a "powerful weapon" in its ability to call or simply threaten a strike, "but, everything considered, it appears that the companies have assumed an unusually supine attitude and have been content to allow needed trucks to lie idle instead of asserting their unquestioned prerogative of hiring in accordance with the national policy enunciated in the Executive Order." The aggrieved black truck drivers were then asked to recount their nearly identical stories of employers willing to hire them and the union standing in the way. Soon after the hearing, the investigation and public censure of the Detroit Teamsters ended along with the war and federal support for the FEPC.[17]

Though the government's investigation failed to change the Teamsters' discriminatory policies, it did reveal much about Hoffa and his union that had little to do with race. Joe Franco, one of Hoffa's closest assistants in the late 1940s, recalled that the stand against the FEPC was unrelated to Hoffa's own feelings about blacks. "In many local meetings, I heard Jimmy telling the members that he would never allow a black man on the highways as an over-the-road driver," Franco remembered. "Underneath it all, it was picking up points with the members." Hoffa had reason to stay on the good side of the rank and file. Investigators for the FEPC learned that several attempts were made by Teamster officials in Ohio to integrate over-the-road routes, but "white opposition and a strike threat" forced the union to abandon the effort. As in the past for Hoffa, the interest of preserving his hold over the union far outweighed any obligations to serve an abstract notion of a brotherhood of man.

Most important for Hoffa's calculations, the protest initiated by Hairston and Simmons in Local 299 did not spread to other locals in the Teamsters Joint Council where black workers constituted significant portions of the membership. Unlike leaders in many other unions during the war, Hoffa did not face extensive black mobilization against discrimination within the rank and file, and so he remained beholden to the interests of the majority white members, particularly those in the vitally important Local 299. For all his bluster and bravado in the face of the government and the press, Hoffa knew that he depended on their loyalty for his position of power. Furthermore, caving in to the FEPC would not only incite the members but also legitimize other government intrusion into his affairs—anathema to the anti-statist

Hoffa. Faced with a choice of either provoking an uprising among the core of the membership or bearing the hostility of the federal government and the press, Hoffa reflexively chose the latter.[18]

"We Have Got to Fight While We Are Strong"

At the same time that Hoffa and the Detroit Teamsters were protecting the interests of their members against the demands of the government, they were receiving an object lesson in the dangers of neglecting those interests. Unrest among Teamster members at Dossin Food Products Company, the Pepsi-Cola bottler, began in the summer of 1943. The company had signed with Teamsters Local 337 in 1940 to avoid dealing with the United Brewery Workers, who had been expelled from the AFL and were then on the verge of affiliating with the CIO. After the Teamsters contract was signed, four organizers from another Teamster nemesis, the Retail, Wholesale and Department Store Employees of the CIO, infiltrated the plant and began agitating among the workers to switch their affiliation to the RWDSE. The drivers at the plant were well paid by industry standards, but Solomon Sniderman, the Teamsters' representative on the regional War Labor Board, was not able to win them pay increases during the war. At a meeting in July 1943 that was attended by Hoffa, Local 337 president Bert Brennan, and representatives of the Retail Workers, a group of employees complained that they "had gotten no contract changes, no wage raises, no vacations, no improvement in deplorable sanitary conditions, no overtime pay." The workers then voted to drop their membership in the Teamsters and join the CIO union. They were advised by the Retail Workers to wait until the Teamster contract with the company expired at the end of February in 1944, at which point they would be welcomed into the CIO.[19]

The CIO's agitation and the Dossin employees' resentment of the Teamsters continued into the winter of 1944. In January, a petition containing the signatures of a clear majority of the workers demanding a termination of the Teamsters contract on the expiration date was delivered to management. The signatories also stated that they would strike if the contract were renewed and would hold the company liable for any dues deducted on behalf of the Teamsters after March 1. Fearing either Teamster retribution or the prospect of bargaining with champions of industrial democracy, the owner of the company, Walter Dossin, refused to accept the petition and then telephoned Trumbull Avenue. A new contract was quickly signed and the four Retail Worker organizers were summoned to Teamster headquarters, where they were tried before the Executive Board of Local 337, found guilty of disloyalty and of violating an agreement with an employer, and expelled. Dossin then fired the four in accordance with the closed-shop contract. Immediately, more than 100 drivers and production workers, representing roughly two-thirds of the workforce, walked out in protest. Shipments of Pepsi to 12,000 retail stores and many of the automobile plants were halted until the Teamsters were able to gather their forces for a counterattack.[20]

As in 1940, when the Brewery Workers shut down Dossin in protest of the first Teamster contract, Hoffa and Brennan organized a replacement force of officers and stewards from every local in the Joint Council to drive the trucks and keep the plant open. Hoffa himself took over one of the company's delivery routes. And, as in 1940, the Teamsters' opponents opted to use Teamster tactics to stop the trucks. Squads of the toughest fighters from the Retail Workers, including former members of the Detroit Police Department, attacked the trucks at the gates and in the streets, taking baseball bats and blackjacks to the heads of the drivers and flinging cases of soda pop onto the pavement.

One of the Teamsters braving the wrath of the Retail Workers was Solomon Sniderman. Local CIO leaders had already protested Sniderman's presence on the War Labor Board and claimed that he had sabotaged the wage requests of CIO unions and was "doing a job on them," but when they learned he was driving a Dossin truck, a full-scale campaign was launched to oust the Teamster from the board. In an indignant article exposing Sniderman's participation in breaking the strike, the *Michigan CIO News* bitterly noted, "Detroit has seen many strange things during the war emergency, but the spectacle of a member of the Regional War Labor Board scabbing on a strike is offered as something new under the sun." As the strike entered its fifth week, the Greater Detroit and Wayne County CIO Council unanimously passed a resolution demanding Sniderman's removal from the board. Fortunately for the CIO, Sniderman was also under fire from the press after being arraigned for an alleged plot to shake down twelve Detroit funeral homes. Several undertakers testified in Wayne County Recorders Court that Sniderman, along with another Teamster business agent and the head of the local florists' association, had threatened to cut off deliveries of funeral supplies unless they made payments to the Teamsters and signed a contract with the union. Sniderman was more sensitive to the political *zeitgeist* than his union colleagues and understood that breaking strikes and extorting mortuaries could not be tolerated in a public official. On April 8, he announced that he would take a leave from the War Labor Board "until such time as my innocence of the serious charges recently placed against me has been established."[21]

As it reached its twelfth week, the battle over 140 soda pop workers escalated into a citywide war between the Teamsters and the CIO. In an act of solidarity with the Retail Workers, UAW shop stewards at converted automobile factories organized teams of workers to block deliveries made by Teamster drivers to the plant cafeterias. Anti-Teamster sentiment was especially strong among Chrysler workers. On Monday, May 15, at the company's Highland Park plant, a Dossin truck driven by a Teamster was overturned as it arrived to make a delivery at the cafeteria. After the company fired sixteen of the workers, including two UAW stewards, for insubordination, all 3,000 of the plant employees walked off the job in protest. The wildcat strike spread to three other Chrysler plants and the Amplex Packing plant, where employees stopped working in sympathy with the fired Highland Park activists. With the Chrysler plants shut down, the Dodge Truck plant was forced to suspend operations through lack of parts and Dodge Main was partially closed by an overpiling of stock. Within forty-eight hours after the truck was overturned at Highland Park, more than 10,000 workers were off the job and seven armament plants sat paralyzed.

On Wednesday, as the UAW rank-and-file rebellion against the Teamsters reached its peak, the Brewery Workers, newly affiliated with the CIO, signed a contract with the Coca-Cola plant located next door to Dossin's on Gratiot Avenue. Fearful that the agreement was a sweetheart deal generous enough to make it impossible to win the Dossin workers from the CIO, Hoffa and Brennan sent carloads of heavies armed with blackjacks and steel chains to force an annulment of the contract. One of the Teamster cars hurtled into a crowd of Brewery Worker organizers, sending one man to the hospital with severe head injuries.[22] Growing desperate that such measures would not prevent them from losing the entire bottling industry to the CIO, Hoffa and Brennan called 10,000 Teamster over-the-road drivers out of work and warned Mayor Jeffries they would "stop every truck moving into the city" as long as the CIO's contract with the Coca-Cola plant stood. "We have got to fight while we are strong," Brennan told the mayor. "If we lose, this is the beginning of the end." The brinksmanship by both sides forced the local War Labor Board to call an emergency hearing and order the attendance of representatives from the Teamsters and the CIO unions, including Hoffa, Brennan, John Gibson, who was then president of the Michigan CIO Council, and Samuel Wolchok of the national Retail Workers organization. At the hearing, the Teamsters agreed to call the highway truckers back to work and recognize the Brewery Workers' contract with Coca-Cola in exchange for the CIO ending the strike at Dossin's. In addition, both sides agreed to cease hostilities until elections to determine representation rights at both plants were held by the National Labor Relations Board.[23]

As the NLRB prepared to conduct the voting, Hoffa took formal measures of his own to forestall the dangers posed by potentially disloyal members of his union. At the June meeting of the Michigan Conference of Teamsters, a motion was passed "that no representative or officer of any local union be allowed to work for, aid, or abet in any way, any association or competitive organization of our local unions." But it was too late. The Teamsters lost the Coca-Cola employees to the Brewery Workers by a vote of 100 to 75. At Dossin, the results were even more disastrous—125 employees voted to be represented by the Retail Workers while only seven cast ballots for the Teamsters. Tobin, stunned by the loss and embarrassed by the Detroit Teamsters' actions, blamed the fiasco on a "subversive conspiracy" by Trotskyists in the RWDSE "to destroy not only our union, but all of organized labor as well." To save face, the IBT president contended that the Detroit Teamsters had attempted to protect the nation from defeat in the war. "Once in control of Trotskyites, war production would virtually cease in the United States," Tobin proclaimed.[24]

More sober analyses came from other Teamster sources. Joseph Padway, the IBT general counsel, attributed the defeats at Dossin and

Coca-Cola to the restrictions placed on the union by the wartime state. "What the CIO does is to await the outcome of an application filed by the Teamsters with the War Labor Board for an increase in wages," Padway wrote to Tobin. "If the War Labor Board acts slowly or turns down the plea for an increase, or if it is granted by the regional board, but appealed to the National War Labor Board, it has its stooges spread vicious propaganda to the effect that it is due to the indifference of the Teamster unions to the interests of the workers that the increase is not granted. To the workers who have waited patiently for the increase, this argument has a strong appeal and it is very easy to arouse their suspicions and cause secession." Hoffa registered a similar complaint when interviewed by A. H. Raskin, the future labor correspondent for the *New York Times*, who was then conducting a survey of industrial conflict in Detroit for the Army. According to Raskin's report, the Teamster leader admitted that "a mood of rebellion and irrationality is sweeping the membership" in the bottling, retail, and warehousing industries, and that he was "finding it impossible to keep his members in line on observance of contract provisions," but only because of the wartime restraints on the union's ability to win good contracts. Hoffa's "insistence that there be no stoppages was simply leading to mass desertion from his union to the CIO Retail, Wholesale and Warehouse Workers, which has been conducting a raid on the Teamsters' jurisdiction in Detroit."[25]

While a union guided by a sense of social responsibility might have accepted defeat after being overwhelmingly rejected by workers in a bargaining unit and ordered by the federal government to relinquish its representation rights, Hoffa and the Detroit Teamsters still considered the employees at the bottling plants to be fair game. They felt entitled to those workers because of their disregard for formal democracy and government authority, but they were also given reason for optimism by a recent weakening of the state regulatory apparatus. In 1943, John Frey, the national AFL's most ardent opponent of the CIO, had persuaded conservatives in the Congress to attach a rider to the NLRB's annual appropriations bill denying funds for the investigation of contracts signed by unions and employers without the consent of workers. Although management at the Coca-Cola plant remained committed to its own sweetheart contract with the CIO, Walter Dossin was still willing to do business with the Teamsters. Shortly after the NLRB election in June, Dossin announced that he regarded himself as bound by the contract he had renewed with Hoffa and Brennan in January. The Retail Workers appealed to the War Labor Board, but the case was deemed to be still under the jurisdiction of the NLRB, which was forbidden by the "Frey rider" from taking action. Once again, the CIO union called its members out on strike, and once again the Teamsters mobilized to keep the plant open. Rather than staff the bottling and delivery operations themselves, however, Hoffa and the Teamster officers formed protective gauntlets around the crews of African-American replacements brought in by Dossin.[26]

The battle at Dossin was the last significant jurisdictional contest between Hoffa's Teamsters and the CIO, and, fittingly, it ended with a demonstration of both the power of competition and the repressive consequences of corporatism. After disregarding the NLRB election results, Walter Dossin and the Teamsters continued to face the dogged opposition of the Retail Workers and scores of disgruntled employees, who maintained a well-staffed picket line outside the plant. To secure his control over the bottling plant workers, Hoffa convinced Dossin, who apparently feared the roughneck Teamsters more than the "industrial democrats" in the CIO, that better contract terms were necessary to hold off the rival union. The resulting pay hike was large enough to cause the Retail Workers and the Michigan CIO to file a complaint with the War Labor Board. Acceding to the CIO's wishes, the WLB fined Dossin $7,509 for increasing wages without board authorization. Despite this intervention by the state against the rewards of competition, both the Teamster contract and the CIO strike continued until the spring of 1945, when the end of the war and the logic of corporatism combined to halt the contest between the unions.[27]

Philip Murray, Walter Reuther, and other national CIO leaders had been frustrated in their efforts to share control of the wartime managerial state, but as the war drew to a close they held fast to their ambitions to become co-managers of a corporatist postwar order. The establishment of such a regime required that these aspiring "labor statesmen" discipline and unify a labor movement still teeming with internal rivalries. Strikes like those caused by the Dossin dispute "were the last thing that anybody that has the welfare of the labor movement and the welfare of the country at heart would want," said Van Bittner, the CIO's representative on the National War Labor Board. In March

1945, the national CIO office persuaded AFL President William Green and Eric Johnston, president of the United States Chamber of Commerce, to sign a "New Charter for Labor and Management." The charter pledged that the union federations along with corporate leaders would cooperate in building a postwar economy of high wages, high employment, and ever-increasing production. Most important for the CIO and the corporations, the agreement promised harmony within and between the classes. Said the *CIO News*, "It's industrial peace for the postwar period!"[28]

CIO leaders in Detroit set out to enforce the new peace pact. In May, Reuther and Michigan CIO Regional Director Gus Scholle called a meeting with Roy Scoggins, the new leader of the Michigan RWDSE, and Hoffa and Brennan to bring an end to the embarrassing and disruptive conflict between the Teamsters and the Retail Workers. At the meeting, both sides agreed to end raiding of companies already organized, which included Dossin and other firms under Teamster sweetheart contracts. Much more than just stopping the soda pop wars, the peace agreement was "intended to establish a pattern of CIO-AFL co-operative and friendly relationships looking forward to the complete elimination of jurisdictional strife between the CIO and AFL." By eliminating the last significant source of external competition for the Detroit Teamsters, however, this corporatist victory deprived thousands of workers of economic leverage and removed a principal motivation for Hoffa's militancy. Workers at Dossin and other companies in the retail, warehousing, bottling, and dairy industries would henceforth have to depend on the goodwill of the Detroit Teamster officers for strong representation of their interests or else oppose the leadership alone.[29]

Perhaps not coincidentally, on June 12, five weeks after the peace meeting with the CIO and ten days after the FEPC hearing, Tobin removed the international's trusteeship over Local 299, thereby allowing elections for the union's officers. For Hoffa, the timing was especially fortuitous. Since most of the Detroit Teamster dissidents were contained in Local 337 and the CIO was effectively barred from trucking, Hoffa was able during the war to build a base of support among the truck drivers in Local 299.[30] In addition to the gratitude he received for protecting the truckers' work environment from integration, Hoffa benefited from the economic standing of the local's members, which had risen steadily since the beginning of the war. Ironically, besides their sense of racial solidarity, much of the good feeling among the membership that lifted Hoffa to the top of the local could not be attributed to the achievements of Hoffa himself. Rather, the buoyant times in the local were due in large part to the benevolence of the federal government. In 1943, when the Central States Area Agreement came due, the War Labor Board granted an 8 percent wage increase to over-the-road drivers covered by the contract, including those in Local 299. The 2,000 cartage drivers, dockmen, and checkers in the local, who made up approximately half of 299's membership and attended union meetings in greater numbers than over-the-road drivers, who were often away on long-distance runs, fared even better during the war. They were awarded five-cent wage increases by the NWLB in 1943, 1944, and April 1945, representing an overall raise of more than 18 percent in the two-year period prior to the union election in June. In contrast, the average wage for automobile production workers during the same period was raised by less than 3 percent. The anti-statist Hoffa rode to the presidency of the local on a wave of government-mandated largesse. In a voice vote of the members present at the local's weekly meeting, Hoffa was elected without opposition.[31]

"You Are With Us or Against Us"

After the war, the state was less helpful to the Teamster leader. Prompted by the massive strike wave of 1945 and 1946, a surge of anti-labor reaction mandated Congress to roll back the unions. In the winter and spring of 1946, the Case bill, which would have severely limited the rights of unions, and included, among other provisions, a complete ban on secondary boycotts, was approved by the House and Senate but vetoed by President Truman. However, it appeared certain that one or another similar bill would eventually be passed into law. In the spring of 1946, as the Congress continued drafting legislation to outlaw coercive organizing tactics by labor unions, Hoffa took the remaining opportunity to launch a secondary boycott campaign aimed at completing the capture of the Detroit food industry. In the process, he was demonized as the "boss" of the Teamsters and a threat to civil society.[32]

In April, Hoffa demanded that all 6,000 Detroit groceries and butcher shops pay five dollars each for "permits" to pick up their orders at wholesale food suppliers, which had been forced to sign contracts with the union in 1941. The permits, called "associate memberships" by the Teamsters, were tantamount to union contracts for the groceries, most of which were staffed entirely by the families that owned them. Faced with the prospect of making payments to the union or having their supplies cut off, the members of the Detroit Retail Meat Merchants Association and the Detroit Retail Grocers Association called emergency meetings with the Teamsters in hopes of fending off the union's attack.

At an assembly of the meat market operators, Hoffa quieted the angry catcalls directed toward him with a blunt ultimatum. "You are with us or against us," he declared. "We are going ahead to organize the stores. The choice is up to you, and no matter how you argue you will be signed up." The association's governing board then encouraged the members to comply with Hoffa's demands. Finally, after Louis Shamie, the president of the grocers association, arrived to announce that his organization had capitulated to the union earlier in the day, the assembled meat merchants voted unanimously to begin contract negotiations with Hoffa. But when the Teamster leader issued his demands, which included two-dollar monthly dues in addition to the permit fees, a closed shop requiring all new employees to join the union, and full compliance with all future Teamster edicts, several of the small shopkeepers began organizing a revolt against the leadership of the two associations. One of the rebels, after hearing of the contract terms, claimed that fewer than half the city's grocers and butchers belonged to either association and warned that an agreement with Hoffa would be used to force all shopkeepers into the union. "If the officers of the association sit down at a table with the Teamsters and sign a contract," he claimed, "they will be dealing in a slave market and selling out the other grocers and meat dealers."[33]

While the leaders of the associations pleaded with Hoffa for time to convince the members to accept the contract, the uprising among the shopkeepers gained some powerful allies. On the same day that the *Detroit News* condemned the "shakedown" as a "grave and fundamental challenge to the authority of law," Mayor Jeffries announced that he had ordered the police department to begin a formal investigation of the Teamsters' organizing tactics. Five detectives were assigned to full-time duty on a special unit charged with determining whether criminal charges of extortion were warranted. Unknown to the press and the mayor, however, one of the detectives assigned to the squad was Albert DeLamielleure, who had been on the unofficial Teamsters payroll for several years. The presence of an ally within the investigation did not stop Brennan, titular chairman of the Detroit Teamsters' political action committee, from expressing his displeasure with the ungrateful mayor, who had benefited from substantial financial support from the union during his reelection campaign in 1945. "I think Jeffries is minding somebody else's business again," Brennan told the press.[34]

Despite Brennan's veiled threat to withdraw support from the mayor in the next election and the union's obstinate refusal to remove or modify the ultimatum, Jeffries's intervention emboldened the previously cowed leaders of the associations to take on the Teamsters. At a meeting called by the executive boards of both organizations, more than 2,000 shopkeepers loudly endorsed a resolution pledging themselves to pay no "tribute" to the Teamsters and vowing to "meet violence with violence and fight fire with fire." Many in the crowd urged that the merchants organize themselves into armed militias to protect themselves from the Teamsters. Hoffa scoffed at the suggestion that his union depended on violence to force the grocers to sign. "That's ridiculous," he sneered. "There is no need for violence of any sort. Our packinghouse dockworkers will simply refuse to serve them and the truckers will not deliver to their places of business. They'll have to join." To help enforce the boycott, carloads of Teamster "permit salesmen" formed blockades around loading docks at packinghouses and produce terminals, physically sealing off the merchants from their supplies.[35]

"Grocers and butchers fight for all of us," proclaimed the *Detroit News* in one of its daily editorials attacking the Teamster campaign. "This ugly exploitation of the presumedly helpless is something, which, if not stopped, will go on fastening its tentacles on Detroit citizens, until at last its grip will be one that can never be shaken loose." Hoffa's Teamsters were depicted as a subversive force no less dangerous than the most insidious radical organizations. "What is confronted is an attempt of the Teamsters, starting with their monopoly of local haulage, to infiltrate the entire economic life of the city," the newspaper warned. "James Hoffa holds the power to cut Detroit's lifeline."

These warnings were echoed in the *Detroit Free Press*, which was usually slightly more sympathetic to labor than its competitor:

> Detroit's citizens are faced with the choice of keeping control of the city's political and economic life in their own hands, or of supinely surrendering that control to a small group of lawless union leaders. . . . The issue involved here transcends even the legal aspects of the union racket. . . . if carried to its possible conclusion, it means that every citizen will be a vassal of the union hierarchy.[36]

The *News* also attacked County Prosecutor Gerald K. O'Brien, who announced that he found no legal basis for prosecuting the Teamsters, and accused him of fearing retribution from the union in the next election. O'Brien had, in fact, received financial support from the Detroit Teamsters during his campaign for County Prosecutor in 1944. "Don't elect men to public office who will let political obligations get in the way of their sworn duty," the newspaper counseled its readers. "Or, if you do, prepare to do without the protection of the law." Calls for criminal charges to protect the merchants even reached Washington, where Clare Hoffman, the Teamsters' chief nemesis in Congress, called for legislation to end the union's "extortion" and "highway robbery."[37]

Despite the protests, Jeffries initially balked at forcing the prosecutor to press charges against the union, claiming there was not sufficient evidence of coercion to warrant an arrest of Hoffa and his business agents. On May 8, however, the escalation of the conflict forced the mayor's hand. The officers of the grocers and butchers associations notified the Teamsters that they would no longer consider the union's demands and would urge their members to refuse to buy the five-dollar permits. In reply, Hoffa issued a terse statement that the "strike is in effect." Union business agents in what the *Detroit News* called "the famous black automobiles of the Teamster picket squads" arrived at the wholesalers to reinforce the blockades. Jeffries, who had recently announced his candidacy for governor and was perhaps less dependent on Teamster support for the statewide race than he had been in his mayoral campaigns, immediately sharpened his rhetoric against the union. The Teamsters' organizing drive had caused "a widespread public clamor to throw the leaders in jail," the Republican candidate acknowledged in a speech to the Kiwanis Club in Monroe. "And maybe before we get through, that's what we will do." The next day, at the request of Jeffries, who had gone over the head of a still reluctant O'Brien, Recorder's Judge Christopher E. Stein ordered a warrant for the arrest of Hoffa on charges of extortion. Jeffries also asked for federal intervention from U.S. Attorney General Tom C. Clark, who ordered an investigation by the FBI.[38]

Undaunted by the warrant, the FBI investigation, or the avalanche of public condemnation, Hoffa entered a plea of innocent to the extortion charge, posted bond, and began carrying out his promise to make the merchants pay, "one by one." Two days after entering his plea, Hoffa personally directed a picket line in front of a grocery store on Second Boulevard owned by Joseph Acho, one of many Syrian immigrants who operated small markets in Detroit. While the pickets marched in front of the store wearing sandwich boards declaring the retailer "unfair to organized labor," Hoffa and Brennan toured the neighborhood in Hoffa's two-tone gray Buick sedan (the only Teamster car that wasn't black), glaring through the windows at shoppers and passing motorists who berated the pickets. By the end of the day, a group of Syrian retail grocers persuaded Acho to negotiate with the Teamsters. The next morning, as Hoffa's menacing visage dominated the front pages of the city's newspapers, the Teamsters shifted the roving strike to a group of Jewish-owned markets along Dexter Boulevard on the West Side. After a few hours of picketing, two of the markets, which belonged to a Jewish retailers association, agreed to terms with the union. Hoffa then announced he would move to the groceries belonging to the Jewish East Side Merchants Association. Meanwhile, the Teamster leader was working through paid agents inside the grocers' nationality groups to pressure the shop owners to capitulate. Within two days, all the Syrian grocers and four Jewish markets agreed to negotiate with the union.[39]

As the Teamster campaign appeared to be gaining momentum in the face of government opposition, the Detroit press spouted its outrage. Assailing "union bosses" for their "unspeakably un-American program of economic piracy," the *News* editorialized that "Here in Detroit, there is loathing for James Hoffa, boss of the Teamsters Union, who is virtually holding a gun at the heads of grocers and meat shop men." The beloved, family-owned corner markets were threatened with extinction by the Teamsters' "brute force." Describing a city "beset by a berserk labor union's determination to reduce it to subjection," the newspaper declared the Teamsters' campaign "downright Fascism." On the House floor, Clare Hoffman presented the Detroit Teamsters as justification for revision of the Wagner Act, while in the Senate, Joseph Ball of Minnesota was gathering evidence from the FBI investigation to support his bill forbidding secondary boycotts.[40]

The grocers themselves charged that the Teamsters' organizing drive was simply a "million-dollar take" designed to fill the union's coffers. But Hoffa soon lowered the permit fee from five dollars to two, while remaining steadfast in his demands that all clerks must be union members and "deliveries to all groceries and meat markets must be made by union drivers, members of the Teamsters' Union." Publicly, Hoffa defended the organizing campaign as a necessary measure to replace jobs lost by Teamsters who had served in the military during the war. "These retailers are taking jobs from Teamsters and we don't intend to let them get away with it," he told the press, suggesting that grocers who picked up their own supplies were in effect scabbing on his members. "The big packing houses have gotten rid of a good many of their trucks during the war years and they are not replacing them. We've got Teamsters out of work. The retailers are scattered and unorganized and they've got to be brought together so that problems like this can be controlled."[41]

In private correspondence with IBT headquarters, however, Hoffa offered a quite different explanation for why he had begun organizing in the retail food industry, a nontraditional jurisdiction for the union. Hoffa claimed in a letter to Tom Flynn that soon after the Teamsters had organized the bulk of the city's warehouses, food wholesalers, "and all allied businesses making deliveries to retail stores," the CIO moved in with a campaign to recruit employees in "the retail stores in and around Detroit." In response, the Teamsters immediately began a counter-campaign "to organize the same type of clerks and personnel, so that we would not wake up some morning and find out that the clerks, being CIO, would be in a position to refuse delivery by an A. F. of L. driver." Hoffa maintained that the CIO's Retail Workers "for the past ten years have used as a spearhead an attempt of raiding Teamsters all over the state of Michigan." Indeed, CIO unions were the first to attempt a secondary boycott campaign against the grocers, and their sole intention was to hurt their rival. During the Dossin jurisdictional battle, organizers for the Brewery Workers, who were then working in alliance with the Retail Workers, spread out to the city's grocery stores and informed the owners that they would stop beer shipments to any store that accepted deliveries made by Teamster drivers.[42]

With this information Dan Tobin might have approved of the campaign to organize the grocers, but the Wayne County judiciary did not. As Hoffa set his sights on the remaining retailers' nationality group, the Polish Federated Merchants, Circuit Court Judge George B. Murphy issued a restraining order against the Teamsters' coercive organizing and announced that he would head a one-man grand jury to investigate the union's activities. The Michigan legislature created the special grand jury, comprising a judge and a prosecutor empowered to subpoena witnesses and sanction recalcitrant witnesses, when a far-ranging system of bribery in Detroit involving the police department, the mayor, and the county prosecutor came to light in 1939. In the 1940s, Michigan courts increasingly depended on the prosecutorial device as a way to circumvent what many perceived to be corrupt local law enforcement agencies. The selection of Murphy to head the Teamsters grand jury, made by a vote of all eighteen Circuit Court judges, was intriguing. Murphy, who shared the New Deal liberal politics of his brother, former Detroit Mayor and Michigan Governor Frank Murphy, had been the perennial choice of the CIO in elections for Wayne County judgeships. As for the selection of the grand jury special prosecutor, more eyebrows were raised when O'Brien excused himself, citing the pressures of his regular duties. Lester Moll, a former Circuit Court judge and chief assistant prosecutor, was chosen by Murphy in O'Brien's stead.[43]

With the Teamster picketing halted by the court order, Murphy spent two weeks sifting through the evidence accumulated by the special detectives squad. On May 28, he emerged from his chambers to announce that he was placing a permanent injunction against the Teamsters' tactics in organizing the retailers and that he was requesting $100,000 from the Wayne County Board of Supervisors to finance the continuation of the grand jury. Asked to explain the need for the funds, Murphy told the board, "In light of what I know now, it is just peanuts in view of the overall picture." He asserted that the preliminary investigation had uncovered a "vicious mess" and a "million dollar racket" perpetrated by the Teamsters. Murphy's request narrowly passed in a vote of the board thanks to the support of George Edwards, the only County Supervisor allied with the labor movement who supported the grand jury. As an organizer at the Kelsey-Hayes Wheel Company in the 1930s, Edwards, a leading member of the Michigan Socialist Party, had been instrumental in building the United Automobile Workers during the UAW's formative years and maintained close ties with the automobile union and the CIO after moving from labor organizing into electoral politics. Despite telegrams from rank-and-file CIO members protesting that "labor needs no grand inquisitor," Edwards steadfastly supported Murphy's request. "I most certainly would oppose any move to stymie the jury by preventing the appropriation measure from coming to a vote," he declared. And while Frank Martel, president of the Wayne County Federation of Labor and a longtime critic of the Teamsters, loudly condemned the grand jury as an attack on the labor movement as a whole, local CIO leaders like Gus Scholle, John Gibson, and Walter Reuther remained silent.[44]

Once the grand jury began its work in earnest, surprisingly little was uncovered about the Teamsters' campaign to organize the grocers and meat dealers, yet much was revealed about Hoffa's methods of accumulating power and avoiding trouble in Detroit, most notably his penchant for bribing those with useful occupations. Sheriff's deputies, the former chairman of the Liquor Control Commission, and even Prosecutor O'Brien's chief investigator were shown to be on the Teamster payroll.[45] The grand jury investigation also revealed that even though he had acquired such an impressive roster of public officials, Hoffa was unable to win the services of Lieutenant Governor Vernon Brown, who was offered a substantial contribution for his gubernatorial campaign in exchange for restoring the union's "friend," Orrin DeMass, to the chairmanship of the Liquor Commission. In the private sector, the Teamster leader developed a team of "Labor Relations Counsels" to assist in the expansion of the union. These former business agents or associates of the Teamsters offered their "services" to businesses undergoing organizing campaigns by the union. The experience of one of the besieged retailers after refusing to sign with the union and being threatened with a boycott on the delivery of his supplies was related through the *Detroit News:*

While the bewildered businessman is still trying to figure out what it is all about he gets a telephone call from a man who identifies himself as a labor relations counsel. He opens the conversation with the observation that, 'I understand you are having labor trouble.'

Upshot of the matter is that the labor relations counsel suggests a solution. If the business man will pay a lump sum equal to what their initiation fees would total if his employees joined the Teamsters Union and if he will each month pay an amount equal to the dues his employees would pay, if they were organized, he will have no more trouble. Of course, on top of this, the employer pays a fee to the labor relations counsel for 'services rendered.'[46]

Not surprisingly, these agents of the Teamsters operated in industries that were the objects of the fiercest competition between the IBT and the CIO. The retail trade was handled by Jacob "Babe" Bushkin, a former poolroom operator with extensive connections to the Purple Gang, whose brother Herman was a business agent with the Teamsters. Bushkin was aided in the grocery campaign by Louis Shamie, the president of the retail grocers association, who had worked with Hoffa and Brennan to organize the markets since 1942, when the Retail Workers were in the midst of an organizing campaign in the Detroit food industry. Arthur Stringari and Morris Nort shared responsibility for bringing automobile dealers into line. During the drive on the grocers, the Teamsters were waging a similar campaign against automobile dealers, which remnants of the United Construction Workers Organizing Committee had been attempting to organize since the great raids of 1941. With their monopoly on carhauling, the Teamsters, through Stringari and Nort, were able to make a convincing claim that they could halt deliveries of new cars from the auto plants until dealers in the area signed a closed-shop contract. Several dealerships were brought under Teamster contracts by this method. Stringari had been an organizer with the AFL city employees union in Detroit before going to work for the Teamsters to head off the UCWOC drive among the auto dealers. Nort's career as a labor relations counsel followed brief stints as an armed robber and automobile salesman. Hotels and restaurants were under the jurisdiction of John Curran, a former business agent for the Teamsters who had been forced to enlist in the army to avoid a prison term for child molestation.[47]

In the summer and early fall of 1946, as the grand jury investigation was filling the front pages of all the Detroit newspapers and it appeared certain that indictments would be handed down, Hoffa's enemies both within and outside the union attempted to take advantage of the opportunity. In July, the Detroit district council of the Retail Workers announced that it would begin a drive to organize all retail grocers and meat markets in the city. Leaders of the RWDSU were no doubt aware of their tremendous advantage over the Teamsters, who were restrained by Murphy's injunction from picketing the retailers, "conspiring to interfere with the free flow of meats and merchandise," conducting boycotts, and even from parking their automobiles near the stores. Faced with the potential loss of 6,000 stores to the CIO, Hoffa and his men did what came naturally to them—they broke the law. Even after indictments were issued charging Hoffa and seventeen other Detroit Teamsters with conspiracy, extortion, and forcible coercion, several grocers came forward to complain that the Teamsters had renewed their organizing drive and asked Murphy to cite the union for contempt of court.[48]

The investigation and indictments also caused trouble for Hoffa within the Joint Council, which he had ruled with virtual impunity since the beginning of the war. An anti-Hoffa faction emerged within Teamsters Local 247, the construction drivers union, and several officers from the local volunteered to testify against Hoffa before the grand jury. In September, shortly after Hoffa appeared in court to answer questions from Murphy and Moll, Frederick Willis, a business agent with Local 247, testified he heard Hoffa threaten to kill Herbert Crimp, the local's vice president, who had given testimony on the grocery organizing drive. Soon reports circulated that the construction local was seeking greater autonomy, possibly through lawsuits, from Hoffa's Joint Council leadership. Yet less than two days after Crimp, Willis, and two other officers from the local were given police protection against possible reprisals, the revolt appeared to fade. Following a special meeting of the Joint Council, officers from all the member locals, including Crimp, who attended the meeting accompanied by his police guard, publicly pledged their loyalty to Hoffa, Brennan, and the entire Joint Council leadership. Crimp claimed the reports of a revolt were exaggerated and said the Teamsters "should wash its dirty linen in the utility room rather than in Briggs Stadium." But whether he had been influenced by intimidation or bribery to make the avowals of loyalty, they did not stop Crimp from attempting to lead an insurgent faction against Hoffa in elections for the Joint Council leadership five months later. By then, however, Hoffa had accumulated too much power to be easily dethroned. Delegates from the member locals voted unanimously to elect him as president.[49]

Despite continued indignation against the Teamsters in the press, the grand jury showed few results as it dragged into 1947. The once-popular investigation came in for a barrage of criticism. Local AFL leaders attacked Murphy for "squandering $100,000 of the taxpayers' money," the net result being only "his re-election to a position for which he lacks both the legal training and the mental poise." The Wayne County prosecuting attorney publicly complained that because of the small amount of evidence uncovered in the cases, he was "not convinced they can be prosecuted successfully." In May, after his fellow judges urged him to terminate the inquiry, Murphy announced that the grand jury would end its investigations and turn over the pending cases to the police and prosecutors for further action. In defense of his work, the beleaguered judge declared that the investigations and indictments had achieved "the stabilizing of labor-management relations."[50]

Indeed, a month later, congressmen who had cited Murphy's investigations in their arguments for the Taft-Hartley bill, voted to enact the legislation over President Truman's veto. Among other measures, Taft-Hartley banned the closed shop, required unions to file financial reports with the Labor Department, and, most important for the Detroit Teamsters, outlawed the secondary boycott. In August, Republican congressman Fred Hartley of New Jersey, coauthor of the new law, singled out Hoffa as a reason for the restrictive legislation and announced that a hearing of the House Labor Committee would be held in Detroit to carry on the work of the Murphy grand jury. Not only had the Teamsters' favorite organizing weapon been taken from them, but the demonization of Hoffa had reached national proportions.[51]

The immediate material effects of the grand jury investigation, however, were far less dramatic. After the state Supreme Court ruled that a key witness could not be required to testify, enthusiasm for prosecuting the case began to wane among Detroit's law enforcement officials. In October, prosecutors dropped charges of conspiracy stemming from allegations that Hoffa had attempted to "fix" a liquor license for a bar owner through his associates in the Prosecutor's office and the Liquor Commission. Amid accusations made by Murphy that the County Prosecutor was dragging his feet on the remaining charges in connection with the grocers organizing campaign because of possible Teamster retribution in an election year, the case remained stalled through 1948. Finally, the state dropped the charge of extortion in exchange for guilty pleas to the lesser charge of violating a state labor law by attempting to organize the grocers through force. In January 1949, Hoffa, Brennan, and thirteen other Teamster officers were ordered to return $7,617 that had been collected from the merchants for permits. In passing sentence, Circuit Judge Ira W. Jayne upbraided the union for its conduct:

> It is too bad that labor controversies cannot be kept out of the arena of intimidation and fighting. It is too bad the only way to settle a labor controversy apparently is by ordeal of battle. The parties to every other personal dispute now submit themselves to the orderly processes of the courts. Labor disputes, probably the most important of any of our personal controversies, are fought out under the regulations of the Dark Ages. We all share in that responsibility.

Once again, the specter of social responsibility was raised against Hoffa and his associates. And while many of their enemies within labor heeded the call to confine the class struggle to "orderly processes," the Detroit Teamsters did not. Soon the struggle between the old, "Dark Ages" culture of the Teamsters and the new culture of social management moved out of the streets and into the offices of government.[52]

Eight

Jungle Politics

He is the biggest small man in Detroit. When you go to Detroit today you hear about Hoffa, but you do not hear a word about Henry Ford. . . . [Hoffa] is pretty nearly civilized now, but I knew him when he wasn't.—DAN TOBIN, 1952[1]

Contrary to Tobin's proclamation, by the time the Murphy one-man grand jury investigation reached its conclusion, Jimmy Hoffa and his union were considered barbaric by nearly every significant social group in Detroit. Officials in city government avoided being associated with the union, the press vilified the "labor czar" and his "goon squads," and letters flooded into City Hall from businessmen, veterans, church groups, women's clubs, and other outraged citizens demanding a crackdown on the Teamsters.[2]

None of this slowed Hoffa's rise in the IBT. His standing within the international had grown considerably since his conflict with Tobin and Flynn early in the war years. Once the war was over, the IBT leadership was far more willing to look past Hoffa's unstatesmanlike conduct and low esteem in the public eye and reward him for his remarkable accomplishments in building the union. By 1947 Hoffa had increased the combined membership of his two locals, 299 and 337, to 13,000, and as negotiating chairman of the Central States Drivers Council brought 125,000 drivers in twelve Midwestern states under the Central States Area Agreement. Perhaps even more impressive, in the late 1940s Hoffa organized a wide swath of the South, a rare feat for the American labor movement.[3]

In the Southern drive, competition once again spurred Hoffa to expand his operations. Beginning in 1939, the Central States Area Agreement ostensibly covered "operations into and out of the territory contiguous to the southern, southwestern, and western boundaries" of the original eleven-state Midwestern region; yet because the Teamsters had little presence below the Ohio River, it was virtually impossible for the union to enforce the contract with trucking companies coming into the central states from the South. Through the war years, several interregional freight firms in the Midwest took advantage of this loophole by moving their headquarters into the South and hiring nonunion drivers to avoid the high wages mandated by the Central States Area Agreement. Hoffa recognized that the only way to stop the runaway firms from bleeding the life out of the CSDC was to organize drivers—or, more efficiently, their employers—in the Southern states.

Moving quickly within the small window between the end of World War II restrictions on organizing and the new restraints imposed by the Taft-Hartley Act in 1947, Hoffa ordered Southern-based carriers crossing into the central states to be boycotted by warehousemen and dock workers unless they added union members to their payrolls. Once Taft-Hartley made secondary boycotts like this illegal, Hoffa innovated. He skirted the law through a standard clause in Teamster contracts allowing members to "refuse to handle 'unfair goods.' " With the Democratic appointees to the NLRB ruling in 1949 that such "hot cargo" clauses were lawful, Hoffa was able to force remaining Southern scab outfits to sign with the union. Hoffa used the unique leverage power of the Teamsters to accomplish what the CIO had failed to do with its more famous "Operation Dixie." By 1958, wages and working conditions for truck drivers in the South were essentially equal to those in the Midwest, an astonishing anomaly in the low-wage, mostly non-union region. A year later, the Landrum-Griffin Act, passed with the Teamsters specifically in mind, closed the last secondary boycott loophole by outlawing the "hot cargo" clause and effectively ended the Southern drive.[4]

Hoffa received ample rewards for his contributions to the growth of the Teamsters. In 1947, "our little sparkplug" from Detroit was elected as a trustee of the IBT at the union's national convention. His nominators expressed admiration for his work in building the South-

James Hoffa (left) being taken into custody in 1940 on charges of violating the Sherman Antitrust Act. Accused of conspiring with a group of businessmen to establish four waste-paper companies under Teamster contracts and then force out non-union competitors, Hoffa and Local 337 president Bert Brennan pleaded no contest to the charges and were each fined $1,000.

Hoffa (left) and Brennan at a hearing called by the War Labor Board in May 1944, soon after the Detroit Teamsters had pulled 10,000 highway truck drivers off the job. The strike was an outgrowth of a city-wide jurisdictional war with the CIO.

John L. Lewis, president of the United Mine Workers, seated, with his brother Dennie, at a UMW convention in the 1930s. In 1939, the Lewis brothers formed the United Construction Workers Organizing Committee, which for more than two years waged a campaign to supplant the Teamsters in the Midwestern trucking industry.

Walter Reuther, leader of the United Automobile Workers, whose efforts, together with Sidney Hillman, to discipline the labor movement during World War II helped eliminate the Teamsters' chief competitors in the CIO. Later, during the U.S. Senate's investigation of Hoffa and labor corruption, Reuther was promoted by Robert F. Kennedy as a contrasting model of responsible unionism.

The handsome patrician G. Mennen "Soapy" Williams was the ideal front man for the group of CIO and liberal activists who set out to wrest control of the Michigan Democratic Party from Hoffa. Williams was elected governor in 1948, after defeating a Hoffa-backed candidate in the primary.

Sidney Hillman in 1940. Hillman's ongoing campaign to merge labor and government shaped much of Hoffa's career.

Hoffa—with his lawyer, George S. Fitzgerald, to his right—being arraigned on charges of extortion in Detroit in May 1946. Hoffa had threatened to stop deliveries to local independent grocery stores if they did not sign contracts with the Teamsters.

George Meany, president of the AFL-CIO, urging the federation at its 1957 convention to expel the Teamsters.

Hoffa and his wife, Josephine, on the podium at the 1957 Teamsters convention after his overwhelming victory in the election for president of the union. At left is Dave Beck, the outgoing president. A portrait of former IBT president Dan Tobin, who aided Hoffa's rise in the union, hangs in the rear. The smiling man at the right is Anthony "Tony Pro" Provenzano, leader of Local 560 in New Jersey, who many years later would be suspected of engineering Hoffa's murder.

Hoffa being carried on the shoulders of delegates after his landslide victory at the Teamsters convention in 1957. IBT secretary-treasurer John English stands at far right.

Robert F. Kennedy, chief counsel of the Senate Select Committee on Improper Activities in the Labor and Management Field, questioning Hoffa, while his brother, committee member Senator John F. Kennedy, looks on.

In one of many such encounters, Hoffa confronts Robert Kennedy during a break in the Senate hearings.

Hoffa responding to questions during the Senate hearings.

Hoffa shaking hands with Teamster truck drivers outside the courthouse in Chattanooga during his trial for jury tampering in 1964.

Having just negotiated the 1964 National Master Freight Agreement, which centralized under his control the union's collective bargaining in highway trucking, Hoffa shows a copy of the contract at a press conference.

ern Conference and sympathy for "what he is going through in the city of Detroit." At the next convention five years later, Hoffa was again praised for his work in building the union's Midwestern and Southern base and was unanimously elected vice-president of the IBT. Harold Gibbons, president of Local 688 in St. Louis, a former socialist who defected from the CIO's Retail Workers to become a major figure in the Central States Teamsters and one of Hoffa's closest allies, attested to the "loyalty and devotion" the Detroit Teamster inspired among the union's officers and members.[5]

Indeed, by the late 1940s Hoffa had gained a remarkable degree of fealty from fellow Teamsters. This was especially true in his home local. In 1949 he was reelected president of Local 299 by a unanimous voice vote at a meeting of the membership. When his election was announced, Hoffa received a raucous standing ovation from the assembled rank and file. Since the removal of the local's trusteeship in 1945, elections for officers as well as some contract ratification votes were conducted at the union's weekly meeting by a voice vote of the members present. By all accounts, these meetings were, after a fashion, democratic—those who attended were allowed to speak their minds, and many did, often in opposition to Hoffa's views. The *Michigan Teamster* even chided members for not showing up at meetings; yet the number of participants was normally fewer than 100 of the local's 10,000 members during this period. Those who did show up were virtually unanimous in their support of Hoffa. An over-the-road driver who regularly attended meetings from 1945 through the 1950s recalled that the members often questioned the union leader's decisions but never his standing:

> Jimmy Hoffa was president and that was it. We never gave it a hell of a lot of thought. What we did give a thought about was am I going to work next week and where's my run gonna be. . . . Everyone I knew thought Hoffa was a great man. . . . When the government came after him a lot of us wanted to take our trucks and run 'em over certain people.[6]

Hoffa's popularity was partly derived from what many in the rank and file considered to be the Teamster leader's straightforward, "no bullshit" communication with them, but his support within the union was rooted in a substantial material base. Soon after escaping the confinement of the National War Labor Board's wage brackets, Hoffa reeled off a string of generous contracts to secure his status among the heart of the union's membership. In 1945, as chairman of the bargaining committee for the CSDC, he negotiated wage increases of 18 to 20 percent for 40,000 highway drivers in twelve Midwestern states. A year later, through use of the secondary boycott and hot cargo clauses, he brought an additional 85,000 drivers into the agreement, which included a minimum hourly rate of $1.25 per hour, a prodigious 56 percent increase from 1941. By 1950 Hoffa had raised the hourly wage rate for highway drivers in the renamed Central States Conference of Teamsters to $1.75, equal to average earnings for automobile workers. He also established a Central States health and welfare program financed entirely by employer contributions. His reward was election as president of the Central States Conference in 1953. In Detroit, his achievements in local cartage were no less impressive. In 1948 Hoffa negotiated a fifteen-cent-per-hour increase for 6,000 drivers, dockmen, and checkers in Detroit. By 1950 local drivers affiliated with 299 had reached wage levels comparable to those of highway drivers and automobile workers.[7]

In addition to good contracts, Hoffa worked continuously to ensure the members' loyalty. While other major union leaders in the postwar period became increasingly involved with the affairs of government and ever further removed from the daily operations of their organizations, Hoffa maintained an unusual intimacy with both his union and its members. Visitors to the Detroit Teamster headquarters were often astonished to find that Hoffa's office opened directly into the hallway, with no reception area shielding him from the rank and file. No appointments were made. Rather, he extended an open invitation to members to come to him with their problems, and as a consequence the corridors of the Teamsters building were frequently filled with men waiting to see him. His dealings with the membership were much like the relationship between the political machine boss and urban immigrants. Hoffa liberally doled out favors, gifts, and jobs to members who knocked on his door. Every Christmas, he handed out wads of cash, at times up to $100, to whoever asked for it. Rolland McMaster, treasurer of the local in the 1950s, once found that Hoffa had given away $48,000 in cash without accounting for it. "The government called me in with our accountant," McMaster recollected, "and says, 'You can't do this.' " But however much the government may have frowned upon this munificence, the members who benefited from it as well as from the union's contracts felt a personal loyalty to Hoffa that would eventually carry him to the top of the Teamster hierarchy.[8]

Soon after his reelection to the presidency of Local 299, Hoffa was reminded of the necessity of providing for his members by a group of disgruntled carhaulers in nearby Flint. In December 1948, 150 members of Local 332 walked off their jobs as drivers for Commercial Carriers, Inc., a company contracted by General Motors to haul new Buicks from Flint to dealers in other cities, in protest against "the loss of the right to negotiate our own wage agreements." The wildcat strikers declared their intention to challenge the control of Hoffa, who with the imprimatur of Tobin had recently centralized all carhauling negotiations in Michigan under his authority. The strike was crushed when seven of its leaders were fired and replaced by drivers supplied by the Teamsters. The union expelled the strike leaders and in collusion with the National Automobile Transporters Association blacklisted them in the carhaul industry. A few months later, the wives of Hoffa and Brennan were given ownership of a new trucking company incorporated in Tennessee named Test Fleet, whose sole business was the leasing of equipment to Commercial Carriers. The deal was arranged by Carney Matheson, legal counsel for NATA. Hoffa and Brennan received considerable revenue from Test Fleet, but their more important acquisition was the cooperation of carhaul employers in eliminating challenges to Hoffa's central authority.[9]

Though faced with determined opposition from both the employer and the union, the carhaul rebels continued to fight. In November 1949, the remaining Commercial Carriers drivers announced their plans to secede from the Teamsters and establish an independent truckers union. But after Hoffa warned that auto dealers and dockworkers under Teamster contracts would not unload cars delivered by an independent union, the uprising dissolved. The Flint carhaulers weighed Hoffa's threat against their desire to participate in collective bargaining and the small possibility of raising their already middle-class wages as a new union and voted 49 to 12 against bolting the Teamsters. The movement for democracy in Flint failed to expand beyond the Commercial Carriers drivers, despite extensive coverage in the Detroit and Flint press. Without the cooperation of auto dealers and dockworkers or a more widespread rebellion among carhaulers, the Flint insurgents possessed no leverage to use against Hoffa. In fact, there was never a significant movement for democracy among the rank and file in unions controlled by Hoffa. The only other call for democratic reform from the rank and file occurred in 1940, when a group of 44 members of Local 299 staged a series of wildcat strikes and demanded that elections be held in the local, which was then under trusteeship. The dissidents abandoned their efforts when they failed to generate a broader uprising among the local's membership.[10]

Participatory democracy may never have been popular among Detroit Teamster members, but they continually exerted their power over Hoffa through the democracy of the market. Members in Detroit, outstate Michigan, Ohio, and Minneapolis had voted with their feet since the late 1930s, when competitors from other unions began successfully recruiting in Teamster jurisdictions and when local leaders in the IBT challenged Hoffa's widening authority. By the end of the 1940s, thousands of members had left Hoffa's unions or allied themselves with more ambitious Teamster officials to find better representation for their dues. But Hoffa was well aware of this. Through his rich contracts he was able to retain the majority of his members, win their votes in union elections, and create a base of support that compelled Tobin to grant him the leadership of the Michigan Conference and the CSDC. Hoffa understood well the power of "the boys who pay me." Like the urban machine boss who appeared to hold total dominion over his constituents but worked continuously to maintain their support, Hoffa knew who held the final authority in his union. In 1953, government investigators who had wiretapped Hoffa's telephone line heard him relate his philosophy of trade union leadership to a colleague. "Treat 'em right and you don't have to worry," he told Johnny "Dio" Dioguardi, a famously corrupt Teamster leader in New York. Hoffa later expanded on this dictum in a televised interview. "The people we have in this union talk about Jimmy Hoffa, what he does for them, what he does daily when they call him," he told David Brinkley. "They're the only ones that are going to defeat me in a convention."[11]

A New Machine

Hoffa's strategy of buying power extended outside his union into local and state governments. As the Murphy grand jury showed, the Teamster leader had purchased the services of officials in several regulatory and law-enforcement agencies. Yet while he received relatively little punishment from the state for these transgressions, Hoffa encountered fierce and sustained attacks on his political power from within the labor movement. In a battle reminiscent of the clashes between urban bosses and good-government progressives earlier in the century, beginning in the early 1940s Hoffa's carefully cultivated and expensive network of political allies was challenged by a group of his rivals in the CIO who sought to bring the New Deal order to Michigan. Ironically, competition from the CIO caused Hoffa to broaden his political ambitions, just as it had forced him to expand the jurisdictional operations of his unions.

Hoffa began involving the Detroit Teamsters in electoral politics during the war years. In 1943, the union endorsed and gave considerable financial support to Edward Jeffries for reelection as mayor of Detroit, in opposition to both the CIO and the rest of the Wayne County Federation of Labor (WCFL), which backed Jeffries' opponent in the nonpartisan race. The following year, the Detroit Teamsters moved their political operations to the state and national levels, and chose the Democratic Party as their point of entry. Teamster locals engaged in partisan politics were restricted to working with the Democrats by the insistence of Tobin, still labor's most vocal ally of the Roosevelt administration, but the Michigan Democratic Party also offered a tempting opportunity for Hoffa. The state party, through a string of defeats to the Republicans and debilitating internal dissension, had been reduced to a nearly empty vessel with no faction holding decisive authority by the end of the war years. At the 1944 Democratic National Convention in Chicago, the Teamsters' chief political operative, Otto Wendell, who had gained notice in Detroit as the "Voice of the Teamsters" on the union's radio program and was a leading member of the Wayne County Democratic committee, busily worked his contacts in the Michigan delegation to lay the groundwork for a Teamster presence in the state party. At the Michigan State Democratic convention in Grand Rapids two weeks later, Hoffa, Brennan, Fitzsimmons, Wendell, and several other officers from Joint Council 43 began developing more intimate relationships with key figures in the party. By the close of the convention the Teamsters had established themselves as an independent political force in Michigan. Evidence of this came in September 1944, when the Democratic State Central Committee, in establishing official liaisons with organized labor, appointed not just one coordinator each for the AFL and the CIO, but a third one for the Teamsters as well.[12]

Conflict between the Teamsters and the CIO in the state party emerged shortly before the Democratic convention in Flint in January 1945. The two rivals were at the time locked in the battle for representation rights over the workers at the Dossin bottling plant. Gus Scholle, the director of the state CIO Political Action Committee (PAC) who had helped organize the fight against the Teamsters at Dossin, was alarmed when Wendell launched a pre-convention campaign for the chairmanship of the state party and secured endorsements from the leaders of the 1st and 14th congressional district organizations in Detroit.

Despite Scholle's wish to commit the CIO to working within the Democratic Party, Sidney Hillman and Philip Murray were still holding the national CIO Political Action Committee to an official nonpartisan policy and forbade Scholle from running CIO officials for positions within the party. "The Teamsters, on the other hand," reported the *Michigan CIO News*, "made no bones about their desire to lay their hands as completely as possible upon the Democratic organization." IBT delegates from across the state flocked to Flint to agitate and cast their votes for Wendell. Hamstrung by the national CIO, Scholle could only instruct his delegates to shun the Teamster even though Wendell was the only labor candidate for the chairmanship. The opposition of the CIO, along with the distaste that many of the regular delegates from middle-class and rural districts held for the Teamsters, forced Wendell to withdraw his candidacy the day before the convention opened. The CIO accused the Teamsters of conspiring with Joseph Bannigan, chairman of the 14th district organization and a member of the Wayne County Prosecutor's office—whose alliances with the Teamsters dated back to the late 1930s—to throw the union's weight behind Bannigan's candidacy for the state chairmanship in exchange for handing the district post to Wendell. Bannigan lost in the vote for the chairmanship to the incumbent, Walter Averill, but the Teamsters continued their push into the Democratic Party.[13]

In local politics, the Teamsters maintained their policy of opposing any candidate backed by the CIO. In the 1945 mayoral election, the CIO shed its formal voluntarist policy and put its full weight behind an effort to elect UAW vice president Richard Frankensteen. As the national PAC and state and local CIO bodies pumped more than $200,000 into the Frankensteen campaign, the Teamsters did not hesitate to endorse the incumbent Jeffries. In a publicly disseminated letter to Jeffries granting him the Teamsters' endorsement, Hoffa, Brennan, and Joint Council 43 president Sam Hurst praised the mayor's honesty and experience but emphasized the dangers posed by the Frankensteen candidacy. "Your opponent does not represent labor as a whole but only a faction of labor," the Teamsters declared. "If elected, he would be responsible only to the Political Action Committee of the CIO, or else an ingrate to the organization responsible for his election. With labor divided as it is today, it is not to the best interests of labor as a whole that a representative of any single labor group be elected to the important office of chief executive of Detroit."[14]

When Frankensteen scored an impressive victory in the primary, the concerted effort of the CIO behind his candidacy caused the Wayne County Federation of Labor to abandon its longtime opposition to Jeffries and finally agree with the Teamsters on the threat of the CIO's entry into politics. Citing "continual raids and controversy with the rival organization" backing Frankensteen, the WCFL gave a full-throated endorsement to Jeffries, whom it had loudly denounced just two years earlier. The federation claimed the CIO was "seeking to gain control of the City Hall in an effort to make it a citadel from which to crush AFL unions." WCFL president Frank Martel, who had publicly ridiculed Hoffa for his endorsement of Jeffries in 1943, began to sound much like the Teamster leader. "Many of our locals are faced with a threat to their very existence," Martel stated. "The first duty of a leader of the American Federation of Labor is to fight to protect the integrity of each AFL union in his jurisdiction. And come what may I shall accept that responsibility." The WCFL's opposition to Frankensteen along with vigorous Teamster campaigning and Jeffries' race-baiting proved to be a winning combination among Detroit's white working class, who reelected the incumbent by a margin of 56,000 votes. Dan Tobin, who took great interest in the election, credited Hoffa's unions with the defeat of Frankensteen. "The Teamsters supported his opponent, Mr. Jeffries," Tobin wrote in an IBT magazine editorial, "not because they were in love with Mr. Jeffries but because they could not afford to support Frankensteen, knowing very well that if he became mayor all the machinery of city government would be directed against the Teamsters."[15]

Following the defeat of the CIO in mayoral politics, both the Teamsters and their rivals concentrated their efforts on the Michigan Democratic Party. The chairmanship of the state party had changed hands several times after Wendell's aborted attempt in 1944, and by the time of the 1947 convention the organization was merely a collection of hostile factions that had been unable to produce a winning candidate for governor since 1940. Into the void stepped John Franco, a wastepaper company executive and chairman of the Oakland County party organization. With the support of Teamster delegates and a caucus of insurgents demanding "new blood and new leadership," Franco won election to the state chairmanship. Though claiming to be a progressive force within the party, Franco was more Hoffa's kind of politician. The new Democratic chairman, a former supporter of Father Charles Coughlin, was rumored to have taken payments for appointments to party offices and was viewed by many as representing "the muscular rather than the idealistic branch of the organization." Franco was held in particular disfavor by a small group of party activists affiliated with Americans for Democratic Action, a liberal anticommunist organization founded in 1947 by ex-New Dealers and social-democratic labor leaders, including Walter Reuther and several of Hoffa's nemeses in the CIO—Allan Haywood, Boris Shishkin, George Edwards, and Samuel Wolchok. While the national ADA was formed to disassociate New Deal liberalism from the Communist Party, the group's activists in Michigan were more concerned with saving the Democratic Party from cronyism than from communism.[16]

One Michigan labor leader affiliated with the ADA who was particularly concerned about the Teamsters' incursion into the state Democratic Party was John Gibson, whose conflict with Hoffa had begun in 1937 during the jurisdictional struggles between Gibson's Dairy Workers union and the Teamsters and had continued through the war years as Gibson rose to the presidency of the Michigan CIO Council. In 1946, part of Gibson's corporatist ambition was fulfilled when he was appointed by President Truman as Assistant Secretary of Labor, but even after moving to Washington he remained preoccupied by Hoffa's disruptive tendencies in his home state. Following the state party convention in 1947, Gibson returned to Michigan to help organize resistance to the Franco-Hoffa alliance. Gibson found common cause with a group of liberal lawyers, businessmen, and unionists who wanted to replace the old-style machine politicians in the party with the modern machine of New Deal liberalism. In addition to Gus Scholle, who took the lead in the political fight against Hoffa, Gibson's chief allies in the labor movement were several ADA activists and sympathizers in Detroit, including Scholle's chief assistant Tom Downs, Helen Berthelot, a telephone operator and the secretary-treasurer of the Detroit local of the Communications Workers of America, and Adelaide Hart, a leading member of the Detroit Federation of Teachers. These union leaders joined forces with Neal Staebler, a liberal businessman from Ann Arbor, and two ADA members who were partners in a Detroit law firm, Hicks Griffiths and G. Mennen Williams.[17]

Perhaps even more than Gibson, Williams was quintessentially anti-Hoffa. A member of two of Michigan's wealthiest and most prominent families, one being the owners of the Mennen toiletries company from which he received the nickname "Soapy," Williams was then serving as a member of the State Liquor Commission, an agency that had been influenced by Teamster dollars for nearly a decade. Williams, like his hero Franklin D. Roosevelt, was guided by a patrician's facile enthusiasm for setting the world right. As a liquor commissioner he turned in a prodigious effort to clean up the scandal-ridden agency. The bowtie-wearing Williams toured the state, visiting bars and liquor stores and exhorting proprietors to adhere to the laws and improve their conduct. According to his official biographer, Williams "encouraged the vendors to run a legitimate business, to show self respect, to contribute to local charities, and generally to do those things which would put the liquor business on a better legal-social plane than it had ever known." His experience in reforming one of the seediest industries in the state—and the seedbed of the Teamsters' milieu—only broadened his political ambitions. But before he could extend "good government" throughout Michigan, the barriers within his party had to be removed. It was natural, then, that when Williams, Griffiths, and Staebler met with Gibson and other liberal labor activists to plan a challenge to the Franco-Hoffa faction, the group chose as its front man the embodiment of everything that Franco and Hoffa lacked—bourgeois respectability, social responsibility, and a sense of duty to reform humankind. After a founding meeting in the basement of Griffiths' house, the new Michigan Democratic Club set out to seize control of the party through a campaign to elect Williams governor.[18]

Through the winter of 1948, the dissident Democrats spread out across the state to organize clubs of liberals that would send delegates to the state party's spring convention. Meanwhile, Scholle worked to bring the Michigan CIO to fully commit its Political Action Committee to rebuilding the Democratic Party as a vehicle for labor-liberalism. In February, Scholle's mission took on greater urgency when Victor Bucknell, a lawyer and leader of the Democratic Party organization in Kalamazoo, declared that he was seeking the party's nomination for governor. By himself, this relatively unknown party official was hardly a viable candidate in the primary, but Scholle knew that Bucknell was backed by Franco, Hoffa, and the considerable war chest of the Detroit Teamsters. With Hoffa's indictments on charges of extortion and violation of state labor laws still pending, the Teamster chief stood to benefit from a friendly governor with the power to grant clemency in criminal cases and thwart further investigations of the union. Thousands of dollars from the IBT treasury flooded into the Bucknell campaign and Teamster members across the state were instructed to vote for Hoffa's chosen candidate, threatening to stymie the liberal insurgency within the party. By the time of Bucknell's announcement, however, the liberals' fortunes had begun to turn for the better.

Critical support for Scholle's endeavor to capture the party came from the national CIO, which by 1948 had rejected the third-party movement behind Henry Wallace. Just before the state CIO convention in March, Walter Reuther, the new UAW president and vice president of the CIO, gave both the approval of the national CIO-PAC and the weighty endorsement of the auto workers union to Scholle's plan. The new policy of creating a political party that would implement the policies and programs of the CIO, "in the state of Michigan in the current political campaign," wrote Reuther, "can best be implemented by concentrating our efforts, and working within, the Democratic Party." Meeting in Lansing on March 13, the state CIO convention adopted a resolution drafted by Scholle that provided both a declaration of war against Hoffa's incipient political machine and an acknowledgment that the CIO intended to make the state Democratic Party its own:

> Progressives and liberals within the Democratic Party have often been outnumbered by conservatives and reactionary elements. The PAC is unanimous in its opinion that the best way of supporting liberalism within the Democratic Party, to conform to National CIO policy and to serve the best interests of Michigan labor, is to join the Democratic Party.
>
> It is our objective in adopting this policy to remold the Democratic Party into a real liberal and progressive political party which can be subscribed to by members of the CIO and other liberals.
>
> We therefore advise CIO members to become active precinct, ward, county and congressional district workers and attempt to become delegates to Democratic conventions.

This gave formal approval to what J. David Greenstone has called "the most ideological, most aggressive, and most ambitious example of labor political action of the time." With the approval of Reuther, UAW activists in Detroit were mobilized to provide the organizational muscle for the campaign. "This realignment of political forces in Michigan could not have been accomplished without the active support of UAW staff and rank and file members," Tom Downs later wrote. "UAW congressional district coordinators provided practical leadership for registration, get-out-the-vote drives as well as recruiting candidates for precinct delegate."[19]

At the May convention of the Michigan Democratic Party, it appeared that the CIO was on the verge of accomplishing its objective when it won the election of several of its members, including Gibson and Scholle, as well as several non-labor liberals from the Michigan Democratic Clubs, as delegates to the national Democratic Party convention to be held in July in Philadelphia. Franco had hoped to take the position of national committeeman, the state party's representative on the Democratic National Committee and liaison with the White House, during the caucus of Michigan delegates in Philadelphia, but the strong showing of the liberals at the state convention persuaded him to relinquish the attempt to expand his power. Before the national convention, it seemed certain that the liberal forces would reelect Cyril Bevan, a bitter opponent of Franco, to the national committeeman position and supplant national committeewoman Violet Patterson, a close ally of Franco, with one of their own. Party observers predicted that if reelected, Bevan would organize a purge of the Franco-Teamster faction.[20]

With his rivals poised to take control of the Michigan Democratic Party, Hoffa attempted a coup of his own. Signaling his intention to insert a strong Teamster presence into state politics, Hoffa succeeded in replacing the two top officials in the Michigan Federation of Labor (MFL) with Teamster members at the federation's convention in May. Elected president of the MFL was Joseph "Red" O'Laughlin, who had led Hoffa's Local 299 in the 1930s before being assigned to Minneapolis in 1941 and who had returned to Detroit to help strengthen the Teamsters within the state federation. Robert Scott, a member of Pontiac Teamsters Local 614, won election as secretary-treasurer. The Teamster candidates won by criticizing their opponents, both Republicans, for failing to lead a fight against the anti-labor Bonine-Tripp Act, known as Michigan's "little Taft-Hartley," and campaigned on the pledge to provide a more vigilant defense of labor's interests against the interventions of the state.[21]

Soon after the MFL convention, Hoffa made a bid to move from state politics into the national political arena. In June, George Fitzgerald, the longtime attorney and public-relations front man for the Detroit Teamsters, announced that he would challenge Bevan for the national committeeman position at the Democratic national convention. In Philadelphia, Gibson and Scholle worked feverishly to line up the state delegates behind Bevan, but when the votes were cast, Fitzgerald stunned the liberals by taking 25 to Bevan's 16. Virtually overnight, Hoffa had gained direct access to the White House and control over more than 400 federal patronage positions in Michigan. Several commentators in the press argued that Bevan's chances were diminished by the revelation of his involvement in an effort to draft

Dwight Eisenhower as the party's presidential nominee over Truman. Fitzgerald himself concurred with this assessment, claiming that his opponent "looked like Brutus to Caesar." The CIO and their liberal partners offered a different explanation for Fitzgerald's sudden ascendancy. Scholle claimed that operatives dispatched to the convention by Hoffa had distributed tens of thousands of dollars to Michigan delegates in exchange for their votes for Fitzgerald. A number of the delegates were alleged to have bought expensive new cars and taken long vacations in Florida after the convention. Whether it was Bevan's political blunder or more illicit machinations that decided the contest, given Hoffa's long record of accomplishments through bribery it would have been out of character for him not to have made such an outlay to tip the scales in his favor. "Hoffa has managed to get control of the Democratic Party in Michigan by having his man made a Democratic national committeeman," sighed the *Detroit Free Press*, a friend of neither Democratic faction. "If Labor wears any chains in this free country they are those placed on it by such Union Pork Choppers as the notorious Jimmy Hoffa."[22]

Once the race for governor began, the differences between the CIO's political motivations and Hoffa's became apparent. Since the fall of 1940, when the semi-syndicalist John L. Lewis left the CIO and corporatists like Philip Murray, Sidney Hillman, and Walter Reuther began to define the goals of the industrial union movement, its leadership had moved with steady, well-conceived purpose toward the moment when it would reveal the full scope of its political intentions. That moment came in 1948. The anti-labor backlash represented by the Taft-Hartley Act and the Communist-backed third-party challenge of Henry Wallace were perceived by the CIO leadership as threats but also as opportunities. The corporatists could demonstrate their hostility to radicalism and use the anti-labor legislation as a pretext for organizing the CIO into a coherent, disciplined force in American politics. The idea of forming an anti-Communist labor party appeared premature, even to those like Reuther who hoped one day to see such a development, and so a strategy of transforming an established party was adopted. At the CIO Executive Board meeting in January 1948, Murray and his allies, over the objections of the outnumbered pro-Soviet faction, committed the CIO to working within the Democratic Party and transforming it into a vehicle for economic planning and the expansion of governmental welfare programs. Immediately after the meeting, a concerted effort was made, from the Washington office to the local Industrial Union Councils and Political Action Committees, to bring the entire organization into line behind liberal Democratic candidates in the 1948 elections. Through the spring and summer, local CIO leaders were instructed to "take a forthright stand in support of National CIO policies" by shunning Wallace and mobilizing their forces in Democratic campaigns in the fall.[23]

Nowhere was the CIO political policy more fully enacted than in Michigan, where Scholle directed a wall-to-wall operation in support of Mennen Williams and his slate. Scholle, Downs, and UAW organizer Ken Morris developed and implemented a strategy to elect CIO members as precinct delegates to the Democratic Party's congressional district and state conventions. Liberal organizations and the Wayne County PAC, which directed all union stewards and officers affiliated with the CIO to run for precinct delegate, accounted for approximately 1,000 of the 1,240 petitions filed for precinct delegate candidates in the county. Thousands of CIO delegate candidates and volunteers worked door to door, distributing flyers featuring an American flag on one side and the name of Williams as the gubernatorial candidate on the other. Of the 1,000 labor-liberal candidates, 720 were elected to the Wayne County congressional district conventions, providing a decisive base of support for Williams in the Democratic primary.[24]

Meanwhile, Jimmy Hoffa was demonstrating the limitations of his commitment to electoral politics. Unlike his ideological CIO opponents, Hoffa had only practical considerations in backing candidates for office. For him the state was not a vehicle through which to expand the New Deal, create a corporatist commonwealth, or make himself into a labor statesman, but rather a hindrance to be overcome. His involvement in the Democratic Party was simply another application of Samuel Gompers's strategy of "punish your enemies and reward your friends," which in this case Hoffa redefined as "punish your enemies and buy your friends." Compared to the thousands of troops enlisted in the CIO's political army, the entire Teamster campaign organization consisted of Hoffa, Brennan, Fitzgerald, and a handful of conscripts from the union's officer corps. Their weapon, rather than door-to-door organizing, was the union's treasury. Such shortcut tactics worked with great effectiveness against employers and rival unions, but success in the politics of government, as Hoffa soon learned, required much more.[25]

One thing it required that the Detroit Teamsters did not have was the CIO's discipline and adherence to a party line. Soon after his election as national committeeman, Fitzgerald began to assert some independence from Hoffa. Seeking to distance himself from what appeared to be a doomed Franco administration, Fitzgerald refused to endorse Bucknell's candidacy despite Hoffa's insistence that he do so. Compounding Hoffa's problems was the entrance into the gubernatorial race of another "old-line" candidate, Burnett Abbott of Albion, a former state official in Democratic administrations in the early 1930s who seemed sure to split not only the conservative vote but the outstate vote as well. Hoffa was furious when Fitzgerald told Abbott's supporters that he would not oppose the third candidate. Some outstate Teamster locals, confused by the signals coming out of Detroit, actually instructed their members to vote for Abbott.

The split between the old-line candidates along with the CIO's mobilization in Wayne County proved to be enough to give Williams the primary victory in August. The liberal candidate won the party's nomination with a plurality of only 8,000 votes but an overwhelming margin in Wayne County. Hoffa's other candidates for state and county offices also went down to defeat to the CIO-ADA insurgents. "By the August, 1948 primary," writes Dudley Buffa, historian of the Michigan labor-liberal alliance, "it was clear that the state CIO-PAC, with remarkable speed and efficiency, had called into being a Wayne County organization fully capable of carrying the day for candidates it supported." Yet Hoffa was not ready to concede. At the state party's fall convention in Flint, the Teamsters provided a vivid display of their desire for political power and their differences with the genteel, "good government" liberals. Hoffa "came into the convention with a flock of hoodlums who became delegates, the Good Lord alone knows how," remembered Adelaide Hart, a music teacher, devout Catholic, and cofounder of the Michigan Democratic Club.

> They put on one of the worst exhibitions I have ever seen at any time or any place. Women were shoved around and subjected to verbal abuse and obscene language.

Hoffa tried to force a nomination for the Attorney General-ship through the convention. Mennen and Hicks opposed him. He threatened Hicks' life in a caucus when he couldn't get his way. The labor movement was ill-served that day. . . .

Hoffa's boys when opposed have performed in an immature, politically irresponsible fashion. . . .

The disrepute in which Hoffa is held among decent, law abiding people makes political companionship unthinkable.

The disruption caused by the Teamster roughnecks did not stop the CIO's machinelike organization from lifting Williams to victory over the incumbent Republican governor, Kim Sigler, whom many had considered invincible prior to the election.[26]

Once in power, however, Williams and his CIO-ADA allies faced opposition from virtually every quarter. The legislature had returned to Republican hands, while Hoffa's faction retained its hold on key positions within the Democratic Party, most importantly the post of national committeeman. The contest between the Fitzgerald-Hoffa faction and the Williams forces grew increasingly bitter. At the party's convention in the winter of 1949, Hicks Griffiths was elected state chairman to replace Franco, who had been shunned by both factions. Suddenly outnumbered in the top leadership, Fitzgerald stepped up his public attacks against his opponents. "I won't sit by and see the Democratic Party become the captive of any one group within it," he declared at a party banquet in Grand Rapids. Fitzgerald warned that domination by "one faction that feels self-ordained to lead the party" would result in "defeat and destruction." In the 1949 mayoral race, Fitzgerald refused to abide by Griffiths's orders for all city Democratic organizations to support George Edwards, chairman of the Detroit Common Council, former CIO organizer, and national officer of the ADA. In a direct snub to the liberal Democrats, Hoffa and Brennan endorsed Albert Cobo, Edwards's conservative Republican opponent in the ostensibly nonpartisan election. As in 1945, the liberal candidate's identification with the "Negro invasions" of white neighborhoods proved fatal for the labor-liberal alliance, as Cobo defeated Edwards in a landslide. Despite once again failing to capture the mayor's office in the Motor City, the CIO continued to gain ground within the state Democratic Party, and by 1950 was poised to complete the purge of the disreputable, retrograde Hoffa and his band of hoodlums.[27]

Faced with the growing presence of the CIO-ADA faction within the state party and his own increasing isolation, Fitzgerald attempted to counter the liberals' organization with one of his own. In February 1950, he announced the formation of the Truman Democratic Club and stocked it with old-line party members who resented the takeover bid by Williams, Griffiths, and Scholle. In retaliation, Griffiths, who was by then directing day-to-day party operations, published a biography of Fitzgerald in the party's newspaper, *The Michigan Democrat*, which ended by listing Fitzgerald's current employment as "counsel for the AFL Teamsters" and noting that he "has been backed energetically as national committeeman by his client, Teamster Head James R. Hoffa." Until then, Hoffa, who was well known across Michigan for his grand jury indictment in the grocers case, had preferred to work behind the scenes. But at the Michigan Federation of Labor convention in June, he made a public stand against a pro-Williams movement within the federation. In conjunction with their satellite union, the Detroit local of the Retail Clerks International Protective Association, and their allies in the Hotel, Restaurant, and Bartenders union, Hoffa and the Teamsters succeeded in blocking a resolution introduced by MFL president Frank Martel, a New Deal liberal and longtime adversary of the Teamsters, granting a blanket endorsement of Williams. More important, two of Hoffa's candidates for top offices in the federation were elected by votes of the delegates. George Dean, a former president of the federation who had recently moved into an alliance with Hoffa, was reelected to the top position, and Robert Scott of the Pontiac Teamsters again took the post of secretary-treasurer. In addition, Frank Fitzsimmons of Local 299 was elected one of ten vice presidents of the federation.[28]

Blood on the Pavement

As the 1950 state elections approached, the struggle between Hoffa's Teamsters and the CIO for control of the Michigan Democratic Party began to resemble their battles for control over union members in the 1930s and 1940s. Both sides focused on the September conventions of the six Wayne County congressional district party organizations, which would provide a plurality of the delegates to the state convention later in the month. Through the summer, the CIO and its ADA allies recruited 3,600 like-minded activists to run for precinct delegate and organized house-to-house calls to gather signatures on the nominating petitions required for candidates to be eligible in the district elections. To the great surprise of the liberal alliance, the Teamsters and their old-line party allies countered by submitting to the Wayne County Clerk more than a thousand petitions for their own candidates. Meanwhile, national leaders of the AFL and CIO, worried that the conflict between the two organizations in Michigan would damage both the Democratic Party and organized labor's political standing, brought Hoffa, Fitzgerald, and Scholle to a "peace conference" in Washington. There, Jack Kroll, head of the national CIO-PAC, and Joseph Keenan, national director of the AFL's League for Political Education, forced the Detroit combatants to agree to maintain a civil competition during the elections. The agreement lasted less than a week.[29]

A few days after the peace conference, the CIO and the ADA claimed that most and possibly all of the Teamsters' petitions for precinct delegates were fraudulent. From the great number of signatures written in the same script and arranged in alphabetical order, the liberals surmised that the Teamsters had copied them out of the telephone book. This theory gained added credence when it was later learned that several of the people listed on the petitions were long dead. The liberal alliance then established "screening committees" in five of the six Wayne County districts to examine the petitions. Neil Staebler, who had replaced Hicks Griffiths as state party chairman, filed suit in circuit court seeking to force the County Clerk to invalidate more than 1,000 allegedly fraudulent petitions. The court refused, ordering that "the eligibility of these persons to act as delegates may properly be determined by the county conventions in their respective districts in the event that they are elected to office." By leaving it to the conventions to decide, the court handed a victory to the CIO-ADA coalition, which controlled four of the six Wayne County districts and was threatening to take over a fifth. The liberals interpreted the court's decision as granting them the right, and the police protection, to bar illegitimate candidates from entering the convention halls. The police department complied, stationing officers at the doors to assist veterans of the UAW's "flying squadrons" fighting force, who were enlisted to fend off the notoriously violent Teamsters.[30]

Skirmishes broke out at five of the six district conventions, as hundreds of delegates backed by the Teamsters and old-line Democrats were blocked from entering or forcibly evicted from the meeting halls. At the 14th District convention, held at the UAW Local 212 hall, seventy-five Teamster delegates led by Fitzgerald fought their way through the doors and demanded to be seated. Several of the delegates who did not make it into the hall were bloodied by the CIO's battalion of guards. During the melee, one of the old-liners yelled, "By God, there's blood on the pavement, by God!" Inside the hall, Nick Rothe, the liberal district chairman, shouted down Fitzgerald's forces from the podium, where instead of a gavel he wielded a large wooden club.[31] After failing to seize the dais from Rothe, Fitzgerald led his delegates out of the convention, declaring, "After this the theme song of the nation should be 'God Save America' instead of 'God Bless America.' " Fitzgerald then struck at his opponents where they were most vulnerable. "I have just watched socialism take over the Democratic Party by Communistic processes," he told the press. The local newspapers, no admirers of the Teamsters but even less sympathetic to the CIO's attempt to dominate the Democratic Party, ran with Fitzgerald's characterization. The *News* denounced "the crude power tactics of Mr. Williams' friends," while the *Free Press* noted the CIO's "Communist techniques of beating down opposition by violence." Accompanying the *Free Press* editorial, under the title "Democracy in Wayne County," a cartoon showed a brass-knuckled giant resembling John L. Lewis but wearing Mennen Williams's trademark polka-dot bowtie, thundering "Shut Up!" and bashing a roomful of convention delegates with an enormous baseball bat.[32]

The red-baiting helped to taint the CIO's political activities, but it did not loosen the hold of the organization's machine on the Wayne County Democratic Party. The "Hoffa-Fitzgerald-Old Gang" faction was overwhelmed in every one of the district conventions. Liberals took over the chairmanship of all six Wayne County organizations and supplied nearly 500 delegates to the state convention at the end of September. Even in the Detroit Teamsters' home organization in the 13th District, which for years had held its conventions in the IBT hall,

George Edwards, champion of both the CIO and ADA and archfoe of the Teamsters, won the chairmanship over the old-line candidate. In the general election for governor, Williams was able to overcome his Republican opponent's use of Fitzgerald's accusation and was able, through diligent campaigning by thousands of CIO activists who fanned out across the state, to eke out reelection. By doing so, the governor and his CIO-ADA supporters not only defeated the formerly dominant Republicans but also finally destroyed the old-line Democrats. At the party's state convention in February 1951, Williams hailed the election results but noted with some bitterness that the defeat of two enemies was necessary for his victory: "These accomplishments were achieved not only by overcoming the attacks of our opponents from without, but also by surviving greater sabotage from within."[33]

The only thing left standing between the CIO-ADA forces and complete control of the state party was George Fitzgerald in the national committeeman position. In 1952, with the consent of the Democratic National Committee, Williams and Blair Moody, Michigan's newly elected U.S. senator, stripped Fitzgerald of his power to select federal patronage appointments in Michigan. Williams then announced that he would do everything in his power to stop the "incompetent" Fitzgerald from winning reelection as national committeeman at the party's national convention in Chicago in 1952. With no hope of winning, Fitzgerald announced soon before the 1952 convention that he was retiring from the post and would not even bother to travel to Chicago. "And I'm not sending regrets," he added.[34]

Fitzgerald's political career was not quite over, however. In 1954, with $56,000 from the Teamsters' treasury, he mounted a campaign for lieutenant-governor in the Democratic primary against the CIO-ADA candidate, Philip Hart. The Teamsters and the Detroit Building Trades Council were virtually alone in backing Fitzgerald. Frank Martel, who by then had accepted the CIO's capture of the Democratic Party and whose feud with Hoffa and his allies had culminated in 1951 with the withdrawal of the Teamsters and the construction unions from the Wayne County Federation of Labor, blasted Hoffa's latest political endeavor as a menacing power-grab. A headline over an editorial in Martel's *Detroit Labor News* read, "Is Hoffa One Heart Beat from Governor?" In the editorial, Martel predicted that should the governor become incapacitated after Fitzgerald were elected lieutenant governor, Hoffa would be "virtually dictator of the State of Michigan." Leaders of the state CIO and ADA were so alarmed by Fitzgerald's candidacy that Williams for the first time abandoned his policy of neutrality in state elections. "To pretend neutrality is repulsive to my conscience," said Williams, who explained that a reversal of his policy was necessary "because this case is out of the ordinary." The governor accused Fitzgerald of helping the Republican ticket in the 1950 election, "and since that time has shown no sign of having changed his views." During the primary campaign, Hart asserted that Fitzgerald "was ordered into the race by forces whose only aim is to defeat Governor Williams" and charged the Teamsters with spending "enormous sums" of money for cynical purposes. "Neither my opponent nor the forces he represents are interested in the Democratic program for Michigan," Hart declared. "They want only to elect a Republican to the governorship in 1954 as they tried to do in 1950." Williams and Hart weren't far from the truth. After Fitzgerald was crushed by Hart in the primary, losing by more than 3 to 1, Hoffa and the Detroit Teamsters abandoned their experiment with the Democratic Party and moved into a friendlier political environment.[35]

Actually, Hoffa's relationship with the Republican Party began in the late 1930s, long before his troubled affair with the Democrats. The Detroit Teamsters' long-standing, illicit friendship with Orrin DeMass, Republican Liquor Control Commissioner, began during the Teamsters' jurisdictional war with the Brewery Workers in 1938. At the same time, the Detroit Teamsters were represented by attorney Emmett Kelly, brother of then Secretary of State Harry Kelly, a Republican who served as governor from 1943 to 1947 and lost to Williams in the 1950 election. In 1940, the same year that Harry Kelly won praise from the Teamsters for abolishing an interstate mileage tax on truck drivers, Emmett Kelly was accused of using his brother's influence to help the IBT establish a monopoly over Detroit's wastepaper recycling and wholesale business. During the 1940s, the Teamsters supported Republicans Edward Jeffries and Albert Cobo in the nonpartisan mayoral elections, but Hoffa was restrained from endorsing Republicans in partisan elections because of Dan Tobin's devotion to the Democratic Party during this period. Tobin's replacement by Dave Beck in 1952 cleared the way for Hoffa's full embrace of the G.O.P. Beck, who voted for Dewey in 1948 and Eisenhower in 1952, shared Hoffa's brand of political voluntarism. So by 1953, Hoffa was able to announce to the press that he was "both a Democrat and a Republican," and by the following year, when Tobin was close to dying, to pledge the endorsement and financial support of the Detroit Teamsters to the reelection of stalwart Republican Homer Ferguson to the U.S. Senate. From there, Hoffa forged a permanent alliance with the Republican Party that proved highly profitable for him personally and for the Teamsters. His rivals in the Michigan and national CIO, meanwhile, were committing themselves fully to the Democrats, a combination that would ultimately doom Hoffa's career.[36]

Nine

The Enemy Within

Now I beseech you, brethren, mark them which cause divisions and offences
contrary to the doctrine which ye have learned; and avoid them.
For they that are such serve not our Lord Jesus Christ, but their own
belly; and by good words and fair speeches deceive the hearts of the
simple.—ROMANS 16:17–18

The demonization of Jimmy Hoffa that began in 1946 with George Murphy's one-man grand jury investigation in Detroit reached its national culmination during the U.S. Senate hearings on Hoffa and the Teamsters from 1957 through 1959. By the end of the hearings, Hoffa's name and face, which previously had been known by few outside Detroit, had taken over television news reports and the covers of major magazines and newspapers across the country. The Teamster leader came to be widely viewed as one of the most dangerous men in America, considered by many to be the chieftain of a vast criminal organization on the verge of seizing control of the national economy.

The Secret Government

The creation of Hoffa as the "enemy within" was enabled by a culture that emerged in the United States well before the Senate Select Committee on Improper Activities in the Labor and Management Field began its hearings. The Murphy grand jury investigation, with its surrounding discourse of Hoffa as the "boss" of a many-tentacled Team-

171

ster conspiracy within the Detroit economy, proved to be merely a local dress rehearsal for a national drama that frightened, entertained, and mobilized much of the American public in the postwar era. While the literature on the culture of anti-subversion in the late 1940s and 1950s has concentrated on the crusade against communism, the parallel campaign against crime has received far less attention.

The hearings conducted by Senator Estes Kefauver's Special Committee to Investigate Organized Crime in Interstate Commerce in 1950 and 1951, which received broader press coverage than the simultaneous trial of Julius and Ethel Rosenberg and higher television ratings than the subsequent Army-McCarthy hearings, brought the image of conspiratorial gangster syndicates into millions of American households. In its report, the committee echoed the charges of both anticommunists and those made by Murphy and the Detroit press against Hoffa's Teamsters:

> ... these criminal gangs possess such power and had access to such sources of protection that they constituted a government within a government in this country and that second government was the government by the underworld ...
>
> This phantom government nevertheless enforces its own law, carries out its own executions, and not only ignores but abhors the democratic processes of justice which are held to be the safeguards of the American citizen.
>
> This secret government of crimesters is a serious menace which could, if not curbed, become the basis for a subversive movement which could wreck the very foundation of this country.[1]

Two years after the Kefauver committee finished its work, Congressman Clare Hoffman formed a subcommittee of the House Government Operations Committee to investigate the CIO's seizure of the Democratic Party in the Wayne County district conventions in 1950. But ironically, Hoffman's attention soon turned to the CIO's defeated opponents in those conventions, Hoffa and the Detroit Teamsters, who were well known to the congressman for their organizing drives among Port Huron milk drivers and Detroit grocers in the 1940s. Hoffman was particularly interested in the activities of Teamsters

Local 985, which was chartered in the late 1940s to organize Detroit's jukebox and vending machine distribution firms. The Kefauver Committee had touched on Local 985 but focused most of its Detroit investigations elsewhere. Hoffman Committee investigators found that the local, in partnership with the Detroit Teamsters' longtime allies in Bartenders Union Local 562 and certain Italian-owned jukebox and vending machine companies, had conducted a campaign of terror against competing distribution companies and local bar owners in an effort to establish a monopoly over the business. The investigators also uncovered Hoffa's first institutional alliance with an Italian crime family.[2]

Hoffa's arrangement with elements of Detroit's East Side criminal organizations emerged out of his longtime effort to control the local liquor industry—made up of an interdependent network of breweries, bars, groceries, liquor stores, and the state Liquor Control Commission—and to defend it from incursions by the CIO. By the end of World War II, most portions of the industry had been captured by the Teamsters or were shared in a truce with the United Brewery Workers and other CIO organizations, yet one relatively small part of the saloon business remained unsettled.[3] The CIO was the first to organize the businesses that supplied vending machines and jukeboxes to local bars when it signed a contract with an association of distribution companies in the late 1930s. Soon after that contract lapsed during the war, Jimmy James, an organizer with the AFL, established the Music Maintenance Workers Union and began organizing jukebox workers with the help of Hoffa and his friends in the Wayne County sheriff's department and prosecutor's office. When the CIO informed the sheriff's department that several AFL pinball machines were illegal gambling devices, Hoffa used his influence with the law-enforcement agencies to stop the seizure of the machines. By the end of the war, James had organized nearly all of the industry's workers, providing himself with a substantial dues base and Hoffa with a bulwark against the CIO, which to the great alarm of the entire IBT was then negotiating affiliation with the national Brewery Workers union.[4]

James's final obstacle to the complete organization of the industry remained a group of businesses secretly owned by Angelo Meli, his brother Vincent Meli, Mike Rubino, Pete Licavoli, and Joe Bommarito, known by the Detroit police as leaders of the city's largest criminal organizations. The president of the largest mob-owned company, Bilvin Distributing Company, was William Bufalino, a recent arrival from Pennsylvania whose law degree, sterling record as a World War II veteran, and relative anonymity in Detroit made him a safe front man for the company. Before the Kefauver Committee began its investigations, it was generally not known that Bufalino was the husband of the niece of Angelo Meli and that Bufalino's brother was Russell Bufalino, underboss of the Joseph Barbara crime family of Pittston, Pennsylvania, one of the most powerful criminal organizations in the northeastern United States. Undaunted by his opponents' connections, in 1946 James revealed in court and to the press the identities of the owners of the Bilvin firm in an attempt to secure an injunction against the company's anti-union campaign among its workers. Nonetheless, Bilvin and other firms owned by Bommarito, Licavoli, Rubino, and the Melis successfully resisted organization.[5]

In 1947, Hoffa abruptly changed tack in his involvement with the jukebox industry. As the mob-owned vending machine companies continued to hold out, Hoffa took over James's union and chartered it as Local 985. Soon, though, Hoffa replaced James with Bufalino as president of the new union. Rumors circulated through bars and jukebox companies that Angelo Meli "paid a considerable amount of money" to Hoffa to place his niece's husband at the head of Local 985. Whether or not that transaction occurred, the alliance with Bufalino and Meli allowed Hoffa to bring the entire industry under a Teamster contract. Scores of bar owners who did not sign with the mob-owned, Teamster-organized firms were subjected to boycotts, picketing, bombings, acid attacks, and vandalism. After a productive start, the organizing campaign was halted by the indictments of Bufalino and six other union members for extortion in the fall of 1953.[6]

In November 1953, Hoffman, along with Kansas Republican Wint Smith, formed a subcommittee of the House Education and Labor Committee, with Smith as chairman, to focus on the Teamsters' Michigan Conference and Central States health and welfare fund. In 1951 Hoffa had placed the fund with the Union Casualty Life Insurance Agency of Chicago. The agency was owned by Allen and Rose Dorfman, the son and wife of Paul "Red" Dorfman, president of the Chicago local of the Waste Material Handlers Union, who had assisted Hoffa and Brennan in their attempt to establish a monopoly over

Detroit's wastepaper recycling and wholesale business in 1940. Red Dorfman was a useful ally to have in Chicago. His friends included the city's mayor and political bosses, President Truman, the leadership of the Chicago Federation of Labor, the new IBT president Dave Beck, and AFL president George Meany. Dorfman was also known by the police for his connections to both the Italian syndicate in Chicago and the Jewish mob in New York, and for the unsolved murder of his predecessor in the Waste Handlers Union. Hoffman's investigators raised questions about Dorfman's character but were especially concerned that his family's company was skimming considerable amounts of money in excessive fees and commissions from the Teamsters' fund.[7]

A few weeks after it began, the investigation conducted by Smith and Hoffman's Education and Labor subcommittee came to a sudden halt. During testimony at a hearing, Smith left the room to take what he said was a long-distance telephone call. When he returned, he announced that the hearings were terminated. In response to questions from the press, Smith pointed to the ceiling and cryptically declared, "The pressure comes from away up there, and I just can't talk about it any more specifically than that." Government investigators later reported that pressure to close the hearings had come from Payne Ratner, a former governor of Kansas and close friend of fellow Kansan Wint Smith, who had been retained as Hoffa's attorney when the hearings began. But syndicated columnist Drew Pearson alleged that the hearings had been called off by Arthur Summerfield, the U.S. postmaster general in the Eisenhower Administration and former leader of the Michigan Republican Party, in exchange for the support that Hoffa gave to Michigan's Republican Senator Homer Ferguson in the 1954 election.[8]

Despite its short life and abrupt ending, the Hoffman and Smith subcommittee succeeded in promoting the idea that the Teamsters were a part of the "secret government" alleged by Kefauver. In its final report the subcommittee claimed that the activities of Local 985 and Hoffa's association with the Dorfmans indicated the existence of a "gigantic, wicked conspiracy to, through the use of force, threats of force and economic pressure, extort and collect millions of dollars" from union members, employers, and the federal government. Yet while these were indeed conspiracies they were far from gigantic and, at least to the vast majority of Teamster members within Hoffa's domain, not very wicked either. Local 985 consisted of only 400 members, representing a tiny portion of Hoffa's empire. Other members in Michigan and the Central States, who did not have health, welfare, or pension programs before Hoffa created them in 1949 and who were enjoying wages that had been increased by more than 50 percent in less than ten years, raised no objections to the violence directed at bar owners and jukebox companies or to the handling of the union's funds.[9]

During the hearings in 1953, Hoffa became convinced that an informant was supplying evidence to the committee from inside the Detroit Teamster headquarters. He telephoned a labor leader in New York, John Dioguardi, whom Hoffa knew to be familiar with wiretapping devices. Dioguardi arranged for an associate to wire the telephones of the Local 299 staff. Hoffa's conversations with Dioguardi were overheard by agents of the New York district attorney's office, who had tapped Dioguardi's telephone. Law enforcement agencies were monitoring Dioguardi, better known as "Johnny Dio," because by the early 1950s he was one of the most notorious gangsters in New York. He had served three years in Sing Sing prison during the 1930s for extortion against trucking companies before gaining notice among New York district attorneys as a major racketeer in the garment industry as both an employer and a union officer. Dioguardi had also captured the attention of a young writer named Budd Schulberg, who was then at work on a screenplay about labor corruption on the New York docks. Using Johnny Dio as the model for the character of a villainous union boss, Schulberg wrote a script that became not only a classic of American cinema but also the ur-text for the crusade against Jimmy Hoffa and corrupt labor unions.[10]

When *On the Waterfront* was released in April 1954, the movement against criminals in organized labor was thrust into the mainstream of American culture. The film, starring Marlon Brando as Terry Malloy, a New York dockworker caught between his conscience and the power of a criminal longshoremen's union, uses corruption in the labor movement to relate a Christian parable of sin, redemption, and manly responsibility. Lee J. Cobb plays the part of the union boss, Johnny Friendly (the Johnny Dio character), as simple, uncomplicated evil. Friendly unflinchingly rubs out anyone, including his closest associates, who threatens the "sweet" deal he gets from the dues his members pay him "to make sure they work steady." After Malloy unwittingly assists Friendly's henchmen in the murder of the "stool pigeon" Joey Doyle, who "ratted" on the union boss to the crime commission, he is confronted by the voices of responsibility, the local priest and Doyle's angelic sister. Edie Doyle, played with blonde purity by Eva Marie Saint, counters Malloy's initial cynicism by asking, "Shouldn't we care about everybody? Isn't everybody part of everybody else?" But the young longshoreman resists "ratting" on the union boss until Friendly has another informant killed in front of Malloy and a group of workers. Father Barry, played by Karl Malden, arrives at the scene of the murder to deliver a sermon that marks the turning point in the plot. "Some people think the Crucifixion only took place on Calvary," he says over the body of the slain man. "They better wise up."

. . . If you don't think Christ is here on the waterfront, you got another guess coming. And who do you think He lines up with. . . .

Every morning when the hiring boss blows his whistle, Jesus stands alongside you in the shape-up. He sees some of you get picked and some of you get passed over. He sees the family men worrying about getting their rent and getting food in the house for the wife and kids. He sees them selling their souls to the mob for a day's pay. . . .

What does Christ think of the easy-money boys who do none of the work and take all of the gravy? What does He think of these fellows wearing hundred-and-fifty-dollar suits and diamond rings—on *your* union dues and *your* kickback money? How does He feel about bloodsuckers picking up a longshoreman's work tab and grabbing twenty percent interest at the end of a week?

. . . How does He, who spoke up without fear against evil, feel about your silence?

Johnny Friendly looks on with a sneer at this performance, as his goons hurl cans and rotten fruit at the priest. Later, Malloy's brother is murdered—crucified on a cargo hook—finally galvanizing Malloy to fight back. He carries a pistol to Friendly's bar with the intent to kill his nemesis, but is dissuaded by Father Barry, who convinces Malloy to seek his revenge by testifying before the crime commission rather than attacking him "like a hoodlum down here in the jungle." After his testimony, Malloy confronts Friendly on the docks by challenging the manliness of the union boss. "Take the heater away and you're nothin'," Malloy shouts at the villain. "Take the good goods away, and the kickback and shakedown cabbage away and the pistoleros away and you're a great big hunk of nothing. Your guts is all in your wallet and your trigger finger!" Goaded into a fight, Malloy attacks Friendly, who cowardly calls on his gang for assistance. After receiving a nearly lethal beating that leaves him bloodied and barely conscious, the heroic dockworker reenacts the scene of Christ struggling to bear the weight of the cross as he staggers forward, leading the longshoremen in defiance against Friendly, onto the loading dock and toward a clean union.[11]

On the Waterfront became one of the most successful films in the history of American cinema, winning eight Academy Awards—including Best Picture, Best Direction, Best Screenplay, and Best Actor—and setting records for box-office ticket sales. Millions of Americans admired the film for exposing the tyranny of corrupt labor unions over helpless workers and providing a compelling tale of good triumphing over evil. One of its admirers was Robert Kennedy, then gaining fame as the earnest and moralistic counsel for Senator Joseph McCarthy's anticommunist Permanent Investigations Subcommittee. Kennedy, a committed Catholic with a zeal for social justice, closely resembled the Father Barry character and likely identified with the crusading priest. Less than three years after the opening of *On the Waterfront*, Kennedy took on the Father Barry role in a real-life reenactment of the Hollywood passion play.

Jeremiah

On the night of April 5, 1956, as newspaper columnist Victor Riesel left Lindy's Steak House in midtown Manhattan, a young man approached him on the street, threw liquid into Riesel's face, and fled. Riesel, unable to cover his eyes in time, was blinded by the liquid, which turned out to be corrosive acid. A few days before the attack Riesel had published a column in which he alleged that businesses and unions in the New York garment and trucking industries were controlled by criminal elements, including Johnny Dio. Riesel immediately accused labor racketeers of ordering the acid attack. Overnight the case became a cause célèbre for the political establishment. Vice President Richard Nixon sent Riesel a letter of support and the New York City and New York State governments both pledged to undertake campaigns to root out "industrial racketeers." Within two weeks after Riesel's blinding, an outraged press had hounded government officials to the point that New York Attorney General Jacob Javits was compelled to state that racketeers had taken control of such a large sector of the economy that consumers in New York were paying a 5 percent "racket tax" for "illegal payments taken out of business by racketeering elements." The *New York Times* editorialized that corrupt influences had spread into the national economy, and that for the country as a whole the amount of money strong-armed out of manufacturers and consumers "may be as much as ten times" Javits's estimate of $50 million in New York.[12]

Attention was suddenly focused on the leaders of organized labor. George Meany, president of the newly merged American Federation of Labor and Congress of Industrial Organizations, was besieged by calls for labor to purge itself of the filth that had crept into its ranks. Letters from outraged citizens poured into AFL-CIO headquarters, suggesting that "any decent man" would not allow such criminal behavior in his own organization. The *New York Times* insisted that "a lot must still be done to give full expression to the anti-corruption program the AFL-CIO wrote into its constitution at its founding convention." But there was widespread doubt that organized labor, though at the apex of its power in the twentieth century, could clean its own house adequately. Riesel himself, in a dramatic performance on the *Meet the Press* television program in which he appeared wearing dark glasses to cover his blinded eyes and bandages on his burned hands, gave a clenched-fist appeal to Congress to form a permanent committee to fight criminals in organized labor. Riesel claimed that Meany and the rest of the AFL-CIO hierarchy lacked the power to do the job without governmental enforcement. The columnist drew a parallel between union gangsters and another menace that had recently gripped the attention of the public:

We have a committee on internal security which goes after the Commies, why not a committee on this kind of corruption? Is there less a danger in this underworld second government to the rank and file, to the public, to the man on the street? If this can happen to me, does anybody think it couldn't happen to anybody else?

President Eisenhower cited the Riesel broadcast in a private conversation with Meany in which he threatened White House action against labor racketeers. The Congress was no less eager to avenge Riesel. Republican Representative Peter Frelinghuysen of New Jersey said on the House floor that the assault raised the question of whether existing legislation was adequate to combat labor racketeering.[13]

The leaders of organized labor wasted no time in coming clean. On May 6, Meany pledged, "just as we have defeated the enemies without, who tried so desperately to destroy the labor movement, so will we defeat the enemies from within whose wrongdoing can undermine the effectiveness of everything good we are trying to accomplish." One month later, the AFL-CIO Executive Council granted authority to the federation's Ethical Practices Committee to conduct autonomous investigations of corruption in affiliated unions and to hire its own staff and counsel. In an approving editorial, the *New York Times* intoned, "the AFL-CIO has done well to heed the call."[14]

Meany built his career by heeding the call of government. Having never led a strike or negotiated a contract, the former president of the New York Federation of Labor raised his stature within organized labor as an effective lobbyist and power broker in Albany. During World War II, Meany served as a permanent AFL representative on the National War Labor Board, often clashing with the board's business representatives but never wavering from total commitment to the war effort, including the no-strike pledge. After the war, Meany emerged as labor's chief ally of the government's anti-communist campaign both abroad and domestically. He secured his future as president of the national AFL at the federation's 1947 convention by red-baiting John L. Lewis and championing union leaders "who feel that they can best represent their membership by complying with the law of the land." So when summoned to the White House to discuss the problem of another kind of outlaw in labor, the archetypal "labor statesman" promised the president that the AFL-CIO would support "any constructive investigation" of corruption by the government and would do all in its power to reform its affiliates. At the August meeting of the Executive Council, Meany followed through on his promise by pushing through the adoption of a measure granting the Executive Council power to expel any union violating the federation's ethical practices code.[15]

Crusader

While momentum was building in Washington for a government purge of criminals from organized labor, Clark Mollenhoff, Washington correspondent for the Cowles Publications, was pressing Robert Kennedy to look into the problem of labor racketeering. But Kennedy was reluctant; he doubted whether the Investigations committee had jurisdiction over labor affairs. Mollenhoff continued to agitate: "Occasionally, I taunted him by questioning his courage to take on such an investigation." Eventually Mollenhoff convinced Kennedy to take a nationwide "survey of the labor scene." This survey involved a trip to the West Coast and Chicago, on which Kennedy and a congressional accountant were guided by muckraking journalists to the worst examples of bribery, extortion, and terrorism by local union officials, most of whom were Teamsters. Kennedy was regaled with stories such as this one, which he later recounted for lurid effect in his account of the investigations, *The Enemy Within:*

> There was the union organizer from Los Angeles who had traveled to San Diego to organize juke-box operators. He was told to stay out of San Diego or he would be killed. But he returned to San Diego. He was knocked unconscious. When he regained consciousness the next morning he was covered with blood and had terrible pains in his stomach. The pains were so intense that he was unable to drive back home to Los Angeles and stopped at a hospital. There was an emergency operation. The doctors removed from his back-side a large cucumber. Later he was told that if he ever returned to San Diego it would be a watermelon. He never went back.

This, according to Kennedy's biographer Arthur Schlesinger, Jr., was "Robert Kennedy's initiation into labor racketeering." It was also his first experience with any part of the labor movement. Kennedy himself admitted that when he heard from Mollenhoff of wrongdoings by Teamster officials, he had "only a vague impression of the Teamsters Union—some notion that it was big and tough."[16]

"The most religious among the sons" of Joseph Kennedy was guided not by knowledge but by a religious imperative. The young lawyer's Christian passion enlarged his concern over organized crime into an obsession. "There are persons so constituted that they can go nowhere without some piece of faith to serve for light," wrote Murray Kempton in 1960. "Robert Kennedy is a Catholic; and naturally he sought his faith there." Kennedy's faith and his attraction to Christlike martyrs drove him into the crusade against labor racketeers. According to Schlesinger, "He came to identify himself with workers who were expelled, beaten, murdered." Labor leaders like Hoffa, "as Kennedy saw it, had corrupted a movement of the oppressed." Confronted by so much evil in such a holy place, Kennedy viewed himself much like Father Barry standing among Johnny Friendly's thugs. "In this spirit, Robert Kennedy became for his journey a Catholic trade unionist," wrote Kempton. "He looked at the labor racketeers as upon men who had betrayed a priesthood." Kennedy saw himself as representing "the survival of the spirit" in a world of immorality.[17]

Sybarites and Statesmen

By the end of 1956, Jimmy Hoffa's associate Johnny Dio had been linked by the New York police to the acid-blinding of Riesel. Hoffa and Dio were also alleged to be partners in setting up various phony Teamster "paper locals" in order to swing the New York Joint Council behind Hoffa's bid for the IBT presidency. Their partner in the scheme was Anthony "Tony Ducks" Corallo, a New York gangster who was then on the Treasury Department's list of major narcotics traffickers. Most inflammatory was the disclosure of Hoffa's attempt to merge the Teamsters with the International Longshoremen's Association, whose gangster-ridden New York locals had been made famous by the New York City Anti-Crime Committee and *On the Waterfront*.

Any lingering doubts about the necessity of reforming the labor movement were wiped away. The *New York Times* reported that elimination of labor racketeers was "of maximum public concern." Riesel, on a speaking tour since his discharge from the hospital, demanded that if labor were to fail to clean its own house, "Congress should step in with Securities and Exchange Commission-type legislation."[18]

In November and December, Robert Kennedy was moving swiftly behind the scenes gathering information on Dave Beck, the former leader of the Western Conference of Teamsters who had replaced Dan Tobin as General President of the IBT in 1952. In the eyes of Kennedy, Beck was a common thief posing as a respected labor leader. Kennedy's Christian ascetic sensibilities were particularly offended by Beck's use of union funds to support a lavish lifestyle. The young counsel was incensed that Beck had built a half-million-dollar mansion in Seattle and a five-million-dollar "Marble Palace" for the IBT's offices in Washington, D.C. The five-story glass-and-white marble headquarters took up a full block just across Louisiana Avenue from the U.S. Capitol. It featured bronze-framed, floor-to-ceiling picture windows, internal columns decorated with Venetian mosaics, a hundred-foot marble lobby, and in the main conference room what official Teamster literature described as "one of the two largest" tables in the United States. In addition to a 474-seat theater in which he showed motion pictures to the staff, Beck had built for himself an office that, according to Kennedy, "was as big as it possibly could have been without being an auditorium." Most galling to Kennedy was that the Teamster president had used union funds for such personal luxuries as "boats and bow ties and diapers and deep freezes and nylons." Beck's replacement as head of the Western Conference, Frank Brewster, was also found to "live a life of luxury" on union money. Brewster was a decent man in the eyes of Kennedy, but he had fallen to the original sin of succumbing to temptation. "His weakness was that he enjoyed living too well, and in the process of so doing, had inherited some of the bad habits of Dave Beck." One product of those habits of decadence was an appalling effeminacy. In the course of his investigations, Kennedy found that Beck had "mothered" his son and made him into an emasculated "jellyfish." Compared to all his crimes as president of the Teamsters, Beck's "attitude toward his son was his worst sin."[19]

By New Year's Day 1957, Kennedy had enough evidence to guarantee that Beck was "about to be utterly and completely destroyed before our eyes." With Kennedy as its chief counsel, the Senate Permanent Subcommittee on Investigations, chaired by Arkansas Democrat John McClellan (who had replaced McCarthy after the 1954 midterm elections produced a Democratic majority in the Senate), prepared to conduct hearings. But after Kennedy subpoenaed Teamster officials to appear before the committee, the men appeared, refused to answer any questions from Kennedy on the ground that the committee had no jurisdiction, and left. Meany was furious that high-ranking officials in the federation's largest union would take such a cavalier attitude toward a Senate committee. He became adamant in high-level AFL-CIO meetings that those refusing to answer questions before a government committee should be purged. On January 28, at an Executive Council meeting attended by Beck, Meany presented a resolution pledging full AFL-CIO cooperation with "proper law enforcement agencies, legislative committees, and other public bodies seeking fairly and objectively to keep the labor movement free from corruption." The labor movement would be free from corruption, but at the price of its independence from the state:

> It is the policy of the AFL-CIO . . . that if a trade union official decides to invoke the Fifth Amendment, for his personal protection and to avoid scrutiny by proper legislative committees, law enforcement agencies, or other public bodies into alleged corruption on his part, he has no right to continue to hold office in his union.

The resolution was carried by a vote of 22 to Beck's 1.[20]

Corporatists from the CIO unions were especially cooperative with the Senate investigation. Walter Reuther, who had through his career sought ever greater participation in state governance, advocated complete submission to Congress and the expulsion of recalcitrant union members. As early as 1945 Reuther had urged labor's compliance with public morality. "I do not believe we can protect the good name of the union movement by attempting to cover up the facts concerning . . . bad practices," he said. "I think it is much better to acknowledge such undesirable practices publicly and to act affirmatively to correct them." Amid the clamor for reform in 1957, Reuther was even more emphatic: "American labor had better roll up its sleeves, it had better get the stiffest broom and brush it can find, and the strongest disinfectant, and it had better take on the job of cleaning its own house from top to bottom and drive out every crook and gangster and racketeer we find." Reuther directed UAW locals to remove any officer taking the Fifth before a congressional committee unless he provided "clear and sufficient evidence that he is beyond a doubt not disqualified." On January 18 the International Executive Board of the UAW, citing that it was "greatly concerned and disturbed by the extremely unfavorable stories appearing in the newspapers," adopted unanimously a resolution calling for "close cooperation" with any "fair and objective congressional committee."[21]

Cleaning the House of Labor

To counter the charges made by subpoenaed Teamsters that McClellan and Kennedy's Investigations subcommittee lacked proper jurisdiction in labor affairs, the Senate, on January 30, 1957, unanimously approved the creation of the broadly empowered Select Committee on Improper Activities in the Labor and Management Field, with an appropriation of $350,000, McClellan as chairman, and Kennedy as chief counsel. The Democratic members were McClellan and Sam Ervin, both conservatives, as well as the liberal Patrick McNamara, a former leader of the Wayne County Federation of Labor, and Robert Kennedy's brother, John Kennedy. Another liberal on the committee was Irving Ives, a Republican from New York with close ties to the labor movement. Besides Ives, the Republican side included three of the most right-wing politicians in Washington: Karl Mundt, Barry Goldwater, and Joseph McCarthy.[22] Sympathizers with labor were outnumbered five to three, but the committee's composition remained relatively unimportant in the investigations, since it was Robert Kennedy's project from beginning to end. Television networks made the investigation especially important when they announced the hearings would be broadcast live, as by that time more than two out of three American households owned television sets. The broadcast of the hearings, according to the *New York Times Magazine*, became "one of the capital's best attractions since the Army-McCarthy hearings."

By the end of the McClellan Committee proceedings, more than 1.2 million households had tuned in live and millions more saw taped excerpts, an enormous audience for a televised program at the time.[23]

The first witnesses were a number of Kennedy's subjects of inquiry on the West Coast, notably in Portland and Seattle. Kennedy very skillfully traced a paper trail, aided by witnesses' confessions, leading from a network of criminals to Frank Brewster, president of the Western Conference of Teamsters. The hearings quickly took on the character of a moral reform meeting. Testimony provided by Jim Elkins, a minor organizer in the Western Conference, indicated that the union was run by the foulest elements in society. Elkins, whom Kennedy considered "one of the three or four best witnesses" to come before the committee, had secretly tape-recorded his conversations with criminals in the West Coast Teamsters.

KENNEDY: Now these tape recordings covered subjects such as prostitution.

ELKINS: They did.

KENNEDY: And abortionists?

ELKINS: Yes.

KENNEDY: Gambling.

ELKINS: Correct.

KENNEDY: Bootlegging.

ELKINS: That is right.

KENNEDY: After-hours joints.

ELKINS: That is right.[24]

With the press full of sensational accounts of the first hearings, leaders of the AFL-CIO shielded their private apprehensions about the spectacle with public pronouncements pledging their continued support of the work of the government. Walter Reuther gave a series of tough speeches pledging to fight alongside the McClellan Committee "until we have driven every crook and gangster out of the labor movement." James Carey, another prominent member of the AFL-CIO Executive Council and the former secretary-treasurer of the CIO, declared that labor racketeers "deserve to be hounded out of the American labor movement as fast, as furiously, and as finally as we can find the means to do it. . . . the undeniable fact is that the house of labor has termites and therefore needs a fumigation."[25]

The largest termite was on the run. Dave Beck knew that Kennedy had enough information to put him in a penitentiary, so the Teamster president spent several weeks in the West Indies and Europe evading the committee's subpoena. Finally, amid growing pressure within the IBT and after securing former U.S. senator James Duff as his attorney, Beck returned to the country to try his luck before the committee. The treatment Beck received by the senators demonstrated that the committee's investigation was not a right-wing enterprise, as some in labor claimed. Indeed, Karl Mundt and Barry Goldwater took pains to defend the Teamster leader. In this exchange, Mundt attempted to flatter Beck into answering the committee's questions while reminding the senators of the Teamster's patriotism:

MUNDT: I remember that, as a former educator, and I watched with great admiration some of the statements you made at that time, one which as I recall had to do with college professors accused of communism who took the fifth amendment. Do you recall that statement?

BECK: I don't recall that particular statement, but for 35 years, Senator, of my lifetime in the labor movement, I don't think there is a man in the United States of America, along with my friend here, Senator McCarthy, who has fought communism harder than I have fought it.

But once Kennedy took over the interrogation and began peppering Beck with questions about his use of union funds for extravagant personal expenses, Beck was forced to retreat behind the Fifth Amendment. In one of the greatest stonewalling acts in the history of congressional hearings, Beck invoked his constitutional right to refuse to be a witness against himself sixty-five times in a single day. By the end of the session, Kennedy had achieved his desired effect. Though none of the allegations against him had been confirmed, Beck and his union were disgraced before a national television audience. Perhaps sensing the nature of Kennedy's motivation, Edwin Lahey, correspondent for the *Chicago Daily News*, wrote the chief counsel to congratulate him on his performance. "If ever Providential justice was ladled out in the Caucus room, you did it that day."[26]

The AFL-CIO president wasted no time deciding Beck's fate in the federation; Meany called a meeting of the Executive Council "about ten seconds after I was told that he had taken the Fifth Amendment." Two days later, the council voted unanimously to suspend Beck as vice president of the federation. He was eventually convicted of larceny and tax evasion and sentenced to five years in the McNeil Island federal penitentiary in Washington State.[27]

Indian Arm Wrestling

While Beck was sweating in the Senate Caucus Room, Jimmy Hoffa was touring the country gathering support from local Teamster officials and rank-and-file members who would serve as delegates to the union's national convention in September. During Beck's presidency, Vice President Hoffa had accumulated a substantial base of power within the IBT by running many of the national union's daily affairs while on his frequent trips to Washington, D.C. By 1957 local officers across the country knew of Hoffa's accomplishments in building the union in the Midwest, and many welcomed him as a replacement for the bureaucratic, uncharismatic Beck. But to help clear his way to the presidency, Hoffa offered money to an attorney and former federal official named John Cye Cheasty to feed information to Kennedy on Beck's misdeeds. Unbeknownst to Hoffa, Cheasty shared Kennedy's moral belief system and immediately informed the chief counsel of Hoffa's proposition. A fellow Irish Catholic, Cheasty told Kennedy, "I believe in right and wrong and that I must answer to God for my conduct. All my life I have regarded good as something to work for, and evil as something to be fought." Cheasty agreed to work with Kennedy and the FBI to ensnare Hoffa.[28]

Meanwhile, Eddie Cheyfitz, one of Hoffa's attorneys, was working to persuade the chief counsel that, as Kennedy said, "after a wild and reckless youth during which he had perhaps committed some evil deeds, Hoffa had reformed." The lawyer convinced Kennedy to have dinner with Hoffa in February. The meeting, held at Cheyfitz's house in suburban Washington, began a long and intense competition in masculinity between the two. Kennedy was particularly interested in Hoffa's physical characteristics. The Teamster's handshake was "strong, firm," but Kennedy was more impressed "by how short he is—only five feet five and a half." According to Kennedy's account, Hoffa spent much of the dinner talking about his life of fighting scabs and police on the streets of Detroit, and about how "always, he had won." In reply, Kennedy mockingly asked whether he should have worn a bulletproof vest to the dinner, "but it seemed to go over his head." Kennedy judged Hoffa's performance during the encounter to be an attempt to cover insecurities about his masculinity. "It seemed to me he wanted to impress upon me that Jimmy Hoffa is a tough, rugged man," Kennedy recalled. "It had always been my feeling that if a person was truly tough; if he actually had strength and power; if he really had the ability to excel, he need not brag and boast of it to prove it. When a grown man sat for an evening and talked continuously about his toughness, I could only conclude that he was a bully hiding behind a facade." In counterposing his own, more genuine manliness, Kennedy closely resembled the heroes of *On the Waterfront*. In his critique of Hoffa's personality, he echoed both Terry Malloy's challenge to the courage of Johnny Friendly and Father Barry's hagiography of the martyred longshoremen:

> It is important to Jimmy Hoffa that he appear the tough guy to the world. But the truth is that the tough ones are not the Jimmy Hoffas, with three hundred lawyers, and hired lieutenants riding in Cadillacs, armed with guns and clubs. The really tough ones are the men in Hoffa's union who have the guts to stand up to him and his hired hands. The really strong ones are the men who get knocked down again and again by Hoffa and who always get up to fight back. The really tough ones are the men Jimmy Hoffa cannot buy and cannot cajole and cannot threaten.

Hoffa's account of the dinner contains the same theme but reverses the outcome. In Hoffa's telling, Kennedy was exposed as the insecure

189

child hiding behind a façade of toughness. In his second autobiography, in a chapter entitled "The Spoiled Brat," Hoffa claims that Kennedy challenged him to an "Indian hand wrestling" contest. "I hadn't heard anything so stupid since I was a kid and another kid put a chip on his shoulder and dared me to knock it off," Hoffa recalled. "I'd knocked it off by flattening the kid. But this from a grown man?" When Kennedy asked if he was afraid to arm-wrestle, Hoffa at first demurred.

Christ! I couldn't imagine a grown man seriously acting like that. But obviously there was only one way to shut him up. So I stood up and peeled off my jacket. I didn't even bother to roll up my sleeve. Meanwhile he had cleared a table and we sat down facing each other, put our elbows together, and locked hands.

"Whenever you're ready," I said, and it was all so damned ridiculous I had to laugh.

I let him strain for a couple of seconds. Then, like taking candy from a baby, I flipped his arm over and cracked his knuckles on to the top of the table. It was strictly no contest and he knew it. But he had to try again. Same results.

He didn't say a word.

He just got up, his face red as fire, rolled down his sleeve, put on his jacket, and walked out of the room.[29]

In March, FBI agents photographed Hoffa handing Cheasty a wad of money in exchange for an envelope containing information on the McClellan Committee. Minutes later, Hoffa was arrested on charges of bribery and conspiracy. A pleased Kennedy greeted the prisoner at the courthouse, and the two continued their jousting. Kennedy remembered an awkward silence, "and then, somehow, we began talking about physical exercise. He had read somewhere that I exercised a lot and that I did push-ups." Kennedy claimed he could do more push-ups. Hoffa agreed: "What the hell weight does it take to lift a feather?" Hoffa's version of the encounter differs from Kennedy's, but contains the same attempt to belittle the manhood of his opponent. "I said, 'Listen, Bobby, you run your business and I'll run mine. You go on home to bed, I'll take care of things. Let's don't have no problems.' He was very unhappy because I called him Bobby. He's a kid, a spoiled kid."[30]

Ten

Remaking the American Working Class

And Jesus went into the temple of God, and cast out all them that sold and bought in the temple, and overthrew the tables of the money-changers, and the seats of them that sold doves. And said unto them, 'It is written, My house shall be called the house of prayer; but ye have made it a den of thieves.'—MATTHEW 21:12–13

Nothing's too good for the working class.—WILLIAM "BIG BILL" HAYWOOD, LEADER OF THE INDUSTRIAL WORKERS OF THE WORLD, WHEN ASKED WHY HE SMOKED EXPENSIVE CIGARS

Immediately after Hoffa's arrest in Washington, leaders of the AFL-CIO denounced the Teamster's activities. Walter Reuther broke the UAW's long-standing alliance with the Detroit Teamsters by announcing that if the bribery charges were upheld, Hoffa should "go to jail." Kennedy was so convinced that Hoffa would be convicted he told the press that if the trial ended in acquittal, he would jump off the Capitol. The trial, which began in June in Washington, D.C., was held before a jury that was two-thirds black. Hoffa and his attorneys, apparently taking note of this fact, radically revised the Detroit Teamster's image among African Americans. To the astonishment of the prosecutors, former heavyweight boxing champion Joe Louis, perhaps the most famous African American at the time, appeared in the courtroom and embraced Hoffa. A black lawyer named Martha Jefferson was brought in from California to assist Hoffa's defense team. During the cross-examination of Cheasty, Hoffa's attorney, the eminent Edward Bennett

191

Williams, implied that the informant had once investigated the National Association for the Advancement of Colored People. The *Washington Afro-American* and other black newspapers published articles portraying Hoffa as a champion of civil rights and denouncing Cheasty and McClellan as racists. As for the facts in the trial, Williams argued that his client believed the money turned over to Cheasty represented legal fees rather than a bribe and that Cheasty had handed Hoffa documents relevant to his own legal affairs. Whether influenced by the appeals for racial solidarity or persuaded by Williams's arguments, the jury returned a verdict of not guilty. At a press conference after the trial, Williams promised to send Kennedy a parachute for his leap off the Capitol.[1]

Incensed by Hoffa's acquittal, Kennedy ordered an investigation of the jurors and found that several had been convicted on charges of drunkenness and possession of narcotics. "Still another had been released from his Government job after refusing to take a lie-detector test on the question of whether he was a homosexual," Kennedy later wrote. "Such people are not prohibited from jury service. But they certainly are persons the Government might find antagonistic to the aims of law enforcement in a criminal court." Even more galling to Kennedy than the questionable morality and manliness of the jurors was Hoffa's assumption that human beings are motivated by self-interest rather than social responsibility, the philosophy "that every man has his price whether it is money, pressure or prejudice."[2]

Shortly after his acquittal, Hoffa announced that he would seek the presidency of the IBT at the union's convention in September. Kennedy responded by calling a new series of hearings that would focus on Hoffa. In making the announcement, Kennedy began to portray the fight against the Teamsters in apocalyptic terms. The intrusion of racketeers and hoodlums into the labor movement was bad enough, he said, but in the Teamsters it posed a threat to the entire nation, for there was "no organization, union or business, that has a greater effect on the community life in this country."[3]

During the Hoffa hearings the patterns of the Beck interrogation were repeated. Republicans on the committee tried to soften the image of a rare asset to their party within the labor movement. Again, the rhetoric of the Cold War was used to accomplish this task:

MUNDT: Basically, do you believe in socialism?

HOFFA: I positively do not.

MUNDT: Do you believe in our private-enterprise system?

HOFFA: I certainly do.[4]

Once the platitudes were over, the liberals, led by Robert Kennedy, fired away at Hoffa on his relationship with Johnny Dio, Tony Corallo, and the New York paper locals. Kennedy had no shortage of circumstantial evidence, and he knew that Hoffa could not afford to take the Fifth as had his artless predecessor. Yet once confronted with irrefutable evidence of his relationships with gangsters, Hoffa resorted to evasive, stumbling wordplay, as in his answer to a question regarding tapes of the phone conversations between Hoffa and Dio that were recorded by the district attorney of New York County:

HOFFA: To the best of my recollection, I must recall on my memory, I cannot remember.

KENNEDY: 'To the best of my recollection I must recall on my memory that I cannot remember,' is that your answer?

HOFFA: I cannot recall the substance of this telephone call, nor place the facts together concerning what it pertains to.

MCCLELLAN: But if these things [the tapes] do not refresh your memory it would take the power of God to do it. The instrumentalities of mankind, obviously, are not adequate. . . .

KENNEDY: You have had the worst case of amnesia in the last 2 days I have ever heard of.[5]

For Kennedy, this was merely the first skirmish in a world-historic war between good and evil. "In our August, 1957 hearings, when the Committee began to spread on the record Hoffa's close ties with racketeers," he recalled, "the nation got its first look at the man who in little more than a month would be elected to succeed Dave Beck as president of the most powerful union in the country—and at the convicted killers, robbers, extortionists, perjurers, blackmailers, safecrackers, dope peddlers, white slavers and sodomists who were his chosen associates." But Hoffa had already lost the critical battle for the sympathies of the television viewers. The young, handsome, articulate Kennedy posed brilliantly as the crusader for good against the squat, uneducated, deceitful Hoffa. Beneath the more cosmic significance Kennedy ascribed to it, the confrontation represented a cultural conflict between the rising, respectable professional class of the prosperous postwar years and the uncultured, unassimilated, and unruly industrial working class of the Depression. Hoffa took note of this after a series of questions from Kennedy about his personal history:

> He had the idea that a union is supposed to operate like a social club. I told him about our union. He asked a lot of personal questions—how I got into the union, how much a labor leader earned, and so on. It was as though he was asking, with my limited education what right did I have to run a union like this?

Unfortunately for Kennedy, on September 30, 1,700 members of the working class who resented the moral impositions of their well-heeled antagonist arrived at the Miami Beach Auditorium for the opening of the IBT convention.[6]

Hoffa's entrance into the convention hall was greeted with a raucous ovation, which by the estimates of the press was greater than the applause for his three rivals combined. A reporter for *The Wall Street Journal* noted the overwhelming support Hoffa enjoyed among the delegates:

> Walk into any hotel in Miami Beach and you see Jimmy Hoffa in one form or another, picture or banner. Or walk along almost any street here and you see cars with bumper stickers reading 'Jimmy for President.' . . . If the public display of Hoffa buttons means anything, Mr. Hoffa doesn't even need to go through the formalities of being elected. Everywhere, Hoffa buttons, three inches in diameter, stare out at you. Some delegates wear papier-mache derbies with vivid signs repeating the slogan, 'Hoffa for President.'

Save for a few dissenters, the delegates appeared to be rallied around Hoffa by the attacks against him. Just two days before the convention opened, the McClellan Committee issued a report detailing thirty-four new charges against the Teamsters' front-runner. Hoffa was accused by the committee of having used the pension and welfare funds of the Central Conference for his own business investments, including a large land development scheme in Florida, and of providing financial assistance to "employers and convicted extortionists." These allegations did not dissuade the Teamster delegates from expressing their loyalty to Hoffa. Nor did Hoffa's recent indictment for perjury by a grand jury in Detroit on charges that he had lied to another grand jury investigating the wiretapping of Local 299's offices. And when a report by the AFL-CIO Ethical Practices Committee calling Hoffa's actions "inherently evil" was read from the rostrum as required by the federation, the delegates shouted it down. Though the report warned that the IBT would be expelled from the AFL-CIO if Hoffa were elected president, the gathered Teamsters struck it from the convention record by what the *New York Times* described as a "roaring vote."

On October 4, Secretary-Treasurer John English, who was viewed by many outside the IBT, including Robert Kennedy, as a man of unimpeachable integrity, stood in defiance of the union's enemies to nominate Hoffa for the presidency. "We are being watched by everybody all over the country," English told the convention. "Yes, they have people here to our left and right from the FBI, the Senate Rackets Committee and probably the American Federation of Labor–Congress of Industrial Organizations watching what we do. . . . We don't care what other people think, we are nominating Hoffa for what he has done for the organization." By the conclusion of the roll-call balloting, the Detroit Teamster had received 73 percent of the vote against his two opponents.[7]

After taking the stage to thunderous applause, Hoffa began his acceptance speech with a brief bow to social responsibility by pledging to lead the Teamsters "to a position of respect and honor in the eyes of the rank and file of labor; in the eyes of the Nation; in the eyes of the world," but then cast the union as an autonomous, embattled entity and called for the members to "close ranks" against the hostile world. To create a loyal fighting force under his command, Hoffa merged his own identity with theirs. "I am your servant by virtue of my office as General President," he declared. "We are Teamsters together, and I pledge to you that your problem is my problem." Hoffa then moved toward an emotional identification with the delegates by describing the personal effects of the Senate investigation:

> To say that I do not feel deeply about the charges that have been made against me would be untrue. To say that it has not been tough would be untrue. I am a family man. I have a wife and children. I am proud of my family, and they are proud of me. They know how I believe in the cause of labor. They know this is my life's work and I am not ashamed to face them at any time for anything I have ever done.

Hoffa placed himself within a tradition of great labor leaders who had persevered against attacks by outside enemies. "We know that men like Samuel Gompers, Dan Tobin, William Green, Phil Murray and others were smeared," he said. "They were ridiculed. They were investigated and persecuted. Yet they kept fighting. . . . I have given 25 years of my life to fighting for this union. I have fought for what I believe is right and good against forces more vicious than you can imagine. I propose to continue that fight as long as I live." After denouncing the McClellan Committee's "destruction of the basic principles of due process and the use of the lawmaking function to smear a man's reputation," Hoffa gave ownership of his victimization to the rank and file:

> I want to say that a great injustice has been done to the individual members of the Teamsters Union. You are the people whose good name has been smeared. And I want to say this to the whole country: The 1,500,000 working American men and women that make up this International Brotherhood of Teamsters are your next-door neighbors. They aren't gangsters. They aren't hoodlums. . . . These people are Americans. I am proud to be one of these people.

After his appeals to their shared identity as embattled trade-unionists and good Americans, Hoffa reminded the members of the material basis of their bond. "Among all the charges, no one has said we have failed to organize," he affirmed. "No one has said we have failed to bring our membership a program of wage gains and improved security never equaled in the history of organized labor."[8]

Hoping his audience was sufficiently roused, Hoffa pointed them toward the enemy without. As during his career in Detroit, the principal foe was neither the government or employers, but "labor statesmen" whose mission was to join the managerial class. The new leaders of the AFL-CIO had not only "surrendered" their independence to the government but were also crippling the labor movement through their slavish attention to public opinion: "Samuel Gompers did not formulate his program by reading the morning newspapers." The threatened expulsion of the Teamsters from the AFL-CIO demonstrated that "a few ambitious men in the top leadership" of the federation were attempting to destroy the IBT. But just as they had fought with determination against the Brewery Workers, the Dairy Workers, the Retail Workers, and the United Construction Workers in Detroit, the Teamsters would fight their rivals within the top ranks of organized labor:

> I say to you that if certain forces succeed in driving us from the united labor movement for their own selfish ends, let me give them this warning. Separation didn't hurt the Machinists. It didn't hurt the Carpenters. It didn't hurt the Mine Workers. And it won't destroy the International Brotherhood of Teamsters. The Teamsters Union will continue to live and grow.
>
> If these people succeed in forcing the Teamsters out of the Federation, and attempt to raid our organization, mark my words, and mark them well, we will be ready to defend ourselves with every ounce of strength we possess.

The chanting, shouting delegates responded to the speech with such boisterous enthusiasm that security guards feared the floor of the auditorium might give way.[9]

Predictably, in Washington, McClellan and Secretary of Labor James Mitchell denounced the Teamster election as a travesty. Kennedy, who was enraged by Hoffa's ascendancy to the Marble Palace, claimed that the selection of delegates had been rigged to eliminate Hoffa's opponents. Kennedy asserted that more than 95 percent of the delegates had been selected illegally or by dubious means. "In short, we could establish that only 4.8 per cent of the delegates who elected Jimmy Hoffa had any clearly legal right to be at the convention and to vote," he later attested.[10]

Kennedy's implication that Hoffa's support within the union did not extend below the top leadership of the IBT was belied by the reception Hoffa received upon his return home.[11] Some two thousand members of Detroit Teamster locals greeted the new president at Willow Run Airport with noisemakers, streamers, and an American Indian headdress for "our big chief Jimmy Hoffa." A year later, after more revelations by the Senate committee, continued unremitting derogatory press reports, and a constant stream of public censure of Hoffa, A. H. Raskin of the *New York Times* found even greater enthusiasm among the members for "their boy." The reporter witnessed a meeting of Local 299 at which Hoffa was carried to the podium on the shoulders of two truck drivers as thousands from the rank and file stood on their feet and cheered. In a direct rebuttal to critics of his amoral approach to trade unionism, Hoffa told the approving audience, "They even criticize me for calling this a business. Well, what do you hire us for, if not to sell your labor at the highest buck we can get?" The assembled members then voted unanimously to continue Hoffa's unchecked control over the management of union funds, the selection of convention delegates, the calling of strikes, and all other union matters.

Raskin, who in the same article condemned Hoffa's view of unions as "cash registers," spent three days before the meeting interviewing members of the local to determine the depth and sincerity of their expressed devotion to Hoffa. Of the nearly two hundred members interviewed, only two mentioned any reservations about their union leader. "The others declared, with every indication of sincerity, that they felt Hoffa had done a stand-out job on wages, welfare, grievances and every other phase of union service," Raskin reported. The members believed the attacks on Hoffa's alleged excesses were in fact an attack on their own prosperity. "They brushed aside the accusations of gangsterism and racketeering as part of an attempt by outside forces to cut Hoffa down to size because he was doing too good a job in defense of the rank and file." One over-the-road driver expressed the feelings of most of the members interviewed by Raskin: "So far as I'm concerned, the union is 100 per cent. Every year that old raise is there, and it has been ever since Hoffa took over." Others also pointed to the benefits they had received from the infamous welfare fund.[12]

"Hoffa's Gotta Go"

The AFL-CIO convention in December 1957 proved to be the defining moment of the corruption crisis. In a meeting of the Executive Council shortly before the convention, Meany invoked the threat of adverse public opinion to press his case for expulsion of the Teamsters:

> There is no question that there were elements, and possibly are elements, with strong underworld connections that have access and companionship even with high officials of the Teamsters Union. If that was allowed to go unchecked on the ground that we had to wait until the law acted; if there were no action taken by the trade union movement itself to try to eliminate those conditions, I am quite sure you all can realize the amount of criticism that we would be subjected to by the press and the public.[13]

When David McDonald, president of the United Steel Workers union, suggested that the Teamsters be given a chance to reform themselves, Meany, in McDonald's words, "slammed his fist down on the table and he said, 'No. Hoffa's gotta go. Hoffa's gotta go.'" McDonald conceded, and "That was that." The council then voted to suspend the Teamsters and recommend to the delegates attending the AFL-CIO convention to permanently expel the IBT along with the Bakery and Confectionery Workers and the Laundry Workers, who had also been singled out by the McClellan Committee. By the time it reached the floor of the convention in Atlantic City, the issue had been decided.[14]

Alex Rose of the Hatters, Cap, and Millinery Workers, who was a leading figure in the AFL-CIO hierarchy, explained in a speech to the delegates the necessity of expulsion by pointing to the new responsibilities of labor in the postwar order:

> In modern society labor cannot stand alone. It must have the sympathy and the good will of public opinion and of the public

at large. It must have the sympathy of the middle class, and it must have the sympathy of the white collar workers and it must have the sympathy of the professional people, because labor and all of these together were responsible for social welfare legislation and this is the only way to avoid anti-labor laws.

Labor had ceded its autonomy and its right to cause social disruption in exchange for the welfare state; its strength was no longer derived from organization at the point of production but through bargaining with other "equal" classes and groups. Here, too, was an admission that as part of this deal labor would lose its place at the bargaining table if it were to overstep its new boundaries. Thus, Rose maintained, Hoffa and his overly desirous cronies had to be dismissed from the polite society of regulated industrial relations:

> All of us who have watched the revelations of the McClellan Committee had good reason to feel very disheartened and very frustrated. . . . But I don't know whether the proceedings of the Teamsters Convention were not even worse from the point of view of labor interests. I think that the behavior, the arrogance, the defiance of the Teamsters Convention has created a climate for all the anti-trust legislation that we fear. . . . It was defiance against public opinion, whose good will needs to survive and grow. This was not defiance as an act of courage. This was defiance as an act of vulgarity and irresponsibility . . . and I think the decisions of this Convention will straighten out and put labor in its proper role and it in its proper light before public opinion.

Though his was the only speech from the floor in favor of expulsion, Rose's argument carried the day—the delegates passed the resolution to expel the IBT by a vote of 10,458,598 to 2,266,497.[15]

Back in Hoffa's home state, the expulsion of the Teamsters reverberated through both labor and political organizations. Michigan was one of eleven states where the merger of the AFL and CIO had not been achieved on the state level. Acting on a resolution adopted by the AFL-CIO Executive Council granting him the power to sanction affiliates that had failed to merge in accordance with the 1955 national agreement, Meany moved against Hoffa's local base of support. Merger in Michigan had been stalled for two years largely as a result of Hoffa's appointment in 1956 as chairman of the Michigan Federation of Labor merger committee. Hoffa refused to hold unity talks with the CIO unless jurisdictional questions were resolved first. When Gus Scholle of the Michigan CIO balked at establishing jurisdictional boundaries before merger, negotiations between the groups ended. Hoffa's intransigence over the jurisdiction issue was understandable, since the Michigan CIO included his bitterest rivals from the 1930s and 1940s and was twice the size of the MFL. In a merged Michigan labor movement, the parent organization of Hoffa's Teamsters would inevitably hold lesser power over critical questions of jurisdiction. But the expulsion of the Teamsters from the AFL-CIO in 1957 allowed Meany to force through merger and destroy Hoffa's power in the statewide organization.

One month after the AFL-CIO convention, Meany sent in two of the federation's vice presidents, Joseph Keenan and L. S. Buckmaster, to establish labor unity in Michigan by any means necessary. When Keenan disallowed a Teamster from participating in merger negotiations, the MFL refused to meet with the Washington emissaries and called for a statewide demonstration against unification. In accordance with the AFL-CIO constitution's "sudden death" provisions, on February 4, Meany canceled the charters of both the Michigan Federation of Labor and the Michigan CIO and issued a charter for a new Michigan labor organization to be established at a special convention. Once formed, the new Michigan AFL-CIO was headed by Scholle and Barney Hopkins, former president and secretary-treasurer, respectively, of the Michigan CIO. George Dean, who as president of the MFL had served as Hoffa's mouthpiece for several years, retired immediately after the dissolution of his organization.[16]

Meanwhile, the Michigan CIO and its liberal allies in state government were making political hay out of Hoffa's national notoriety. In 1956, the public relations director for the Democratic State Central Committee advised John Swainson, liberal candidate for the state senate, to instruct "all persons assigned to phoning on get-out-the-vote activity, or otherwise engaged in this activity, to spell out whenever opportunity presents itself that you are the anti-Hoffa candidate." And in 1958, the reputation of Republican congressman William Broomfield from Oakland County was severely damaged by allegations that he had secretly received contributions from the "Teamster Boss" during his 1956 election campaign. Broomfield was one of seven Republican members of the Michigan congressional delegation who attended a dinner with Hoffa the night of his arrest in the Cheasty affair. In 1958, when ten out of twelve Michigan Republican congressmen helped to defeat a bill sponsored by John Kennedy and Irving Ives that was the first legislative initiative to come out of the McClellan Committee investigations, Governor Mennen Williams publicly demanded an explanation for why they "voted the way Hoffa wanted them to vote." To the *Detroit Free Press*, Hoffa had become the "political bogeyman" of Michigan.[17]

Sacrifices of Citizenship

As the McClellan Committee hearings continued through 1958, the crusade against labor racketeering took on far greater significance than the removal of criminals from unions. Much was revealed about the activities of Hoffa and other labor leaders under investigation, but more importantly, the hearings, the discourse surrounding them, and the resulting interventions of the federal government represented an attempt to replace the working class of the jungle with a new working class appropriate for civilized society.[18]

Robert Kennedy believed civilization depended upon the moral strength of its men, and that therefore the corruption of the labor movement represented a crisis of both manhood and spirituality in American society. In his view, a movement of the righteous poor had been seized by men who were degraded and emasculated by the sin of covetousness. Their desire for luxury had made them soft, cowardly, and self-serving. As a latter-day Christ, Kennedy would drive them from the marble palace and restore it as the temple of the poor.

Kennedy's investigations revealed Hoffa's shakedowns and coercive organizing of businesses, the sweetheart contracts, the payoffs to government officials, the network of hoodlums in the Detroit Teamster locals, the collaboration with the Dorfman, Meli, and Bufalino families, the loans made from the Central States Pension Fund to unsavory characters, and the permitted control by major criminals of Teamster locals in New York, Chicago, and Philadelphia.[19] But to Kennedy the most serious crimes were Hoffa's business speculations financed by union funds. Kennedy was appalled by Hoffa's ownership, through his wife, Josephine, of the Test Fleet trucking company and showed special interest in the amount of money the Teamster president had gained from it:

KENNEDY: Has this been a profitable operation?

HOFFA: You have the record. I think you could say that it was.

KENNEDY: Well, I am asking you the question.

HOFFA: Since it is not my company, I can only say that I think it was.

KENNEDY: It was. You do not know. Your wife has not let you know how much money she made?

HOFFA: I think I know how much she made.

KENNEDY: Approximately, how much do you think she made in that company since it was set up?

HOFFA: I can't tell you, offhand, but a guess. I can give it to you this afternoon, if I can get it.

KENNEDY: We have some figures here.

HOFFA: Read them off, brother.

Kennedy did read off the figures. After an initial investment of $4,000, Hoffa's and Bert Brennan's wives made a net profit after taxes of $155,000.[20]

"It often seemed to me that Jimmy Hoffa was more of a businessman than a labor leader," Kennedy remarked. "He had a wide variety of personal business interests. In fact, he had even more than his predecessor, Dave Beck." One of those business ventures was far less successful than the Test Fleet arrangement. In 1955 and 1956 Hoffa and other Detroit Teamster officers had encouraged union members to purchase lots of land near Orlando, Florida, that would be developed into a retirement community called Sun Valley. Hoffa had put up

$500,000 from the Local 299 treasury as collateral for a bank loan to the project's developer, Henry Lower, who had given Hoffa the option to buy 45 percent of the property at a cut-rate price. When Lower used the loan for other purposes, Sun Valley went bankrupt and the bank refused to return Local 299's money. According to Kennedy, this "sordid story" was evidence that Hoffa, like the sacrilegious money-changers in the temple of God, had sacrificed the welfare of others to his own self-interest. "Time and again the committee has found Hoffa to be faithless to the members of his own union," stated the committee's second interim report. "He has betrayed these members so frequently that it has become abundantly clear that Hoffa's chief interest is his own advancement and that of his friends and cronies—a great number of whom are racketeers."[21]

Of great significance to Kennedy was the decadent culture of the Teamster hierarchy and its resemblance to an earlier example of profligacy:

> We listened to testimony from the dregs of society. We saw and questioned some of the nation's most notorious gangsters and racketeers. But there was no group that better fits the prototype of the old Al Capone syndicate than Jimmy Hoffa and some of his chief lieutenants in and out of the union.
>
> They have the look of Capone's men. They are sleek, often bilious and fat, or lean and cold and hard. They have the smooth faces and cruel eyes of gangsters; they wear the same rich clothes, the diamond ring, the jeweled watch, the strong, sickly-sweet-smelling perfume.[22]

This passage closely resembles Father Barry's description of "the easy-money boys who do none of the work and take all of the gravy . . . these fellows wearing hundred-and-fifty-dollar suits and diamond rings." But to Kennedy, this life of luxury had not only corrupted these men but feminized them as well. During the hearings, Kennedy also played the role of Terry Malloy by challenging the manliness of the racketeers and gangsters who sat before him. Sam Giancana, one of the most famous and feared criminals in the country, was brought before the committee to testify about his involvement with coin-machine unions in Chicago. Kennedy was repulsed by the cowardice of the "chief gunman for the group that succeeded the Capone mob," who had feigned insanity to evade the draft during World War II. During his testimony Giancana hid behind dark sunglasses and when asked by Kennedy whether he disposed of his enemies by "having them stuffed in a trunk," snickered derisively before taking the Fifth Amendment.

KENNEDY: Would you tell us anything about any of your operations or will you just giggle every time I ask you a question?

GIANCANA: I decline to answer because I honestly believe any answer might tend to incriminate me.

KENNEDY: I thought only little girls giggled, Mr. Giancana.[23]

Kennedy noticed a similar unmanly habit in Hoffa's performance before the committee. "Now and then, after a protracted, particularly evil glower," Kennedy recalled, "he did a most peculiar thing: he would wink at me. I can't explain it. Maybe a psychiatrist would recognize the symptoms." And during a line of questioning concerning the criminal histories of several Detroit Teamsters, Kennedy charged that Hoffa's lack of courage had allowed corruption to take hold of the union:

KENNEDY: Are you frightened of these people, Mr. Hoffa?

HOFFA: I am not frightened of anybody, Mr. Kennedy, and I don't intend to have the impression left, as has been stated publicly, that I am controlled by gangsters. . . .

KENNEDY: You have people in Detroit, at least 15, who have police records. . . . I say you are not tough enough to get rid of these people, then.[24]

Though the crisis of masculine morality in the labor movement had been made visible, in Kennedy's view its roots lay in the decaying society at large. In a speech at Notre Dame University in 1958, Kennedy identified the new affluence in American society as the source of labor corruption. His reading of American history convinced him "that the great events of which we are proud were forged by men who put their country above self-interest—their ideals above self-profit." But amid the decadence of the postwar boom, America had lost its moral bearing and its manhood. "It seems to me imperative that we reinstill in ourselves the toughness and idealism that guided the nation in the past." In *The Enemy Within*, published two years later, Kennedy continued to link corruption with materialism and the decline of manliness. "The revelations of the McClellan Committee were, in my estimation, merely a symptom of a more serious moral illness." America had not yet been lost, "But that corruption, dishonesty, and softness, physical and moral, have become widespread in this country there can be no doubt." The book concludes with an extraordinary jeremiad for modern America:

> The great events of our nation's past were forged by men of toughness, men who risked their security and their futures for freedom and for an ideal. The foot soldiers at Valley Forge, the men who marched up Cemetery Hill and those who stood by their guns at the summit, the men who conquered the West, the Marines who fought at Belleau Woods and at Tarawa did not measure their sacrifices in terms of self-reward. And because of what they and countless others like them achieved, we are now a powerful and prosperous country.
>
> But have the comforts we have bought, the successes we have won, the speeches that we make on national holidays extolling American bravery and generosity so undermined our strength of character that we are now unprepared to deal with the problems that face us?
>
> . . . It seems to me imperative that we reinstill in ourselves the toughness and idealism that guided the nation in the past. The paramount interest in self, in material wealth, in security must be replaced by an actual, not just a vocal, interest in our country, by a spirit of adventure, a will to fight what is evil, and a desire to serve.[25]

Even though it had fallen the farthest into sin, the labor movement did offer Kennedy hope for redemption. In Walter Reuther and the UAW, Kennedy discovered a model by which to rebuild the house of labor. After Republicans on the committee agitated for an investigation of a long and violent strike by the UAW at the Kohler company in

Wisconsin, Kennedy began meeting with leaders of the auto union and found them to match his idea of ascetic manliness.

> I was impressed with the difference between these officials of the UAW and the men Jimmy Hoffa and Dave Beck surrounded themselves with in the Teamsters Union. It was a striking contrast—one I noted again and again as I came in contact with other UAW officials. These men wore simple clothes, not silk suits and hand-painted ties; sported no great globs of jewelry on their fingers or their shirts; there was no smell of the heavy perfume frequently wafted by the men around Hoffa.

Kennedy learned that Walter Reuther lived an exemplary Spartan life. Like Kennedy, the UAW president never smoked, very rarely drank, and often berated his associates who succumbed to such pleasures. The McClellan Committee accountant found that Reuther took home a modest salary of $20,920 and refused to allow the union to pay for such things as business dinners or even laundry charges of $1.50, a far cry from Hoffa's annual take of $50,000 and limitless expense account. All proceeds from Reuther's speeches and writings had been turned over to his own nonprofit charity, the Reuther Labor Foundation. And in marked contrast to Hoffa's far-flung business ventures, Reuther had made only one investment—$1,000 in Nash-Kelvinator stock in 1948 that had earned him a net profit of $1.26 when he sold it eight years later.[26]

Reuther derived his asceticism from the logic of corporatism, which dictated limits on labor's aspirations. By accepting responsibility for social management, corporatist labor leaders also accepted the obligation to police their desires and those of the workers they represented; demands for wages could not be set so high as to put employers out of business or threaten national security, and their own salaries would provide the example of self-restraint and sacrifice for a social good. During World War II, Reuther took the lead in taming the material desires of workers through his "Victory Through Equality of Sacrifice" program, whereby unions would renounce not only the right to strike but also premium pay for overtime work. When AFL unions refused to abandon premium pay demands in their bargaining with employers, Reuther cajoled a reluctant President Roosevelt into signing an executive order banning all premium pay for the duration of the war. After the war, when a movement for a thirty-hour workweek at forty hours of pay gained enormous popularity among the UAW rank and file, Reuther attacked it as "irresponsible," a childish demand for a "Santa Claus," and a communist attempt to "weaken the position of America in the total world picture at a time when that happens to be the most important objective." According to Reuther, unions should not be considered as vehicles for material gain. "If the labor movement is not an instrument of social change, it is nothing," he said in an attack on union leaders who shared Jimmy Hoffa's economistic philosophy. "And when it fails to be that kind of a creative, constructive instrument for social change and is just dealing with pressure group things—getting more—then I think it fails totally in its responsibilities." Reuther was particularly scornful of Hoffa and others who had sacrificed their social responsibility for material gratification. These men had "made it and they are very comfortable, and when you try to get people to do things that disturb their comfort, . . . they're not going to feel very pleasantly about you."[27]

Though inspired by different sources, the Christian Kennedy and the corporatist Reuther found that their missions were essentially the same. Both were contemptuous of materialism and self-indulgence, and both took it upon themselves to curb such base and disruptive impulses in the service of social harmony. Kennedy worked his entire life to bring his morality to America, from his crusades against communists and racketeers in the 1950s to his marches with farm workers in the late 1960s. Likewise, Reuther had virtually no life outside his quest to create a well-ordered society. In *Who's Who in Labor*, he listed his outside interests as "wood & metal craft work; development of economic and production plans." Reuther and Kennedy recognized their common bond during the course of the McClellan Committee's investigations. John Kennedy said later of his brother, "He might once have been intolerant of liberals as such because his early experience was with that high-minded, high-speaking kind who never got anything done. That all changed the moment he met a liberal like Walter Reuther." During the committee's investigations, Reuther led the fight for the expulsion of the Teamsters from the AFL-CIO and applauded the work of Kennedy as a service to both the labor movement and society as a whole. In return, both John and Robert Kennedy did everything they could to help Reuther make his case against the attacks of the committee's Republican members. And in 1960, Reuther cemented the relationship by throwing the full weight of the UAW behind the presidential campaign of John Kennedy. The Teamsters, of course, endorsed Richard Nixon.[28]

As the McClellan Committee investigations appeared to be winding down in late 1958 and early 1959, calls for legislative action reached an apocalyptic crescendo. "No family in this country can escape the repercussions," McClellan told *Time* magazine. "All of our lives are too intricately interwoven with this union to sit passively by and allow the Teamsters under Mr. Hoffa's leadership to create such a superpower in this country—a power greater than the people and greater than the Government." On *The Jack Paar Show*, Kennedy called the Teamsters "probably the most powerful institution in the United States next to the federal government." He insisted that "unless something is done" about labor racketeering, "this country is not going to be controlled by the people but is going to be controlled by Johnny Dio and Jimmy Hoffa and Tony 'Ducks' Corrallo." The national media helped broadcast these dire warnings. *Newsweek* ran a cover story entitled "Senate Probe or No Senate Probe: The Hoodlums Ride High in Labor." Alongside a full-page photo of Hoffa sitting in his office in Washington, his outstretched hand reaching toward the Capitol building outside his window, a caption asked, "In the Palm of His Hand?" Legislators inside the Capitol responded in the negative.[29]

The first to take action was John Kennedy, who began drafting legislation that would remake the American labor movement in the image of Walter Reuther. The senator consulted with George Meany, who assented to some sort of government supervision of union finances but angrily attacked Kennedy's proposal to impose government regulation on internal union politics. On the other hand, the Kennedys found Reuther to be amenable to a wide array of regulatory measures: "control of union funds, democracy within the unions, limitations on trusteeships, and the rest—he supported all of these in principle." The resulting bill, co-sponsored by Irving Ives, received half-hearted support from the AFL-CIO Executive Council but full endorsement from Reuther, the UAW, and most of the CIO unions. The Kennedy-Ives bill required unions to hold regular elections by secret ballot and to file comprehensive financial reports with the Labor Department. McClellan succeeded in adding an amendment granting union members a "bill of rights," which brought the state even further into the labor movement. The amendment not only granted members the right to seek court interventions against their union officers at any time, but also authorized the Attorney General or the Secretary of Labor to obtain court injunctions correcting union malfeasance. This provoked Meany and other former AFL leaders to withdraw their support of the bill. The Kennedy-Ives-McClellan measure passed the Senate by a vote of 90 to 1 over official AFL-CIO opposition but with the continued support of Reuther and much of the former CIO leadership.

In the House, Republican Robert Griffin of Michigan and Democrat Philip Landrum of Georgia drafted a measure that included all of the Kennedy bill's provisions but added several restrictions intended specifically for the Teamsters. The Landrum-Griffin bill prohibited felons from holding office within five years of incarceration, and, most important for the IBT, banned the principal means by which Hoffa had built the Detroit Teamsters, the Central Conference of Teamsters, and the Southern Conference of Teamsters since the 1930s. The bill outlawed picketing to force employers to recognize a union, and closed loopholes in the Taft-Hartley Act that allowed secondary boycotts, including the "hot cargo" clause by which the Teamsters could refuse to handle an employer's goods until he signed a recognition contract. In short, Landrum-Griffin took from the Teamsters their unique ability to expand through unmediated coercion against employers. The last vestiges of jungle unionism would soon be gone.[30]

The Kennedys expressed some reservations about the Landrum-Griffin bill, but after it passed the House, John Kennedy voted for the final version with its major provisions intact in conference committee. With President Eisenhower's signature, the Labor Management Reporting and Disclosure Act became law in early September 1959. Citing "the passage of effective labor legislation by the Congress—the purpose to which we have pointed two years of effort," Robert Kennedy resigned as chief counsel of the special investigating committee.[31]

The merger of Christian morality and corporatist ideology that drove the crusade against Hoffa and the Teamsters was codified in the so-called Landrum-Griffin Act, whose purpose as stated in its preamble was to enforce "the highest standards of responsibility and ethical conduct" in industrial relations. By limiting their control over union coffers, the law forced Hoffa and his colleagues to curb their unseemly appetites for wealth. It attempted to bring social responsibility to the labor movement by enforcing the right of members to participate in the management of their unions and by barring irresponsible elements from holding office. The bans on the coercive forms of organizing, which many scholars have considered merely a "gratuitous" attack on labor by right-wing Congressmen, were actually wholly consistent with CIO corporatism as well. It is significant that during the drafting of the Landrum-Griffin bill Reuther did not attend meetings with members of Congress that were called by the AFL-CIO to protest the prohibitions on organizational picketing and "hot cargo" clauses.[32]

The UAW president had good reason to allow the Teamsters' forms of organizing to be abolished. Reuther's corporatism required social responsibility not only from labor leaders but from ordinary workers as well. The notion of "industrial democracy" that was central to both corporatism and Reuther's original faith of socialism served as recognition that workers would have to be voluntary participants in their own organization and management. As Reuther put it, "We want a disciplined organization. We believe that in a union, as in an army, discipline is of first rate importance. There can be no question of that whatsoever." But Reuther acknowledged that an army of conscripts could not win this war against social disorder. His proposals for a fully regulated economic system were designed around what Nelson Lichtenstein has called "counterplanning from the shop floor up." Workers managing their own industries would need skill and discipline, but because responsible self-management required maintaining high levels of worker output and upward limits on wages, they also needed self-restraint in the service of a greater cause. The methods used by Hoffa to sweep tens of thousands of workers into the labor movement by forcing employers to sign recognition contracts—rather than by mobilizing, organizing, and disciplining the workers themselves—subverted Reuther's vision. By the late 1950s virtually all Teamster members in Hoffa's Midwestern and Southern domains had been brought into the union without their active participation, and, other than a handful of scattered dissidents and competitors for Hoffa's position, most happily declined to share in the management of the union.

Their loyalty to the Teamsters—their own brand of solidarity—came not from devotion to a cause greater than the union, but from the benefits they received from it. Walter Reuther and Robert Kennedy declared this attitude shameful; Landrum-Griffin made it illegal.[33]

To corporatists and moralistic liberals, Hoffa was the Antichrist of greed. But to the Teamster rank and file, the government repression that ultimately crushed his power made him a martyr for the fulfillment of their desires.

Eleven

Crucifixion of an Antichrist

My father drove a truck delivering bread and later became an organizer in the Bakery Drivers' Union. He dug Jimmy Hoffa (so do I).—JERRY RUBIN, *DO IT! SCENARIOS OF THE REVOLUTION*[1]

When Robert Kennedy was appointed by his brother as United States Attorney General in 1961, Jimmy Hoffa remembered, "I knew that my worst days were still in front of me." His prediction proved correct. As Attorney General, Robert Kennedy launched the largest governmental campaign against organized crime in U.S. history. He coordinated the activities of twenty-seven federal agencies to assist the Organized Crime and Racketeering Section of the Justice Department's Criminal Division and added forty-five attorneys to the fifteen already working in the section. Between 1961 and 1963 the annual rate of convictions by Organized Crime and the Tax Division nearly quadrupled. During this period no group faced greater government attacks than Kennedy's chief target during the McClellan Committee investigations.

"Get Hoffa"

Walter Sheridan, a lead investigator for the McClellan Committee who held a nearly fanatical hatred for Hoffa, was put in charge of a special unit within the Organized Crime Section devoted to labor rackets. What became popularly known as the "Get Hoffa" squad enlisted sixteen attorneys and some thirty FBI agents to watch, investigate, and

213

prosecute the Teamster president. "Under the Kennedys," wrote Victor Navasky, "the U.S. government considered itself at war with Jimmy Hoffa and the Teamsters." By the fall of the first year of the Kennedy administration, thirteen federal grand juries were receiving testimony on the activities of Hoffa and his associates. Several Teamster officials soon went to prison, including Local 299 secretary-treasurer Rolland McMaster, who was convicted on charges of taking payoffs for keeping a trucking company non-union. Yet Hoffa proved to be more elusive, requiring six years of litigation to put behind bars.[2]

Robert Kennedy believed the best chance to incarcerate his nemesis was Hoffa's indictment for mail fraud in the Sun Valley scheme, which had been handed down during the final months of the Eisenhower Administration. While Kennedy and his staff were poring over the records in the Sun Valley case, their efforts received ample promotion from the continued sensational press coverage of Hoffa and Kennedy's *The Enemy Within*, which reached the best-seller list soon after its publication in 1960. Unfortunately for the labor movement, the results of Kennedy's crusade against Hoffa also helped to recast all of organized labor in the image of the Teamster "boss." According to the Gallup Poll, pro-union sentiment had reached an all-time high just prior to the beginning of the McClellan Committee hearings, when 76 percent of the public registered their general approval of labor unions, while only 14 percent disapproved. By 1961, the percentage of people polled who approved of labor unions had dropped to 63 percent while those who disapproved jumped to 22 percent.[3]

The popular conception of the labor movement as run by thieves and thugs had a deleterious effect on the organizing efforts of various unions. The National Association of Manufacturers and the United States Chamber of Commerce initiated a ferocious anti-union drive during the McClellan hearings and used as one of its selling points the issue of union corruption. State Chamber of Commerce organizations distributed a pamphlet, entitled "Preventive Medicine," recommending that employers "discuss with employees the fact that unions abound with racketeers and corrupt elements." Reports from field organizers to the AFL-CIO headquarters noted a direct correlation between the hearings and worker resistance to unionization, and recounted many instances of anti-union workers referring directly to Teamster leaders by name.[4]

In stark contrast to Hoffa's infamy outside the Teamsters, the IBT convention in 1961 served as both a public repudiation of the government's attacks on the union and the apotheosis of the General President. Before the convention, Hoffa ordered all locals to strictly adhere to Landrum-Griffin guidelines so as to forestall any charges of a rigged election. For good measure, he tape-recorded the nomination and election of delegates from Local 299 and instructed other locals to follow suit. Even Hoffa's lone opponent for the presidency, Milton Liss of Newark, New Jersey, declared that he had been treated with "full fairness" during the election process. On the day the convention opened, an airplane trailing a banner with the message "Re-Elect Hoffa" circled overhead as more than 2,000 delegates, nearly all wearing Hoffa campaign hats and saucer-size buttons, flooded into the Deauville Hotel in Miami Beach. After Hoffa was nominated by John English, who called the incumbent "the man with the most guts in America," the delegates responded with a fifteen-minute ovation and a continuous chant of "Hoffa, Hoffa, Hoffa." Liss subsequently withdrew his candidacy after receiving only fifteen votes out of the first thousand cast, allowing Hoffa to be elected by acclamation. The delegates then mocked the government's attempts to impose Spartan living on their leaders by passing with roaring unanimity a resolution raising Hoffa's salary to $75,000—the highest of any American union official at the time—and adding a provision that "all expenses of the General President and General Secretary-Treasurer shall be paid by the International Union." Elected as the three trustees of the union, with the responsibility to audit the IBT finances, were two convicted felons and William Presser, who was under indictment for destroying records subpoenaed by the McClellan Committee. Finally, by another unanimous vote, Hoffa and all other Teamster officers were declared innocent of all charges of "malfeasance, misfeasance, and non-feasance" brought against them in Congress and the courts over the previous four years.[5]

Among the Teamster rank and file, anti-government sentiment merged with devotion to Hoffa. Robert Kennedy had long been the target of the members' insults as a "pantywaist" and "hatchet man" bent on taking away the comforts they had gained from the union, and in Hoffa they saw their hero, their provider, and a paragon of manliness. In December 1962, David Brinkley took an NBC television crew to visit Local 299 in Detroit during the election for the local's officers, "to see how Hoffa holds on, how the members look and what they say." Hoffa's opponent was a carhaul driver named Ira Cooke, whom many in the local considered to be an agent of Robert Kennedy. On the sidewalk outside the union headquarters, Brinkley's camera caught an impromptu rally for Hoffa, who had flown in from Nashville, where he was on trial for his involvement in the Commercial Carriers and Test Fleet companies. Teamster members crowded around Hoffa to shake his hand, slap his back, and wish him luck in the trial and the election. "If we had three or four more Hoffas in this country, that would be all we need," one man told the camera. "He's really the man." Another member directly addressed the incumbent: "Mr. Hoffa, I thought that Sampson was a giant. But you's a labor giant!" When Hoffa remarked that Cooke was a "proxy" for Kennedy, one member asked, "Jimmy, did you say Bobby was here by proxy or he's a doxy?" Seizing the opportunity to broadcast another swipe at his adversary's masculinity, Hoffa replied, "He's worse than that—he's a touch football player." In the election for local president, Cooke received 230 votes to Hoffa's 3,615.[6]

Trust

But while the Teamster rank and file carried him on their shoulders, Hoffa was spending much of the time he had out of court creating a monopoly that would stifle their interests for years to come. After rising to the General Presidency, Hoffa used his new power to convince, cajole, and in some cases force locals and regional conferences to negotiate trucking contracts that were modeled after the Central States over-the-road and local cartage agreements. Hoffa also demanded that all new contracts expire on the same date in 1964 and include the following clause: "The parties in this Agreement accept the principle of a National Over-the-Road Agreement and are willing to enter into negotiations for the purpose of negotiating such National Agreement."[7]

It was not long, however, before Hoffa found that preparing most of the country's trucking employers for nationally centralized collective bargaining was far easier than overcoming the more imposing obstacle of demanding and militant members within the union.

The most vexing center of worker demands was the San Francisco Bay Area, where in 1959, after a six-week strike, Teamster locals had won the highest cartage wage scale in the country. On a tour of the Western Conference in 1961, during which he convinced most locals to submit to his bargaining authority, Hoffa attended meetings of the Bay Area locals to persuade them to drop their "uncooperative" ways and allow him to negotiate for them within a national collective bargaining arrangement. Sounding oddly like Robert Kennedy and Walter Reuther, Hoffa argued that the "excessive" demands of a few threatened the welfare of the many. He promised that he would eventually bring their wages up, but that he needed to end competition within the union in order to establish a united front against the employers. Hoffa intended to stop the practice of locals "trying, for some unknown reason, to advance their own personal interests to see that they are the highest hourly rated individuals in the area." But at each of the Bay Area locals he visited, the rank and file booed and shouted down the General President and voted to bar him from bargaining for them.

Soon after his failed West Coast swing, Hoffa used his overwhelming support at the IBT convention to push through a change in the union's constitution requiring all locals in a regional conference to bargain as a collective unit if a majority of the region's locals agreed to an area-wide contract. The only opposition from the floor of the convention came from representatives of the Bay Area locals and from the Baltimore and Newark Joint Councils, who also believed they could do better as independent bargaining units. Most of the rest of the country, however, had experienced substantial economic improvements in their contracts after allowing Hoffa to take control of their negotiations and were only too happy to accept his plans to centralize all of the union's bargaining under his control. After a delegate from Local 70 in Oakland rose to denounce Hoffa's "machine," the hall shouted in near-unanimity to expunge the remark from the convention record.

Soon after the convention, Bay Area locals threatened to strike their employers for a wage increase well above what Hoffa was seeking to negotiate for the national agreement. In July, when the owners appeared to be on the verge of capitulating, Hoffa threatened to sabotage the operations of any company that met the locals' wage demand. Against the rebel unions Hoffa threatened to order other locals to drive through their picket lines and even send in scabs from Teamster locals outside the region. Ultimately, Hoffa's enormous leverage power forced the Bay Area unions to surrender not only to a lower wage increase but also to Hoffa's bargaining authority. But in many other parts of the country Hoffa was forced to dramatically drive up the demands of local unions, both to bring their wages up to the level of the Central Conference model for the national agreement and to quell outbursts of rank-and-file rebellion against lax local officials.

In the early 1960s, members in Los Angeles and Philadelphia, angered by local union leaders who had signed sweetheart contracts for grossly substandard wages and failed to prosecute grievances against employers, threatened to bolt the Teamsters for the AFL-CIO. Hoffa's intrusion into local bargaining was more welcome in Los Angeles than in the Bay Area, since he promised—and delivered on his promise after conducting negotiations with local employers in 1961— to raise the city's trucking rates to Detroit levels. In Philadelphia, Hoffa took even more dramatic action. In 1963 he demoted Ray Cohen, the head of Local 107, whose membership appeared ready to vote to decertify the IBT in an impending NLRB election and join the AFL-CIO, and brought in an army of organizers to process longstanding grievances. After a slew of grievance claims were won by the union, the members voted by a large margin to retain the Teamsters as their bargaining representative. Soon after the election, Hoffa coerced the Philadelphia employers through a variety of work-stoppage threats to accede to a 43-cent increase, making the city's truck drivers among the highest-paid Teamsters in the country.[8]

Having cleared his path toward the national centralization of collective bargaining in trucking, Hoffa began organizing employers into a single negotiating unit as the common expiration date for the industry's contracts approached. On January 16, 1964, he and a team of employers meeting in Chicago reached agreement on a thirty-eight-month National Master Freight Agreement covering 450,000 intercity and local cartage truck drivers. Several "riders" to the contract allowed for higher wages in several cities where militants and anti-Hoffa dissidents remained powerful, including New York and Los Angeles, but Hoffa did achieve far greater uniformity than had existed in the plethora of local and regional contracts that existed previously. For most of the members covered by the agreement, the across-the-board increases of 28 cents per hour over three years and three-quarters of a cent per mile constituted a substantial increase over their previous contracts, while a small minority received less than they would have under decentralized bargaining. In their 1965 study of Hoffa's collective bargaining history, the economists Ralph James and Estelle Dinerstein James concluded that "certain groups were inevitably hurt—e.g., local cartage workers in San Francisco-Oakland, and highway drivers on a few of the more lucrative Eastern trip-rated runs. But most truck-freight workers have higher wages today because of Jimmy Hoffa."[9]

Hoffa's campaign to eliminate intra-union competition on the national level was a virtual repetition of what he had accomplished in Michigan during World War II. In both cases he argued—and demonstrated—that centralization would raise the floor for wages and improve the economic standing of large sections of the IBT that lagged behind the standards of the Detroit Teamsters. But Hoffa's actions also proved that centralization required curbing the upward pressure on wages from more ambitious locals such as those in San Francisco and Oakland and thereby lowering the ceiling as well. By assenting to Hoffa's monopolistic mission, Teamster members attained a middle-class standard of living in exchange for a limit on their desires. The key to Hoffa's success and popularity within the IBT was that the members who benefited from his intervention greatly out-numbered those who suffered from it.[10]

Ambitious Teamster members found that virtually the only effective means to break through the ceiling imposed by the powerful General President was the threat of secession. "The moral of the story," wrote James and James, "if the Teamsters in a local area want Hoffa to obtain a disproportionately high wage increase for them in the next bargaining session or if they want improved servicing grievances and job security, they can apparently ensure this by developing a vociferous AFL-CIO minority." Indeed, the power of members to vote with their feet in a market of competing unions had forced Hoffa to provide for their material desires from his earliest years with Local 299 in Detroit through his presidency of the IBT. Unfortunately for the members, their leverage power was curtailed by the declining interest of Hoffa's rivals in competing for them.[11]

As we have seen, by the time of Hoffa's ascendancy to the IBT presidency, corporatists and "labor statesmen" in the service of social responsibility had destroyed much of Hoffa's external competition. In 1941, Walter Reuther and Sidney Hillman demonstrated their commitment to forging a unified and disciplined wartime labor force by conspiring to crush John L. Lewis's challenge to the Teamsters' control over trucking. At the close of the war, in preparation for unification of the labor movement and its concerted entry into governmental politics, Reuther and his counterparts in Detroit forced through a peace agreement between Hoffa's Teamsters and their CIO archrivals the Retail Workers and their subsidiary the Dairy Workers. Three years later, the Retail Workers virtually collapsed as a result of an internal civil war between the union's large communist faction and the national leadership. The CIO transferred much of the union's traditional retail jurisdiction to the Amalgamated Clothing Workers of America, leaving the Retail Workers eviscerated and demoralized and in no position to renew the union's organizing drives against the Teamsters and their satellite union, the Retail Clerks. Ironically, a dissident faction from the Retail Workers' warehousing division, which had been the chief bane of the Detroit Teamsters, transferred to the IBT during the Retail Workers' factional strife, and several of its officers, including Joe Konowe, who had led many of the jurisdictional battles against the Teamsters in Detroit, eventually joined Hoffa's staff in Washington.[12]

Perhaps not coincidentally, Hoffa's home locals 299 and 337 stopped growing in the 1950s and actually began to lose membership in the 1960s. This was a sea-change in two unions whose combined membership had expanded from 3,000 in 1938 to more than 20,000 in the 1950s. The stagnation of Local 299's growth was no doubt a product of the completion of the organization of trucking in the Midwest as well as the destruction of its rivals, but the flat growth rate of Local 337 in the 1950s was almost certainly linked to the peace pact with the Retail Workers and the splintering of the CIO union. Local 337 had grown by more than 600 percent from 1938 to 1947, the years when its rivalry with the Retail Workers had forced the Teamster local to expand into the warehousing, retail, food, and bottling industries. Over the subsequent ten years, when only the Brewery Workers remained as a significant rival, the local expanded by just 43 percent. It then stopped growing at all.[13]

Even after the expulsion of the Teamsters from the AFL-CIO,

efforts to renew competition with the IBT were frustrated by federal law and the reluctance of the federation's top leadership to take on Hoffa's union. The Landrum-Griffin Act of 1959 greatly restricted jurisdictional raids by declaring illegal "forcing or requiring any employer to recognize or bargain with a particular labor organization as the representative of his employees if another labor organization has been certified as the representative of such employees." And after a group of delegates to the 1959 AFL-CIO convention called for the creation of a new trucking union, Meany quashed the idea by insisting that even if the federation were able legally to establish such a dual organization, its drivers would not be allowed to make deliveries in cities controlled by the Teamsters.

Another motion to compete with the IBT came during an AFL-CIO Executive Council meeting in 1961, when Joseph Beirne of the Communications Workers of America proposed the creation of an umbrella local for defectors from Hoffa's union. Again, Meany opposed committing the federation to an organizational battle with the expelled union. This time, the AFL-CIO president claimed that dissident Teamsters would only be replaced by men "with long criminal records." When Beirne's motion came to the floor of the AFL-CIO convention a few days later, several federation leaders, including Walter Reuther, expressed frustration with Meany's unwillingness to compete with the IBT. Nonetheless, the federation president succeeded in blocking the establishment of a rival trucking union. Meany later recalled that Hoffa's support among the rank and file had made it impossible for the AFL-CIO to mount a successful campaign against the Teamsters. "The biggest obstacle we had to overcome was loyalty to the union," Meany told his biographer. "We would get the younger members, but we couldn't get the older members. They would say, 'It's our union; it may not be all we want, but it's our union. You're not going to destroy it.' "[14]

"Free Hoffa"

In the crowning irony of Hoffa's life, just as he was finally establishing a permanent monopoly over the union, his power was taken away. The Test Fleet trial in Nashville had ended in a hung jury, but Robert

Kennedy's Justice Department attorneys had uncovered evidence that Hoffa had attempted to buy votes from some of the jurors. In the winter of 1964, after another grand jury handed down an indictment on charges of jury-tampering, Hoffa went to trial again, this time in Chattanooga, where the judge had moved the proceedings because of pre-trial publicity in Nashville. Testimony from Edward Partin, a Louisiana Teamster official who had worked as an informant for Kennedy and Sheridan during the Nashville trial, proved decisive for the jury in Chattanooga, who found Hoffa guilty of the felony charge on March 4, 1964. During the sentencing hearing, the judge told Hoffa that he had been convicted "of having struck at . . . the very basis of civilization itself, and that is the administration of justice." He then sentenced the Teamster president to eight years in prison and a fine of $10,000. Kennedy was pleased with the conviction but wanted a longer term of incarceration. After pushing for another grand jury indictment for Hoffa's involvement in the aborted Sun Valley deal, the Attorney General received his wish. Just seven weeks after his conviction in Tennessee, Hoffa went on trial in Chicago for defrauding the Central States Pension Fund, which he had instructed to issue $500,000 of Local 299's portion of the fund as collateral for bank financing of the deal. On July 26, Hoffa and several of his coconspirators in the case were found guilty of conspiracy and mail and wire fraud. The judge sentenced Hoffa to five years in prison, to run consecutively after his sentence for jury-tampering. The Teamster leader faced thirteen years behind bars.[15]

A year after his conviction in Chicago, while he and his attorneys were waiting to hear a court's decision on their appeal, Hoffa attended a testimonial dinner given in his honor in New York City. The speeches elevated the Teamster president to epic martyrdom. In addition to the expected praise bestowed on Hoffa by the top leadership of the union, Cecil B. Moore, president of the Philadelphia chapter of the National Association for the Advancement of Colored People, praised Hoffa for the high-paying jobs he had won for black workers. "He's just about like Jesus Christ who died on the Cross," said Moore. "Bobby Kennedy was on one side, some informers from the Teamsters on the other." Had he been present, Robert Kennedy might have reminded Moore of the apostle John's warning of an "antichrist" who deceives the simple-minded.[16]

Hoffa and his attorneys—whose proliferation gave rise to the term "Teamster Bar Association"—spent the better part of 1965 and 1966 filing appeals in various courts, only to be denied at every attempt. After the Supreme Court turned down his final appeal, Hoffa appointed three of his oldest and most loyal comrades to take on his duties. Dave Johnson, who had worked as a business agent for Local 299 since the early 1940s, was selected to run the local. Robert Holmes, one of the original Kroger "Strawberry Boys," who had succeeded Bert Brennan as president of Local 337 after Brennan died of cancer in 1961, was chosen to oversee the Michigan Conference of Teamsters. And for the top position in Washington, Hoffa selected Frank Fitzsimmons, the longtime officer of Local 299. On March 7, 1967, Hoffa entered Lewisburg Federal Penitentiary in Pennsylvania to begin serving his combined sentence of thirteen years.

Immediately after his imprisonment, a "Free Hoffa" movement spread through the Teamster rank and file. Bumper stickers, buttons, and patches demanding the release of the "political prisoner" appeared across the country. Even many rank-and-file dissidents wore "Free Jimmy" paraphernalia. Every Christmas, thousands of cards bearing holiday greetings from Teamster members flooded into Lewisburg for the facility's most famous resident. One Massachusetts local arranged for an airplane to fly over the prison on every one of Hoffa's birthdays trailing a banner reading "Birthday Greetings Jimmy Hoffa." Even non-Teamsters joined the cause. A building trades union leader in Michigan collected 250,000 signatures of people from all walks of life on a petition demanding Hoffa's release.[17]

As the 1971 IBT convention approached and Prisoner Number 33-298 NE entered his fourth year at Lewisburg, A. H. Raskin of the *New York Times*—a Hoffa critic for decades—conducted a survey of Teamster members across the East and Midwest and found that Hoffa's stature had become nearly mythic. Raskin discovered that if he were released, Hoffa would find his power within the union to be greater than ever:

Pick your way through the huge over-the-road truck terminals in any big city; wander among the tractor-trailers at the container ports; talk to the haulers of meat and bread and beer, the men who knife through the metropolitan traffic moving everything from diamonds to structural steel. Ask them whom the convention should pick to head their union, and almost invariably the answer will be: "Hoffa."

A Chicago driver interviewed by Raskin echoed the sentiments of many when he described Hoffa as a martyr for the members' material gains: "He was in there fighting for us all the way; that's why the big guys hated him." Another member, a long-distance driver from New York, reflected the amoral economism so loathed by Hoffa's enemies in labor and government. "Hoffa did steal from us, but he also gave us a hell of a lot," the man said, undoubtedly cognizant that the pension fund Hoffa had been convicted of plundering was paying some of the most generous union retiree benefits in the country. "For what he did for the driver, I'd take a chance on him again. If he robbed a little, what the hell." This libertine attitude may account for Hoffa's popularity among younger members of the 1960s counterculture both within and outside the union. Raskin found "a bearded longhair" Teamster from Jersey City agreeing with "a World War II marine with American decals all over his truck" that Hoffa should run the union. " 'He was the right guy, he was,' " said the hippie trucker. And when Jerry Rubin included an ode to his Teamster father and Hoffa in *Do It! Scenarios of the Revolution*, it appeared that two otherwise hostile generations of rebels had found a common antihero.[18]

Fall

Hoffa's legacy to the union contradicted his reputation. Since nearly all of the IBT's external competition had been eliminated and many of its internal dissidents constrained by centralization, the men who replaced Hoffa as leaders of the union were handed not only enormous salaries and private jets, but also virtual monopoly control over two million members. It was then perhaps all but inevitable that these successors would be something less than firebrands of the class struggle. Fitzsimmons, who assumed the official title of General President after Hoffa resigned in 1971 to encourage his parole, was provided with little of the incentive that had driven Hoffa to produce good contracts and be accountable to the members. To be sure, Hoffa had embezzled and squandered union funds and allowed outright criminals to establish bases of power within the union. But with rival unions always lurking and militant dissidents threatening secession, he was compelled time and again to provide for the members and discipline Teamster officers, like Ray Cohen in Philadelphia, whose blatant disregard for the members threatened to destabilize the union's control over them. But Hoffa's final victory in achieving a centralized monopoly took from the new leadership any such motivation.

The renewals of the National Master Freight Agreement negotiated by Fitzsimmons were so poor that they prompted major wildcat strikes of truck drivers in 1967 and 1970, the first such rebellions in the history of the IBT. And because of the absence of a viable alternative union, when dissidents dissatisfied with the new leadership's lack of militancy emerged in the 1970s, they had nowhere to go, and were forced to sacrifice their jobs and their physical safety to put pressure on the leadership. If not for the efforts of Hillman, Reuther, Meany, and the state to eliminate interunion competition, the dissidents who braved the wrath of the union leadership would have possessed a weapon far more powerful than the fists and steel chains used against them.

When Hoffa was granted clemency by President Nixon and released from prison just before Christmas in 1971—the final return on Hoffa's investments in the Republican Party—he found a union that was imploding. The terms of the clemency barred Hoffa from union activities until 1980, and so he was forced to remain on the sidelines while rebel rank-and-file groups appeared in almost every major city, violent power struggles consumed the union leadership, and the IBT began a slow decline in membership and economic achievements. Most ominously for Hoffa, Fitzsimmons's laxity had allowed powerful criminal organizations to expand their control over large sections of the union, particularly in New York, New Jersey, Cleveland, and Kansas City.

The most famous mob-controlled outfit was Local 560 in Union City, New Jersey, whose president, Anthony "Tony Pro" Provenzano, was also a "caporegime," or captain, of the Genovese crime family. In exchange for providing a base of support for Hoffa in the contentious New Jersey IBT, Provenzano was assisted in his rise to the vice-presidency of the international union. Provenzano had been convicted of extortion and served his sentence in Lewisburg with Hoffa. According to the provision in the Landrum-Griffin Act barring felons from holding union office until five years after their incarceration, Provenzano was due to return to his positions in the Teamsters in 1975. He counted on the normally amenable Fitzsimmons to offer no objections. Hoffa was less pleased with the prospect, since he and Provenzano had fallen out over the latter's insistence that he have free access to the Central States Pension Fund. After being convicted in part for his improper management of the fund, Hoffa was now more circumspect about the Teamsters' business dealings with figures such as Tony Pro. During their time at Lewisburg, Hoffa reportedly said to Provenzano, "It's because of people like you that I got into trouble in the first place."

So in 1973, when Hoffa filed appeals in federal court seeking to overturn the restriction on his union activities and began campaigning to return to the Teamster presidency, Fitzsimmons and Provenzano faced a threat to their power for the first time since Hoffa had gone to jail. As a "Bring Back Jimmy Hoffa" movement gathered steam in 1974 and early 1975, it appeared the hero of the rank and file was heading for a collision with the men who had grown comfortable in power in his absence. On July 30, 1975, Hoffa arrived alone at the Machus Red Fox restaurant in suburban Detroit for a meeting with Provenzano and Anthony Giacalone, the leader of Detroit's largest criminal organization, who had received considerable lucre from the Central States Fund under the Fitzsimmons administration. Provenzano and Giacalone had asked for the meeting ostensibly to arrange for a power-sharing arrangement should Hoffa resume the presidency of the union. A short while after the time of the appointment, Hoffa called his wife from the restaurant to tell her that he had been "stood up." After that brief telephone conversation he was never heard from again. As of this writing, no one has been charged with Hoffa's murder, and the case is still open with the FBI.[19]

Epilogue

Resurrection

Restore Teamster Power!—JAMES P. HOFFA CAMPAIGN SLOGAN, 1996

After his disappearance and apparent murder, it appears certain that Hoffa's career as a myth will have a longer life than the man himself. Through a plethora of nonfiction books, short stories, novels, magazine articles, television programs, films, jokes, rumors, and even poems, Hoffa, or at least his representation in popular culture, has become the most famous labor leader in American history. Interestingly, the Hoffa symbol enjoys far greater prestige than did Hoffa himself. Since his death, and, perhaps more significantly, since the death of Robert Kennedy and his crusade against organized crime, Hoffa has more often been portrayed as a tragic champion of the working class than as a subversive authoritarian. Two of the best-known depictions of his life, the films *F.I.S.T.* and *Hoffa*, both present him as a courageous and benevolent union leader who risked his life against employer goon squads to serve his members and was forced by the exigencies of those battles into a fatal alliance with organized crime.[1]

Hollywood's portrayal has matched Hoffa's reputation among much of the Teamster rank and file. This became apparent again in the 1990s, when Hoffa's son was drafted by leaders of the Detroit Teamsters to run for the presidency of the IBT. James P. Hoffa's campaign to become the bearer of his father's legacy began, fittingly, as a rebellion against the federal government. After the Justice Department used a racketeering suit to force the IBT to sign a consent decree mandating federal oversight of the union's financial activities and elections, Ron

227

Carey, a New York local president with a reputation as a reformer, was elected in 1991 as General President in the union's first-ever balloting of the entire membership. Carey's victory depended on the support of Teamsters for a Democratic Union, an insurgent faction led by members of a small Trotskyist organization with ancestral links to Farrell Dobbs and the Communist League of America, which had become a major force within the union since its founding during the anti-Fitzsimmons movement of the early 1970s. Immediately after his election, however, the reform president faced opposition from "old guard" elements who loathed TDU and opposed Carey's cooperation with the federal overseers.[2]

Beginning shortly before the national contract with United Parcel Service expired in the summer of 1993, the old guard launched a vigorous public relations campaign against Carey and the new IBT administration, charging the international with fiscal irresponsibility and alleging that Carey had owned a large amount of UPS stock and had long-standing ties to Mafia bosses in New York. But by the time negotiations for renewal of the National Master Freight Agreement began in December of 1993, the old guard had added a lethal weapon to its arsenal. While Carey and his negotiating team opened talks with employers over revisions of the national contract that had been instituted by Jimmy Hoffa in 1964, James P. Hoffa was announcing to the media that he intended to challenge Carey in the 1996 election for the IBT presidency. The junior Hoffa had been an attorney for most of his adult life, often representing his father's old locals in Detroit. But after Carey's election in 1991, Larry Brennan, who had succeeded his father, Bert Brennan, as president of Local 337 and later became head of the Michigan Conference of Teamsters, appointed Hoffa to an administrative position with the Michigan Conference so that he would be eligible for union office. Brennan and his colleagues despised the liberal culture and fealty to the Democratic Party that Carey had brought to the Marble Palace, but the principal motivation for pushing the junior Hoffa to run for president of the union was a distinctly Hoffa-like hatred of the government and especially of its intrusion into union affairs. They hoped that once in office, the new Hoffa would lead a movement to overturn the federal supervision of the union.[3]

As the Hoffa election campaign began in earnest in 1996, it became clear that Carey's opponents had the numbers and the organization to prevail in the contest. At the IBT convention in July, Hoffa forces were so powerful that Carey was forced to resort to authoritarian parliamentary tactics to thwart his opposition's attempts to strip him of power through constitutional amendments. Despite their inability to overcome Carey's tactics, Hoffa delegates were able to use the convention as a national platform to present their candidate's irresistible slogan: "Restore Teamster Power!" That slogan, along with Hoffa's charges that Carey had negotiated concessionary contracts with UPS and the freight employers, proved to be highly effective among the membership. The slogan spread to locals across the country, appearing on T-shirts, street signs, and bumper stickers. It became clear that the message and the power of the Hoffa name tapped into a widespread desire among the rank and file for a leadership that would fight the employers for a bigger share of the pie. The slogan's appeal also showed that Carey had not satisfied that desire. "From what you hear, Teamsters had it better when Jimmy Hoffa was around," said one UPS driver. "We were strong." Even the *New York Times*, in an editorial endorsing Carey, acknowledged that he had "yet to prove he can turn the teamsters' economic fortunes around by organizing new members and negotiating rich contracts." Despite Hoffa's almost total lack of union experience and the national media's mocking coverage of "Junior's" campaign, Carey managed to poll only sixteen thousand more votes than his opponent out of nearly half a million ballots cast. Without the $700,000 in embezzled union funds that were later revealed to have been used for the Carey campaign's direct mailings, it is entirely plausible to assume that Hoffa would have won in 1996.[4]

But fortunately for Teamster members at UPS, the embezzlement scheme and the tenacity of the old guard enabled them to fight for the impressive contract they won in the summer of 1997. Immediately after the election, Hoffa's chief advisors, Richard Leebove and George Geller, began investigating the Carey campaign's finances. By March of 1997 they had presented the federal overseer with sufficient evidence to prove that the Carey campaign had stolen union money. Between March and the expiration of the UPS contract in July, Carey teetered within inches of losing the presidency, and survived during that period only because he had the sympathy of the overseer, Barbara Zack Quindel, who was closely associated with the pro-Carey New Party and with Citizens Action, which had been implicated as the money-laundering agent in the embezzlement scheme. Quindel refused to take action before the UPS contract deadline, perhaps hoping that a victory over the company would help Carey in the re-election she would have to mandate. With his chief campaign aide indicted and the operative responsible for overseeing the money-laundering furnishing investigators with information on the scheme, Carey knew that his victory in the 1996 election would be overturned and that his only chance would be to survive long enough to run in the reelection. And if he were to make it to the reelection, he would need to have something to sell to the membership.[5]

Having forgone the opportunity to strike UPS on the expiration of the previous contract in 1993, Carey could not afford that luxury in 1997. Creating a dramatic confrontation with the company was the only chance he had to stay in power. And once he called the strike, the embattled union president revealed what it meant to him. The night the walkout started, in an interview on *The NewsHour with Jim Lehrer*, Carey placed the blame on his real enemy, not UPS. "Jimmy Hoffa introduced the concept of part-timers," Carey said in response to Elizabeth Farnsworth's question about why the issue was so important. The man who allegedly "permitted the company" to institute part-time jobs, who was now a specter threatening to take away his power, forced Carey to call the strike. The nationwide walkout resulted in one of the most impressive settlements in Teamster history, with UPS granting an enormous across-the-board wage increase and an agreement to convert 10,000 part-time jobs into full-time, full-benefit positions. Though many at the time credited the militancy of Ron Carey and the new "democratic culture" of the union for the victory, it was produced instead by the myth of Jimmy Hoffa, the power of competition, and the hunger and courage of the rank and file.[6]

Shortly after the UPS settlement, Quindel overturned Carey's election based on the overwhelming evidence she had received from Geller and Leebove, and in July 1998, the former hero of Teamster democracy was expelled for life from the union by the federal board of monitors. That fall, James P. Hoffa easily defeated his opponent, Tom Leedham of TDU, in the election for general president.

Will the new Teamster president match his father's militancy? The evidence suggests that even the less-talented junior Hoffa, facing a restive membership and a powerful opposition, would have had no choice but to take on employers with the full force of the union's power. Hoffa's willingness to call a national strike against the nonunion Overnite Transportation freight company in 1999—the largest trucking walkout by the Teamsters in decades—was surely caused at least in part by the presence of a relentlessly hostile TDU and his need to have something to show the membership in the next union election.

For union members who want higher wages, less work, and better benefits and working conditions, the histories of the careers of Jimmy Hoffa, Ron Carey, and the junior Hoffa suggest that a strategy of perpetual opposition to the union leadership, regardless of who holds it, might be more effective than attempting to become the union leadership. According to this analysis, democracy is best viewed as an instrument of leverage with which to force the bureaucracy to perform, not as a means to install a new bureaucracy. The primary interest of any leader, whether the most self-interested careerist or a lifelong revolutionary, must be to maintain power. The growing conservatism and declining commitment to democracy by reformers after their assumption of leadership—from Lenin to Mandela to Ron Carey—provides ample evidence of this. Without effective opposition, a leader has no immediate incentive to serve the interests of his constituents over his own interests. If Leedham and TDU had won the recent IBT election, the movement behind Hoffa likely would have faded away.[7] This would have been the worst possible outcome for the Teamster membership, since it would have eliminated any source of opposition within the union and created the kind of one-party institution well known for its lack of accountability.

And so it appears that if TDU maintains its dissident stance, and if the members continue to demonstrate their desires, the junior Hoffa will be forced to deliver the goods. Unfortunately, the socialist leaders of TDU, who intended the group to be "a revolutionary cadre organization based in the working class," are unlikely to relinquish their desire for control of the union. As stated more publicly by national secretary Ken Paff, the objective for TDU is "to organize the rank and file until we have OUR OWN POWER." The group's leaders hope to fulfill the vision of Eugene Debs in which workers participate in their own management—first in their union, then in their industries, and finally in a collective political economy. This ideology differs from the corporatism of Hillman and Reuther only in that it calls for a more complete self-management of labor. Whereas the CIO leaders ultimately settled for a share of power with capital, revolutionary socialists demand total sovereignty. But the ideology of the TDU leadership has generated even less enthusiasm among the American working class than has corporatism. While TDU has grown tremendously since its founding, the remnants of the Trotskyist organization that spawned it remain microscopically small. Perhaps if the Teamster rank-and-file movement can outlive its current leadership, it will one day abandon its self-defeating quest for hegemony in favor of a continuous advocacy of the members' aspirations against the constraints imposed by the union leadership.[8]

As for the Teamster rank and file, many of those who voted for Hoffa seem to think that he was predetermined to be a militant representative of their interests. A freight driver in New Jersey repeated the assumption often heard during the 1996 and 1998 elections. "I'd like to get back to the days when the Teamsters really had power," he said. "When Jimmy Hoffa Jr. came through here, I told him if he's half the man his father was, he's good enough for me." The junior Hoffa may indeed restore Teamster power, but as with his father, that will depend less on the character of the man than on the forces that create him.[9]

Notes

Introduction

1. Quoted in Ralph C. James and Estelle Dinerstein James, *Hoffa and the Teamsters: A Study of Union Power* (D. Van Nostrand, 1965), 51.
2. This handful includes Dorothy Sue Cobble, *Dishing It Out: Waitresses and Their Unions in the Twentieth Century* (University of Illinois Press, 1991); Mark Erlich, *With Our Hands: The Story of Carpenters in Massachusetts* (Temple University Press, 1986); Grace Palladino, *Dreams of Dignity, Workers of Vision: A History of the International Brotherhood of Electrical Workers* (IBEW, 1991); Howard Kimeldorf, *Reds or Rackets? The Making of Radical and Conservative Unions on the Waterfront* (University of California Press, 1988); Craig Phelan, *William Green: Biography of a Labor Leader* (SUNY Press, 1989); and Christopher L. Tomlins, "AFL Unions in the 1930s: Their Performance in Historical Perspective," *Journal of American History*, Vol. 65, No. 4 (March 1979).
3. This is not to deny the long history of exclusionary practices by the AFL and its constituent unions, including the Teamsters. Yet many women, African-American, Latino, and Asian workers became members of AFL unions despite the discrimination.
4. The National Education Association grew to more than two million members in the 1990s, but many of its affiliates operate more as professional organizations than as collective-bargaining unions.
5. Selig Perlman, *A Theory of the Labor Movement* (Augustus M. Kelley, 1928), 5.
6. See David Brody, "The Old Labor History and the New: In Search of an American Working Class," in Daniel J. Leab, *The Labor History Reader* (University of Illinois Press, 1985), 4.
7. Biographies of Hoffa and other works about him include the following: Charles Ashman and Rebecca Sobel, *The Strange Disappearance of Jimmy Hoffa* (Manor Books, 1976); James M. Barker, *One of a Kind* (Seven Js Publishing, 1971); James Clay, *Hoffa! Ten Angels Swearing: An Authorized Biography* (Beaverdam Books, 1965); Joseph Franco and Richard Hammer, *Hoffa's Man: The Rise and Fall of Jimmy Hoffa as Witnessed by His Strongest Arm* (Prentice Hall, 1987); James R. Hoffa and Donald I. Rogers, *The Trials of Jimmy Hoffa: An Autobiography* (Henry Regnery, 1970); James R. Hoffa and Oscar Fraley, *Hoffa: The Real Story* (Stein and Day, 1975); *The Name Is Hoffa* (International Brotherhood of Teamsters, Joint Council No. 13, 1956); Ralph C. James and Estelle Dinerstein James, *Hoffa and the Teamsters: A Study of Union Power* (D. Van Nostrand, 1965); John Bartlow Martin, *Jimmy Hoffa's Hot* (Fawcett, 1959); Dan E. Moldea, *The Hoffa Wars: Teamsters, Rebels, Politicians and the Mob* (Paddington, 1978); Clark R. Mollenhoff, *Tentacles of Power: The Story of Jimmy Hoffa* (World, 1965); David W. Salmon,

The Jimmy Hoffa I Knew (David W. Salmon, 1995); Walter Sheridan, *The Fall and Rise of Jimmy Hoffa* (Saturday Review Press, 1972); Arthur A. Sloane, *Hoffa* (MIT Press, 1991); Lester Velie, *Desperate Bargain: Why Jimmy Hoffa Had to Die* (Reader's Digest Press, 1977).

Books with a chapter or section on Hoffa include the following: Steven Brill, *The Teamsters* (Pocket Books, 1978); Melvyn Dubofsky and Warren Van Tine, eds., *Labor Leaders in America* (University of Illinois Press, 1987); Allen Friedman and Ted Schwarz, *Power and Greed: Inside the Teamsters Empire of Corruption* (Franklin Watts, 1989); Paul Jacobs, *The State of the Unions* (Atheneum, 1963); Robert James, *The Informant Files: The FBI's Most Valuable Snitch* (Electronic Media, 1994); Robert D. Leiter, *The Teamsters Union: A Study of Its Economic Impact* (Bookman Associates, 1957); Sidney Lens, *The Crisis of American Labor* (A. S. Barnes, 1959); Robert F. Kennedy, *The Enemy Within* (Harper & Brothers, 1960); Arthur M. Schlesinger, Jr., *Robert Kennedy and His Times* (Houghton Mifflin, 1978); Nathan Shefferman with Dale Kramer, *The Man in the Middle* (Doubleday, 1961); Sidney Zagri, *Free Press, Fair Trial* (C. Hallberg, 1966).
8. Hoffa uses the term "Depression City" in his autobiography, *The Trials of Jimmy Hoffa: An Autobiography* (Henry Regnery, 1970), 68.

One

American Soil

1. Quoted in Rosa Luxemburg, "The Junius Pamphlet," in *The Mass Strike: The Political Party and the Trade Unions* (Harper & Row, 1971), 111.
2. James Weinstein, *The Decline of Socialism in America, 1912–1925* (Monthly Review Press, 1967), 27.
3. Quoted in Nick Salvatore, *Eugene V. Debs: Citizen and Socialist* (Cornell University Press, 1982), 306–307.
4. Salvatore, 3–177 *passim.*
5. *Ibid.,* 312, 315.
6. Osmond LaVar Harline, "Economics of the Indiana Coal Mining Industry," unpublished Ph.D. dissertation, Indiana University, 1958, 102; William Travis, *A History of Clay County, Indiana* (Lewis Publishing Company, 1909), 451–452; Clay County Records, CH-4, 64, 90, Indiana Historical Library, Indianapolis.
7. Travis, *A History of Clay County,* 113–131; "Brazil, Indiana—City Directory," Brazil Public Library Annex, Brazil, Indiana; Clay County Historical Society, *Clay County, Indiana History, 1880–1984* (1985); *Brazil Daily Times,* November 7, November 11, 1913, January 3, 1917; "A Salute to Brazil, Indiana," *The Gazette,* June 23, 1978, clippings file, Clay County, Indiana Historical Library; "History of Clay County," *Valley: The Magazine of the Terre Haute Tribune-Star,* July 4, 1982. James Hoffa was arrested for running a gambling house in 1921. See *Brazil Daily Times,* April 14, 1921.
8. "First Christian Church" [pamphlet], Brazil, Indiana (1966), Indiana Historical Library; Hoffa, *Trials,* 13–15.
9. "Essay: Our Town," Brazil Public Library Annex; *Clay County Enterprise,* April 1, June 10, 1914; Jim Clay, *Hoffa! Ten Angels Swearing* (Beaverdam Books, 1965), 28–32, 39–40.
10. Clay, 41; Harline, 103, 105; "James R. Hoffa: Revisited," *Daily Clintonian,* February 30, 1998; David R. Bennett, "The Football Coaching Career of Paul 'Spike' Kelly,

An Indiana Legend," unpublished Ed.D. dissertation, University of South Carolina, 1995, 37–40; Louise Booth, *Clinton on the Wabash* (1994), Clinton Public Library, Clinton, Indiana; "Fights Part of Clinton's History," *Terre Haute Tribune-Star,* January 20, 1985; *Daily Clintonian,* January 4, 1923. In 1917 the Socialist Party candidate for mayor of Clinton won 11.3 percent of the vote. See Weinstein, 176.

11. Clay, 42–43.

12. Steve Babson, *Working Detroit: The Making of a Union Town* (Adama Books, 1984), 23–24, 35, 45, 48–49.

13. Olivier Zunz, *The Changing Face of Inequality: Urbanization, Industrial Development, and Immigrants in Detroit, 1880–1920* (University of Chicago Press, 1982), 297–307, 344–347; Clay, 44–45.

14. Clay, 47–48; Hoffa, *Trials,* 29.

15. "David Brinkley's Journal: Inside Jimmy Hoffa," NBC Network, April 1, 1963, transcript in Folder 30, Box 10, John Herling Collection, Archives of Labor and Urban Affairs, Wayne State University.

Two

Jungle Unionism

1. "Manifesto of the Communist Party," in *Karl Marx and Frederick Engels: Selected Works* (International Publishers, 1970), 44.

2. Robert Conot, *American Odyssey* (Wayne State University Press, 1986), 258–260; Alan Brinkley, *Voices of Protest: Huey Long, Father Coughlin and the Great Depression* (Vintage, 1983), 93; Babson, 53–57; B. J. Widick, *Detroit: City of Race and Class Violence* (Wayne State University Press, 1989), 43–44; Anthony J. Badger, *The New Deal: The Depression Years, 1933–1940* (Hill and Wang, 1989), 20–21.

3. Helen Hall, "When Detroit's Out of Gear," in Melvin G. Holli, ed., *Detroit* (New Viewpoints, 1976), 172.

4. A friend told Hoffa that the food business was depression-proof because "people have to eat, no matter what." Hoffa, *Trials,* 38–40 (quote on page 38).

5. *Ibid.,* 40.

6. Robert Holmes, interview with the author, Farmington Hills, Michigan, June 17, 1998; Hoffa, *Trials,* 45.

7. Hoffa, *Trials,* 45.

8. Irving Bernstein, *The Lean Years: A History of the American Worker, 1920–1933* (Penguin, 1966), 335–336.

9. U.S. Bureau of Labor Statistics, *Handbook of Labor Statistics* (U.S. Government Printing Office, 1975), 390. In 1931 only 1.6 percent of the workforce was involved in a work stoppage; In 1930 the percentage was 0.8, the lowest figure ever recorded in the United States.

10. U.S. Bureau of Labor Statistics, *Monthly Labor Review,* Vol. 34, No. 6 (June 1932), 1355–1356.

11. Hoffa, *Trials,* 46.

12. *Ibid.,* 45.

13. Clay, 53.

14. Holmes interview; Hoffa, *Trials,* 42.

15. *Trials,* 46.

16. *Ibid.*, 46–49.

17. *Ibid.*, 51.

18. "Robert Holmes: '50 Years and Still Going Strong,'" program, Robert Holmes Scholarship Fund Benefit Dinner, February 11, 1988; Holmes interview.

19. Hoffa, *Trials*, 53–54; James R. Hoffa, *Hoffa: The Real Story* (Stein and Day, 1975), 33; Clay, 58; *Teamsters Local 337 News: 40th Anniversary*, March 1977, 6.

20. Hoffa, *Trials*, 60; Hoffa, *Real Story*, 34.

21. Holmes interview; *Teamsters Local 337 News: 40th Anniversary*, 6.

22. *40th Anniversary*, 6.

23. Hoffa, *Trials*, 64.

24. Holmes interview.

25. *Ibid.*; *Teamsters Local 337 News: 40th Anniversary*, 6.

26. American Federation of Labor, *Report of Proceedings, 1934*, 453; James and James, *Hoffa and the Teamsters*, 14–15.

27. Hoffa in his memoirs claims that he was fired after he threw down the crate intentionally to protest the foreman's constant heckling. Hoffa, *Trials*, 66; Hoffa, *Real Story*, 34–35.

28. Hoffa, *Trials*, 67; Hoffa, *Real Story*, 35

29. Holmes interview; Moldea, 19.

30. Irving Bernstein, *Turbulent Years: A History of the American Worker, 1933–1941* (Houghton Mifflin, 1971), 218–229.

31. *Ibid.*, 252–298.

32. Farrell Dobbs, *Teamster Rebellion* (Monad Press, 1972), *passim*, 178–179; Bernstein, 229–252.

33. National Labor Relations Board, *Rules and Regulations and Statements of Procedure: National Labor Relations Act and Labor Management Relations Act* (U.S. Government Printing Office, 1987), 299–300.

34. Two of the best examples of this interpretation are Steven Fraser, *Labor Will Rule: Sidney Hillman and the Rise of American Labor* (Cornell University Press, 1991), 330–333, and Christopher Tomlins, *The State and the Unions: Labor Relations, Law, and the Organized Labor Movement in America, 1880–1960* (Cambridge University Press, 1985), 145–147. However, neither of these authors follows the interpretation to its logical conclusion of rejecting the corporatist strategy. A more consistent analysis can be found in Jonathan C. Cutler, "A Slacker's Paradise: The Fight for 30 Hours' Work at 40 Hours' Pay in the United Automobile Workers, 1941–1966," unpublished Ph.D. dissertation, City University of New York, 1998.

35. Nelson Lichtenstein, *The Most Dangerous Man in Detroit: Walter Reuther and the Fate of American Labor* (Basic Books, 1995), 47–73, 144–145; Fraser, 40–76, 126–127, 259–262.

36. Here the term "corporatism" is used as defined by Philippe Schmitter: "a system of interest representation in which the constituent units are organized into a limited number of singular, compulsory, noncompetitive, hierarchically ordered and functionally differentiated categories, recognized or licensed (if not created) by the state and granted a deliberate representational monopoly within their respective categories in exchange for observing certain controls on their selection of leaders and articulation of demands and supports." Philippe Schmitter, "Still the Century of Corporatism," in *Trends Towards Corporatist Intermediation*, Philippe Schmitter and Gerhard Lehm-

bruch, eds. (Sage Publications, 1979), 13. See also Cutler, "A Slacker's Paradise," 10–11.

37. Babson, 22, 89.

38. *Michigan Teamster,* July 1946.

39. Robert D. Leiter, *The Teamsters Union: A Study of Its Economic Impact* (Bookman Associates, 1957), 58–61; James and James, *Hoffa and the Teamsters,* 16–17.

40. James and James, *Hoffa and the Teamsters,* 70.

41. International Brotherhood of Teamsters, *Proceedings of the Twelfth Convention* (1930), "Report of the General President," 18–23; Nathan P. Feinsinger, *Collective Bargaining in the Trucking Industry* (University of Pennsylvania Press, 1949), 26; Clay, 69; James and James, *Hoffa and the Teamsters,* 91.

42. National Automobile Transporters Association, "Automobile Transport Industry: National Facilities," in the G. Mennen Williams Papers (Gubernatorial), Box 32, "Transportation Study Commission," Bentley Historical Library, University of Michigan; Robert Farrell, President, National Automobile Transporters Association, telephone interview with the author, August 25, 1998. The industry continued to expand rapidly through the 1930s, to a high of 4.5 million units transported in 1940.

43. *Detroit Labor News,* November 9, 1934.

44. *Detroit News,* June 28, 1934; April 4, 1935; April 21, 1935; November 11, 1935; August 11, 1936.

45. Agreement "between undersigned employers and the so-called Teamsters' Union," September 13, 1934, National Automobile Transporters Association, Detroit, Michigan.

46. Memorandum and clippings, undated, "National Automobile Transporters Association," Box 7, National Labor Board, 1933–34, Region VIII (Detroit), Records of the National Labor Relations Board, Record Group 25, National Archives, College Park, Maryland; *Detroit Labor News,* October 12, 1934.

47. *Detroit Labor News,* October 19, 1934, November 9, 1934. Organizers for the other locals in Joint Council 43 were not exactly model citizens either. In 1935 business agents for Local 155 kidnapped four milk drivers who refused to join the union and held them prisoner in the Joint Council's headquarters. *Detroit News,* April 20, 1935.

48. *Teamsters Local 337 News: 40th Anniversary,* 6–7; Holmes interview; Hoffa, *Real Story,* 35.

49. Local 337's number came from the date of its charter, March 1937.

50. *Detroit News,* August 11, 1936.

51. Moldea, 22; James and James, *Hoffa and the Teamsters,* 71.

52. For a discussion of the relative autonomy of locals within the IBT during Tobin's presidency, see Leiter, 58–61.

53. *Detroit News,* December 23, 1936.

54. In 1960, after 25 years of regulation, more than 17,000 interstate for-hire carriers were operating under ICC permits, and 80 percent of these reported an annual gross revenue of less than $200,000. See James and James, *Hoffa and the Teamsters,* 96–97; U.S. Public Law, No. 255, 74th Congress, Section 204 (a) (I)-(3), 206, 209, 211; David Brodsky and J. Almyk Lieberman, *Handbook of Interstate Motor Carrier Law* (Milbin Publishing, 1937), 119–120; William R. Childs, *Trucking and the Public Interest: The Emergence of Federal Regulation, 1914–1940* (University of Tennessee Press, 1985), 139–140.

55. Hoffa stood five feet, five inches tall, weighed on average 180 pounds, and was well known for his physical strength.

56. Merlin Bishop, "The Kelsey-Hayes Sit-in Strike," Box 1, File 30, Walter P. Reuther Collection, Archives of Labor and Urban Affairs, Wayne State University; Sidney Fine, *Sit-Down: The General Motors Strike of 1936–1937* (University of Michigan Press, 1969), 130–132; *Detroit Labor News*, December 18, 1936; Richard T. Frankensteen, interview with Frank Cormier and William J. Eaton, June 22, 1968, Frank Cormier Collection, John F. Kennedy Library, Boston, Massachusetts.

The connection between Reuther and Hoffa may have been facilitated by Merlin Bishop, a UAW organizer at Kelsey-Hayes who had been a member of Teamsters Local 247. See *Detroit Labor News*, October 19, 1934.

57. Detroit Police Department, Criminal Record No. 59527, James R. Hoffa, Clare E. Hoffman Papers, Box 86, "James R. Hoffa," Bentley Historical Library, University of Michigan; *Detroit News*, April 5, 1938; Margaret Collingwood Nowak, *Two Who Were There: A Biography of Stanley Nowak* (Wayne State University Press, 1989), 126. The charge of "disturbing the peace" was dropped when the complaining police officer did not appear at Hoffa's arraignment in Recorder's Court.

58. Stephen Norwood, "Ford's Brass Knuckles: Harry Bennett, The Cult of Muscularity, and Anti-Labor Terror, 1920–1945," *Labor History*, Vol. 37, No. 3 (Summer 1996), 387.

59. Douglas Fraser, interview with the author, Detroit, Michigan, June 17, 1998; Rolland McMaster, interview with the author, Fenton, Michigan, June 19, 1998; Holmes interview.

60. U.S. Bureau of Labor Statistics, *Handbook of Labor Statistics* (U.S. Government Printing Office, 1975), 390.

61. *Detroit News*, April 5, April 10, April 11, April 17, 1937; Babson, *Working Detroit*, 89.

62. U.S. Census of the Population, 1940, Vol. III, *The Labor Force*, Part I, Table 77; Richard D. Leone, *The Negro in the Trucking Industry* (University of Pennsylvania Press, 1970), 25–32 (the Midwest was defined as comprising Illinois, Indiana, Iowa, Kansas, Michigan, Minnesota, Missouri, Nebraska, North Dakota, Ohio, South Dakota, and Wisconsin); Leiter, 44.

63. U.S. Bureau of Labor Statistics, *Monthly Labor Review*, Vol. 44, No. 5 (May 1937), 1252; McMaster interview.

64. James Harold Thomas, "Trucking: History and Legend," unpublished Ph.D. dissertation, Oklahoma State University, 1976, 87.

65. *Detroit Labor News*, March 12, 1937; McMaster interview.

66. McMaster interview; Detroit trucking companies' contract, in the possession of Rolland McMaster.

67. *Detroit Labor News*, March 12, 1937, March 19, 1937; McMaster interview.

68. *Detroit Labor News*, March 5, 1937.

69. *Detroit Labor News*, July 16, 1937; *Detroit News*, July 15, 1937.

70. McMaster interview; Farrell Dobbs, *Teamster Power* (Monad Press, 1973), 183.

71. *Detroit News*, July 11, July 13, 1937.

72. *Detroit News*, July 16, 1937.

73. *Detroit News*, July 17, 1937.

74. *Detroit News*, August 18, August 19, August 20, August 22, August 23, August 27, 1937.

75. *Detroit Labor News*, March 26, 1937.
76. *Detroit News*, September 1, 1937.
77. *Detroit News*, September 2, September 13, September 14, 1937; Holmes interview.
78. "George S. Fitzgerald Announces Candidacy," press release, May 30, 1954, Neil Staebler Collection, Box 26, "George Fitzgerald," Bentley Historical Library, University of Michigan; *Detroit News*, June 24, 1929, November 30, 1962.
79. Tom Downs, interview with the author, Lansing, Michigan, June 18, 1998.
80. *50 Years: Local 337, 1937–1987*, in the possession of Robert Holmes.
81. U.S. Senate, Select Committee on Improper Activities in the Labor or Management Field, *Investigation of Improper Activities in the Labor or Management Field: Hearings*, 13492–13493; Clare E. Hoffman Papers, Box 84, "Detroit Teamsters," undated memorandum, Bentley Historical Library, University of Michigan; *50 Years: Local 337, 1937–1987*.
82. *50 Years: Local 337, 1937–1987*.
83. James and James, *Hoffa and the Teamsters*, 82.

Three

The Limits of Brotherhood

1. Quoted in Philip S. Foner, *History of the Labor Movement in the United States: Volume 3: The Policies and Practices of the American Federation of Labor, 1900–1909* (International Publishers, 1964), 210. Foner misidentifies Carrick as "M. P. Garrick."
2. The Communist Party's policy of establishing "Red Unions" outside established, "reformist" unions ended in 1934, when the Comintern in Moscow decided that the revolutionary labor organizations should disband and join the AFL. In March of 1935 the CPUSA officially dissolved its "dual unionist" Trade Union Unity League. Harvey Klehr, *The Heyday of American Communism: The Depression Decade* (Basic Books, 1984), 132–133.
3. Farrell Dobbs, *Teamster Rebellion* (Monad Press, 1972), 35, *passim*.
4. Elizabeth Faue, *Community of Suffering and Struggle: Women, Men, and the Labor Movement in Minneapolis, 1915–1945* (University of North Carolina Press, 1991), 50–52, 215 n.14.
5. *Ibid.*, 111.
6. Constance Ashton Myers, *The Prophet's Army: Trotskyists in America, 1928–1941* (Greenwood Press, 1977), 31–33, 53–55; James P. Cannon, *The History of American Trotskyism: Report of a Participant* (Pathfinder Press, 1944), 73, 98–110, 106–107, 228–229.
7. According to Dobbs, Local 574 was chartered "around 1915." *Teamster Rebellion*, 38.
8. Dobbs, *Teamster Rebellion*, 29–35, 38, 40–41, 47–57.
9. *Ibid.*, 58–190.
10. Dobbs, *Teamster Power* (Monad Press, 1973), 69–70.
11. *Ibid.*, 70–75, 125–126, 145–148.
12. James Harold Thomas, "Trucking: History and Legend," unpublished Ph.D. dissertation, Oklahoma State University, 1976, 66–77.
13. United States Federal Coordinator of Transportation, *Hours, Wages, and Working Conditions in the Intercity Motor Transportation Industries* (U.S. Government Printing Office, 1936), 119; Dobbs, *Teamster Power*, 169.

14. Colin Gordon, *New Deals: Business, Labor, and Politics in America, 1920–1935* (Cambridge University Press, 1994); U.S. Federal Coordinator of Transportation, *Hours, Wages, and Working Conditions*, 113–114.

15. Dobbs, *Teamster Power,* 174–176, 180–181.

16. Sloane, 25.

17. Detroit Police Department, Criminal Record No. 59527, James R. Hoffa, Box 86, "James R. Hoffa," Clare E. Hoffman Papers, Bentley Historical Library, University of Michigan; *Detroit News,* January 30, February 5, February 17, March 19, 1938; Hoffa describes "snappers" in *Trials,* 87.

18. *Detroit News,* March 1, March 2, 1938.

19. Lichtenstein, *The Most Dangerous Man in Detroit,* 65–66, 78–79, 123.

20. Roger Keeran, *The Communist Party and the Auto Workers Unions* (Indiana University Press, 1980), 80–81.

21. "It was from the intellectual that the anti-capitalist influences in modern society emanated. It was he who impressed upon the labor movement tenets characteristic of his own mentality: the 'nationalization' or 'socialization' of industry, and political action, whether 'constitutional' or 'unconstitutional,' on behalf of the 'new social order.' " Selig Perlman, *A Theory of the Labor Movement* (Augustus M. Kelley, 1928), 5.

22. See chapter 2 for an account of Local 299's use of bombs to unionize Michigan carhauling.

23. Carhaul firms in Michigan shipped cars to dealers across the country.

24. Hoffa, *Trials,* 92.

25. Dobbs, *Teamster Power,* 182–183.

26. Robert Farrell, President, National Automobile Transporters Association, telephone interview with the author, August 25, 1998; J. R. Halladay, *Partner in Progress: The Story of the American Trucking Associations* (ATA, 1994), 1–3.

27. Dobbs, *Teamster Power,* 185.

28. *Ibid.,* 186–187; John Lewis Keeshin, *No Fears, Hidden Tears: A Memoir of Four Score Years: The Autobiography of John Lewis Keeshin* (J. L. Keeshin, 1983), 155; Dobbs, *Teamster Power,* 203–204.

29. *International Teamster,* October 1938, 12; Dobbs, *Teamster Power,* 204–209.

30. Dobbs, *Teamster Power,* 212–217; Moldea, 28.

31. "Narrative Summary of Local #383, Sioux City, Iowa," General Drivers, Helpers, and Inside Workers Union, Local 574, "Minneapolis Teamsters Strike, 1934: Selected Documents, 1928–1941" [microfilm], Minnesota Historical Society, Minneapolis.

32. Letter dated November 2, 1938, International Brotherhood of Teamsters, Chauffeurs, Warehousemen and Helpers of America, Papers, Series 1, Box 27, Folder 5, State Historical Society of Wisconsin, Madison.

33. Dobbs, *Teamster Power,* 221–232.

34. James and James, *Hoffa and the Teamsters,* 98–99.

35. Nuala McGann Drescher, "International Union of United Brewery, Flour, Cereal, Soft Drink and Distillery Workers of America," in Gary Fink, ed., *Labor Unions* (Greenwood Press, 1977), 39–42; Foner, *History of the Labor Movement in the United States,* Vol. 3, 211.

36. The International Brotherhood of Teamsters was formed in 1903 out of the merger of the Team Drivers International Union and the rival Teamsters National Union.

37. Robert Scott Bowers, "The International Brotherhood of Teamsters and a Theory of Jurisdiction," unpublished Ph.D. dissertation, University of Wisconsin, 1951, 51–125; Philip Taft, *The A. F. of L. from the Death of Gompers to the Merger* (Harper and Brothers, 1959), 461–465; Leiter, 86–89.

38. Civil Case 483, *Frank Ford, Jr., et al., v. International Union of United Brewery, Flour, Cereal, and Soft Drink Workers of America, et al.*, Records of the U.S. District Court, Eastern District of Michigan, Southern Division (Detroit), Civil Records, Civil Case Files, 1938–1969, Record Group 21, National Archives, Great Lakes Region, Chicago, Illinois; *Detroit News*, January 22, 1939.

39. *Detroit News*, January 22, February 6, February 11, 1939; *Detroit News* photographs and captions, January 20, January 21, 1939, *Detroit News* Library, Detroit, Michigan.

40. *Detroit News*, January 22, 1939.

41. *Detroit News*, December 12, December 20, December 29, 1938.

42. *Detroit News*, June 30, 1937.

43. *Detroit News*, January 22, 1939.

44. *Detroit News*, January 24, 1939.

45. Civil Case 483.

46. See chapter 2 for a biographical sketch of Bennett and an account of the trusteeship of Local 299.

47. *Detroit News*, January 29, 1939.

48. Frank X. Martel to William Green, January 30, 1939, Series 1, Part 1, Box 18, "Teamsters International Union 1939," Wayne County AFL-CIO Collection, Archives of Labor and Urban Affairs, Wayne State University.

49. Civil Case 483; *Detroit News*, February 5, 1939.

50. For an example of Hoffa's extravagant use of profanity, see Joseph Franco with Richard Hammer, *Hoffa's Man: The Rise and Fall of Jimmy Hoffa as Witnessed by His Strongest Arm* (Prentice-Hall, 1987), xiii.

51. *Detroit News*, March 13, 1939.

52. Telegram from William Green to Frank X. Martel, January 30, 1939, Series 1, Part 1, Box 18, "Teamsters International Union 1939," Wayne County AFL-CIO Collection, Archives of Labor and Urban Affairs, Wayne State University.

53. *Detroit News*, February 17, February 19, 1939.

54. *Detroit News*, February 19, March 2, 1939.

55. Matthew Josephson, *Union House, Union Bar: The History of the Hotel and Restaurant Employees and Bartenders' International Union (AFL-CIO)* (Random House, 1956); *Detroit News*, March 2, March 6, 1939; McMaster interview.

56. U.S. Senate, Select Committee on Improper Activities in the Labor or Management Field, *Investigation of Improper Activities in the Labor or Management Field: Hearings*, 5291–5295; *Detroit News*, April 10, May 11, 1937. Herman's nephew Frank Kierdorf, who was hired by Hoffa as a business agent for Local 332 in Flint, gained notoriety in 1958 when he accidentally set fire to himself while firebombing a cleaning-and-dyeing business. As he lay near death in a hospital bed, a prosecuting attorney told him he should confess to the crime before he met "your Maker, your God." In response, the grotesquely burned Teamster whispered, "Go fuck yourself." See Sloane, 116.

57. Quotes from J. David Greenstone, *Labor in American Politics* (Knopf, 1969), 30; and Foner, *History of the Labor Movement in the United States*, Vol. 3, 284.

58. Greenstone, *Labor in American Politics*, 50.

59. See chapter 2 for a discussion of the Detroit Teamsters' non-statist organizing strategies.

60. The relationship between DeMass and the Teamsters came to light during a grand jury investigation of the union in 1946. *Detroit News*, July 6, July 7, August 12, 1946.

61. *Detroit News*, October 3, October 9, October 10, 1939; *Michigan CIO News*, October 30, 1939; *Detroit Labor News*, January 5, January 12, January 19, January 26, February 2, February 9, February 16, February 23, March 1, March 8, March 15, April 12, April 26, 1940.

62. Detroit Police Department, Criminal Record No. 59527, James R. Hoffa, Box 86, "James R. Hoffa," Clare E. Hoffman Papers, Bentley Historical Library, University of Michigan; George S. Fitzgerald, interview with Daniel Bell, "James Hoffa," B2–60, Daniel Bell Papers, Tamiment Library, New York University; Ray Bennett, letter to Tom Flynn, April 23, 1943, quoted in James and James, *Hoffa and the Teamsters*, 85. Other accounts claim that Hoffa was arrested eighteen times during the twenty-four-hour period.

63. McMaster interview.

64. Frank Donner, *Protectors of Privilege: Red Squads and Police Repression in Urban America* (University of California Press, 1990), 57; *Detroit News*, September 8, 1940.

65. John Herling, undated manuscript, pp. 21–22, Box 33, Folder 5, "Who Shot Walter Reuther?" John Herling Collection, Archives of Labor and Urban Affairs, Wayne State University; McMaster interview; Detroit Police Department, Criminal Record No. 59527, James R. Hoffa, Box 86, "James R. Hoffa," Clare E. Hoffman Papers, Bentley Historical Library, University of Michigan; see chapters 6 and 7 for discussions of the Teamsters' links with the Wayne County Prosecuting Attorney's office.

66. See chapter 2 for a biographical sketch of Fitzgerald.

67. "George S. Fitzgerald Announces Candidacy," press release, May 30, 1954, Neal Staebler Collection, Box 26, "George Fitzgerald," Bentley Historical Library, University of Michigan.

68. "All the benefits of our grand jury will cease at midnight next Dec. 31," Fitzgerald said in a speech to the East Side Women's Democratic League, "unless the intelligent Democratic voters realize that four out of six of the candidates for prosecutor are supporting McCrea [a candidate for police superintendent who had been indicted by the grand jury] and worked with him until the indictment." *Detroit News*, August 25, 1940.

69. *Detroit News*, September 12, 1940; McMaster interview.

70. Criminal Case 25959, *United States v. Wholesale Waste Paper Company, et al.*, Records of the U.S. District Court, Eastern District of Michigan, Southern Division (Detroit), Criminal Records, Criminal Case Files, 1851–1969, Record Group 21, National Archives, Great Lakes Region, Chicago, Illinois.

71. Arnold to Richardson Wood, October 19, 1940, Thurman W. Arnold Papers, University of Wyoming Library, Laramie, Wyoming. I am grateful to Alan Brinkley for providing me with a copy of this letter. A full discussion of Arnold's antitrust campaign against labor unions and the reaction against it can be found in Alan Brinkley, *The End of Reform: New Deal Liberalism in Recession and War* (Knopf, 1995), 118–120, and Ellis W. Hawley, *The New Deal and the Problem of Monopoly: A Study in Economic Ambivalence* (Princeton University Press, 1966), 430–446.

72. The Roosevelt Administration launched its antitrust assault early in 1938. See Brinkley, *The End of Reform*, chapter 6.

Four

The Wages of War

1. Christopher L. Tomlins, "AFL Unions in the 1930s: Their Performance in Historical Perspective," *Journal of American History*, Vol. 65, No. 4 (March 1979), 1037; Walter Galenson, *The CIO Challenge to the AFL: A History of the American Labor Movement, 1935–1941* (Harvard University Press, 1960), 459; Tomlins's analysis belonged to what was known as the "organizational synthesis," a critique of institutional dynamics that was in vogue within certain circles of historians in the 1970s. See Louis Galambos, "The Emerging Organizational Synthesis in Modern American History," *Business History Review* 57 (1983), 279–290, and Brian Balogh, "Reorganizing the Organizational Synthesis," *Studies in American Political Development* 5 (1991), 119–172.

2. One of the unfortunate casualties of the rise of the "new labor history" was the discussion of the effects of rival unionism. Before the 1970s, jurisdictional competition and the resultant growth of the unions involved were prominent in the narratives of the best labor history texts, including Irving Bernstein, *The Turbulent Years: A History of the American Worker During the Great Depression* (Houghton Mifflin, 1970), and Walter Galenson's two greatly underappreciated works, *The CIO Challenge to the AFL* and *Rival Unionism in the United States* (American Council on Public Affairs, 1940). An even less appreciated but highly interesting discussion of inter-union competition is George W. Brooks, *The Sources of Vitality in the American Labor Movement* (New York State School of Industrial and Labor Relations, 1964), 29–33. Jonathan Cutler was the first to revive the issue in later years. See Cutler, "A Slacker's Paradise," chapter 13.

This is not to suggest that inter-union competition is the only cause of union militancy. As will be seen, competition between factions *within* unions and sometimes ideological convictions also spur militancy among union leaders.

3. Robert Scott Bowers, "The International Brotherhood of Teamsters and a Theory of Jurisdiction," unpublished Ph.D. dissertation, University of Wisconsin, 1951, iv.

4. *Official Magazine, I.B.T., C., S. and H. of A.*, March 1936, April 1936, July 1937.

5. Chapter 3 contains a fuller explanation of leapfrogging.

6. Bruce Nelson, *Workers on the Waterfront: Seamen, Longshoremen, and Unionism in the 1930s* (University of Illinois Press, 1988), 220–221.

7. Galenson, *CIO Challenge to the AFL*, 475.

8. *Ibid.*, 476–477.

9. *Official Magazine, I.B.T., C., S. and H. of A.*, March 1936, April 1936.

10. Undated memorandum, Box 86, "James R. Hoffa," Clare Hoffman Papers, Bentley Historical Library, University of Michigan.

11. *Detroit News*, April 23, 1937; Bruce Nelson, "Autoworkers, Electoral Politics, and the Convergence of Class and Race: Detroit, 1937–1945," in Kevin Boyle, ed., *Organized Labor and American Politics, 1894–1994: The Labor-Liberal Alliance* (SUNY Press, 1998), 126; *Detroit News*, June 28, 1937; McMaster interview.

12. Fraser, 233; J.B.S. Hardman, "Postscripts to Ten Years of Labor Movement," in Hardman, ed., *American Labor Dynamics in the Light of Post-War Developments* (Harcourt Brace, 1928); "Biographical Sketch of Mr. John W. Gibson," Papers of John W. Gibson, Box 45, Harry S. Truman Library, Independence, Missouri. An excellent critical explication of labor corporatism can be found in Cutler, "A Slacker's Paradise," introduction, and in Cutler and Stanley Aronowitz, "Quitting Time: An Introduction," in Cutler and Aronowitz, eds., *Post-Work* (Routledge, 1998).

13. *Detroit News*, August 9, August 31, 1939.

14. Various leaflets, Gibson Papers, Box 1, "Dairy Industry"; *Detroit Labor News*, March 7, May 2, August 29, 1941; competition between the two unions over one of the dairies, the Johnson Milk Company, continued into the war years and took a new turn in 1943. This will be covered in chapter 5. See *Retail, Wholesale, and Department Store Employee*, September 1, 1943.

15. Melvyn Dubofsky and Warren Van Tine, *John L. Lewis: A Biography* (Quadrangle, 1977), x.

16. Dubofsky and Van Tine, *John L. Lewis*, chapter 14, *passim*; Galenson, *CIO Challenge to the AFL*, 521–523.

17. Robert H. Zieger, *The CIO, 1935–1955* (University of North Carolina Press, 1995), 134, n415.

18. Bertrand Russell, *A History of Western Philosophy* (Simon and Schuster, 1945), 780.

19. *Detroit News*, February 6, 1939, February 12, 1940.

20. *Michigan CIO News*, January 15, January 22, 1940; Lichtenstein, *The Most Dangerous Man in Detroit*, 50–51, 102, 123; Fraser, 344–346.

21. Hoffa, letter to Tom Flynn, May 15, 1946, quoted in James and James, *Hoffa and the Teamsters*, 79.

22. *Detroit News*, July 12, 1940; *Detroit Labor News*, July 19, July 26, August 2, August 9, 1940; *Official Magazine, I.B.T., C., S. and H. of A.*, September 1940; various letters, Mayor's Papers, 1940, Box 14, "UV," Burton Historical Collection, Detroit Public Library; Lichtenstein, *The Most Dangerous Man in Detroit*, 179–180.

23. *Detroit News*, August 4, 1940; *Detroit Labor News*, August 9, August 30, 1940.

24. William Green, letter to Dan Tobin, December 30, 1940, Office of the President, AFL, Copy Books, Reel 31, George Meany Memorial Archives, Silver Spring, Maryland.

25. Walter Galenson points out the important difference between a jurisdictional dispute involving two members of the same federation and a conflict in which the two unions share no organizational commonality: "A jurisdictional dispute, which is to be sharply distinguished from a rival union controversy, is one between competing labor organizations acknowledging allegiance to a common parent. The important additional element is the existence of an agency to which the dispute may be referred for settlement." Galenson, *Rival Unionism in the United States*, 1–2.

The Brewery Workers were suspended by the AFL in 1941 and joined the CIO in 1946. Nuala McGann Drescher, "International Union of United Brewery, Flour, Cereal, Soft Drink and Distillery Workers of America (UBW)," in Gary Fink, ed., *Labor Unions* (Greenwood Press, 1977), 41.

26. *Teamsters Local 337 News: 40th Anniversary*, March 1977, 12–13, in the possession of Robert Holmes; *Detroit News*, January 31, December 3, December 14, December 15, December 20, December 23, 1940, February 12, March 21, May 8, 1941; *Official Magazine, I.B.T., C., S. and H. of A.*, December 1940.

Five

The Price of Peace

1. Quoted in *Detroit News*, October 22, 1941.

2. Lewis supported Wendell Willkie against Roosevelt in 1940, then followed through

on his promise to resign from the CIO presidency if Roosevelt won. Murray was subsequently selected to replace him.

3. *Michigan CIO News*, February 7, 1941; Ronald States, "Philip Murray and the Subordination of the Industrial Unions to the United States Government," in Melvyn Dubofsky and Warren Van Tine, eds., *Labor Leaders in America* (University of Illinois Press, 1987), 234–257; Lichtenstein, *The Most Dangerous Man in Detroit*, 130. Lichtenstein quotes UAW vice president George Addes as recalling that "Murray felt Thomas was his boy. He could lead Thomas around by the nose."

4. *Detroit Labor News*, May 3, 1940; *Retail, Wholesale, and Department Store Employee*, February 28, 1941, March 31, 1941; *Michigan CIO News*, March 21, 1941.

5. *Detroit News*, March 24, March 26, 1941; *Detroit Labor News*, March 28, 1941; G. V. Branch, letter to Edward J. Jeffries, Jr., January 27, 1942, Mayors' Papers, 1942, Box 10, "Unions" folder, Burton Historical Collection.

6. *Retail, Wholesale, and Department Store Employee*, March 31, May 31, 1941.

7. *Retail, Wholesale, and Department Store Employee*, April 30, 1941.

8. *Detroit Labor News*, May 2, 1941.

9. *Michigan CIO News*, February 28, 1941; Leroy H. Schramm, "Union Rivalry in Detroit in World War II," *Michigan History*, Vol. 54, No. 3 (Fall 1970), 204.

10. *Detroit News*, June 20, 1937; John A. Zaremba to John W. Smith, telegram, March 16, 1940, Mayors' Papers, 1940, Box 14, "UV," Burton Historical Collection, Detroit Public Library; Schramm, "Union Rivalry in Detroit in World War II," 205; Alan Clive, *State of War: Michigan in World War II* (University of Michigan Press, 1979), 20–22; photos, May 12, May 14, May 19, 1941, *Detroit News* Library.

11. *Detroit Labor News*, May 16, May 23, 1941; *Michigan CIO News*, May 30, 1941.

12. The Trotskyists in 544 had belonged to the Communist League of America, which merged with other Trotskyist sects to form the Socialist Workers Party (SWP) in 1938. In March 1941 the leaders of 544 formally resigned from the SWP but remained close to the party.

Ralph C. and Estelle James, "The Purge of the Trotskyites from the Teamsters," *The Western Political Quarterly*, Vol. 19, No. 1 (March 1966), 6–7; John Geary, telegram to Daniel J. Tobin, June 10, 1941, International Brotherhood of Teamsters, Chauffeurs, Warehousemen and Helpers of America, Papers, Series 2A, Box 44, Folder 3, State Historical Society of Wisconsin, Madison.

13. *Northwest Organizer*, June 12, June 19, 1941.

14. Daniel J. Tobin to "R. G. Thomas," June 13, 1941, IBT Papers, Series 2A, Box 44, Folder 3.

15. *Minneapolis Times*, June 20, 1941, quoted in *Northwest Organizer*, June 26, 1941.

16. *Northwest Organizer*, June 26, 1941.

17. James and James, "The Purge of the Trotskyites," 9–10; Farrell Dobbs, *Teamster Bureaucracy* (Monad Press, 1977), 169–246.

18. See *Ibid.*

19. "Telephone Conversation with Joe Casey, General Organizer, Minneapolis," June 24, 1941, IBT Papers, Series 1, Box 12, Folder 11.

20. Associated Industries of Minneapolis, *News Letter*, July 28, 1941; Report of Alfred P. Blair, Labor Conciliator, September 18, 1941; "Statement in Behalf of General Drivers Union Local 544, A.F.L. Showing Why Thirty-Day Strike Limitation Clause Provided for by Sections 6 and 7 of the Minnesota Labor Relations Act Should Not Be Invoked"; all in IBT Papers, Series 2A, Box 44, Folder 3.

21. *Detroit News*, July 7, July 21, July 22, 1941; *Detroit Labor News*, September 26, November 21, 1941, January 9, 1942; McMaster interview.

22. *The Retail, Wholesale and Department Store Employee*, June 30, July 31, August 31, 1941; *Michigan CIO News*, June 13, July 4, 1941; *Detroit News*, July 5, July 6, July 7, August 12, 1941.

23. *The Retail, Wholesale and Department Store Employee*, August 31, September 30, October 31, November 30, December 31, 1941; *Detroit Labor News*, September 12, September 19, September 26, October 10, October 17, October 24, November 7, November 21, December 19, 1941; *Detroit Free Press*, September 17, 1941; *Detroit News*, October 17, 1941.

24. James and James, *Hoffa and the Teamsters*, 82; *Official Magazine, I.B.T.C.W. and H. of A.*, October 1941.

In the fall of 1941 the Detroit Teamsters also faced intense jurisdictional competition from an AFL union, the Brotherhood of Railway and Steamship Clerks, who matched the ferocity and physical courage of the Teamsters in defending their hold over workers at the Railway Express Agency. See undated memorandum, "Unions" folder, Box 12, Mayor's Papers, 1941, Burton Historical Collection, Detroit Public Library; *Official Magazine, I.B.T.C.W. and H. of A.*, December 1941; *Detroit Evening Times*, September 6, 1941; *Detroit News*, September 30, October 4–9, October 14–16, October 19, October 21–22, October 31–November 9, 1941.

25. *Detroit News*, August 25; *Detroit Labor News*, August 29, 1941.

26. In September, the Teamster international office transferred Red O'Laughlin to Minneapolis to help guard against the return of the Trotskyists. Though Hoffa had already emerged as the leading figure in Local 299, O'Laughlin's transfer cleared the local of any potential competitors. See *Official Magazine, I.B.T.C.W. and H. of A.*, October 1941.

27. *Detroit News*, September 5, 1941; *Detroit Evening Times*, September 5, 1941; *The Industrial Organizer*, September 11, 1941.

28. *Detroit Labor News*, September 12, 1941; McMaster interview.

29. Moldea, 37–38, 150–170.

The June 1943 issue of the *Michigan Teamster*, the official organ of Detroit Joint Council 43, refers to Johnson as "our new B.A. [Business Agent] of Local 299." McMaster interview; Franco, 71–76. Among the scholarly works that accept Moldea's claim are Sloane, 32, and Lichtenstein, *The Most Dangerous Man in Detroit*, 273.

Few serious scholars of the Kennedy assassination link Hoffa to the killing, and Gerald Posner persuasively refutes the theories that the Teamster was involved. See Posner, *Case Closed: Lee Harvey Oswald and the Assassination of JFK* (Random House, 1994), 363–364, 456–457, 460–461.

30. Briglia was a business agent with Local 51 and Galbo was a business agent with Local 337. The other Teamsters reported to have been arrested or hospitalized were Sol Sniderman, George Coats, Bennett Belcher, Rolland McMaster, Thomas Burke, Edgar Johnson, Orville Matheney, Sam Calhoun, James Clift, and Morris Coleman. See *Detroit News*, July 21, November 1, November 2, 1941; *Michigan CIO News*, July 31, 1941.

31. *Detroit News*, September 27, September 28, October 1, October 14, 1941.

32. Moldea, 37–38; *Detroit Times*, September 13, 1941; *Detroit News*, September 21, October 10, October 11, 1941. In a closed session of the UAW International Executive Board, UAW president R. J. Thomas and Joseph Pagano of the Wayne County CIO

Council claimed the Teamsters were using "imported gangsters" and did not mention the East Side gang. The normally tight-fisted Tobin provided Local 299 with a $1,300 monthly subsidy from the IBT treasury for the fight against the UCWOC. James and James, "The Purge of the Trotskyites from the Teamsters," 11.

33. *Congressional Record*, March 31, 1943, A1549; *Detroit Labor News*, January 30, 1942; McMaster interview; George Geller, interview with the author, Detroit, Michigan, June 16, 1998; *Michigan Teamster*, November 1943; Franco, 67, 80–83.

34. McMaster interview; *Detroit News*, September 10, September 21, 1941; UAW-IEB minutes, Chicago, September 15, 1941, UAW-IEB Collection, Archives of Labor and Urban Affairs, Wayne State University.

35. McMaster interview; *Detroit News*, September 11, 1941; James and James, "The Purge of the Trotskyites," 13.

36. Lichtenstein, *The Most Dangerous Man in Detroit*, 154–193, *passim*, 505 n6; *Detroit News*, September 16, 1941.

37. *Detroit News*, September 21, 1941; UAW-IEB minutes, Chicago, September 19, 1941.

38. *Detroit News*, September 27, September 28, 1941.

39. Fraser, 487–488; U.S. Congress, Senate, Special Committee to Investigate the National Defense Program, *Hearings*, 77th Congress, 1st session pursuant to S. Res. 71, 1941, 2492–2493.

In 1942, Currier's lumber workers voted to join the Carpenters' union and the drivers elected to be represented by Teamsters Local 247. *Detroit Labor News*, May 22, May 29, 1942.

40. *Detroit News*, October 22, 1941; James and James, "The Purge of the Trotskyites from the Teamsters," 12–13.

41. Minutes of meeting of Central States Drivers Council, September 22, 1941, Series 2D, Box 120, Folder 4, IBT Papers; *Detroit News*, November 4, 1941; J. L. Keeshin telegram to Daniel Tobin, November 6, 1941, Series 5, Box 8, Folder 4, IBT Papers; *Detroit Labor News*, November 21, November 28, 1941; *Official Magazine, I.B.T.C.W. and H. of A.*, December 1941.

42. Lewis had demanded that the UMW's closed shop contract with independent mining companies be extended to the so-called "captive mines" owned directly by the large steel corporations.

43. National Defense Mediation Board, "In the Matter of Central States Employers' Negotiating Committee and Central States Drivers' Council, Decision," December 29, 1941, Series 2D, Box 120, Folder 5, IBT Papers; *Detroit Labor News*, January 9, 1942.

Six

A New Man of Power

1. J. B. S. Hardman, "Problems of Labor Organization," in Hardman, ed., *American Labor Dynamics in the Light of Post-War Developments: An Inquiry By Thirty-two Labor Men, Teachers, Editors, and Technicians* (Harcourt Brace, 1928), 96.

2. In 1942, Detroit Joint Council 43 consisted of Locals 51 (bakery drivers), 155 (dairy drivers), 243 (delivery van drivers), 247 (building materials drivers), 271 (beer drivers), 285 (laundry and linen drivers), 299 (local cartage, carhauling, and highway drivers),

337 (food and beverage drivers and warehousemen), 372 (newspaper drivers), 614 (Pontiac general drivers), and 663 (garbage truck drivers).

3. *Detroit News,* October 19, November 3, November 9, 1941; *Detroit Labor News,* November 7, November 14, 1941; *International Teamster,* January 1942.

4. *Detroit Labor News,* January 9, January 29, 1942; *International Teamster,* June 1942.

5. *The Retail, Wholesale and Department Store Employee,* January 31, April 30, 1942.

6. Anton Jakobs, president of the butchers local, denied that his union was "taken over by the Teamsters under duress," saying that the merger was undertaken "because of duplication of membership and effort." Jakobs later worked as an organizer for the Teamsters in the grocery industry. *Detroit News,* February 1, 1942.

7. Don W. Olson, letter to Edward Jeffries, January 13, 1942, G. V. Branch, letter to Edward J. Jeffries, January 27, 1942, Edward J. Jeffries, letter to John C. Lehr, January 30, 1942, Mayors' Papers, 1942, Box 10, "Unions" folder, Burton Historical Collection, Detroit Public Library; Tom Flynn, letter to Bert Brennan, March 20, 1942, Series 2A, Box 11, Folder 8, International Brotherhood of Teamsters, Chauffeurs, Warehousemen and Helpers of America, Papers, State Historical Society of Wisconsin, Madison; *Detroit News,* January 30, January 31, February 1, February 2, February 3, February 4, February 5, 1942.

8. Tom Flynn, letter to Bert Brennan, March 20, 1942, Series 2A, Box 11, Folder 8, IBT Papers; Tom Flynn, letter to John Gillespie, May 27, 1942, Series 2A, Box 7, Folder 27, IBT Papers.

9. Ray Bennett, letter to Dan Tobin, May 15, 1942, quoted in James and James, *Hoffa and the Teamsters,* 72, 78, 80–81.

10. On May 29, 1942, the UCWOC officially affiliated with District 50 of the United Mine Workers, which caused the CIO a week later to dissolve the organization. On the demise of the UCWOC, see James and James, "The Purge of the Trotskyites," 12–13; CIO press release, June 11, 1942, Collection of the CIO Secretary-Treasurer, Box 51, "Construction Workers" folder, Archives of Labor and Urban Affairs, Wayne State University; *Detroit Labor News,* July 17, 1942; Tom Flynn, letter to John Gillespie, May 27, 1942, Series 2A, Box 7, Folder 27, IBT Papers.

11. Robert Holmes, letter to Thomas Flynn, April 22, 1942, Series 2A, Box 11, Folder 8, IBT Papers; Daniel J. Tobin, letter to Philip Murray, May 28, 1942, Series 4, Box 3, "Congress of Industrial Organizations 1939–1946" folder, IBT Papers; Allan S. Haywood, letter to Daniel J. Tobin, June 2, 1942, Series 4, Box 4, "CIO" folder, IBT Papers; Daniel J. Tobin, telegram to Philip Murray, June 4, 1942, Series 4, Box 3, "CIO" folder, IBT Papers; Daniel J. Tobin, letter to Allan S. Haywood, June 8, 1942, Series 4, Box 3, "CIO" folder, IBT Papers; Allan S. Haywood, letter to Daniel J. Tobin, June 13, 1942, Series 4, Box 3, "CIO" folder, IBT Papers; Thomas Flynn, letter to Allan S. Haywood, July 14, 1942, Series 4, Box 3, "CIO" folder, IBT Papers; August Scholle, letter to Allan Haywood, June 24, 1942, IBT Papers; Allan S. Haywood, letter to Daniel J. Tobin, June 26, 1942, Series 4, Box 3, "CIO" folder, IBT Papers.

12. *International Teamster,* July 1942.

13. Hardman, *American Labor Dynamics,* 167.

14. Arthur J. Goldberg, "Labor in a Free Society: A Trade Union Point of View," Speech at Industrial Union Department Conference, May 3, 1958.

15. Tom Flynn, letter to John Gillespie, October 6, 1942, Series 2A, Box 7, Folder 27, IBT Papers.

16. James Hoffa, letter to Tom Flynn, February 26, 1942, quoted in James and James,

Hoffa and the Teamsters, 73–74; Tom Flynn, letter to J. C. Brayton, March 4, 1942, Series 2A, Box 11, Folder 3, IBT Papers; James Hoffa, letter to Tom Flynn, December 14, 1942, quoted in James and James, *Hoffa and the Teamsters*, 74.

17. Ray Bennett, letter to Tom Flynn, December 8, 1942, quoted in James and James, *Hoffa and the Teamsters*, 75.

18. *Michigan Teamster*, March 1943; Holmes interview; McMaster interview; Bert Brennan, letter to Thomas Flynn, March 5, 1942, Series 2A, Box 11, Folder 8, IBT Papers; *Detroit News*, July 21, November 2, 1941.

Sniderman was appointed to the Trucking and Transportation panel of the regional War Labor Board. See Edwin E. Witte, telegram to Lloyd Garrison, October 18, 1943, "Correspondence with Region XI," Trucking Commission, National War Labor Board, Record Group 202, National Archives and Records Administration, College Park, MD.

19. During the war, overtime was paid to over-the-road drivers only in Washington, Oregon, Pennsylvania, and New England and on a few routes in the Midwest. The two wartime Central States Area agreements handed down by the NDMB and the NWLB did not include overtime provisions, which meant that most employers could compel their drivers to work long hours without having to pay additional wages. See "Directive Order, Case No. 4648, Case No. 4448," February 7, 1944, p. 5, "Central States—Government Inquiries," Dispute Cases, Trucking Commission, National War Labor Board, Record Group 202, National Archives.

20. For a discussion of the "social ecology" of wartime strikes, see Nelson Lichtenstein, *Labor's War at Home: The CIO in World War II* (Cambridge University Press, 1982), 110–135.

21. "Joint Meeting of the Central States Drivers Council Executive Board and Ohio Highway Drivers Council Committee, April 21, 1943," Series 2D, Box 120, Folder 6, IBT Papers.

22. The National Defense Mediation Board was replaced by the National War Labor Board in the winter of 1942.

23. James and James, *Hoffa and the Teamsters*, 120–122.

24. "Directive Order, Case No. 4648, Case No. 4448," February 7, 1944, "Central States—Government Inquiries," Dispute Cases, Trucking Commission, National War Labor Board, Record Group 202, National Archives.

25. Dexter L. Lewis, telegram to William H. Davis, June 16, 1944, "Central States," Dispute Cases, Trucking Commission, NWLB, Record Group 202, National Archives; Dexter L. Lewis, letter to Editorial Department, *Milwaukee Journal*, August 7, 1944, Series 2D, Box 121, Folder 3, IBT Papers; A. F. Hudson, letter to Daniel J. Tobin, December 4, 1945, Series 2D, Box 122, Folder 1, IBT Papers.

26. AFL and CIO "peace committee" press release, December 2, 1942, Series 4, Box 3, "CIO" folder, IBT Papers; *Retail, Wholesale, and Department Store Employee*, August 1, 1943.

27. *Michigan Teamster*, January 1943; *International Teamster*, March 1943.

28. *Retail, Wholesale, and Department Store Employee*, January 1, February 1, June 1, August 1, 1943; *Michigan Teamster*, April 1943.

29. *Retail, Wholesale, and Department Store Employee*, April 1, 1943; *Detroit News*, September 17, September 18, 1942.

30. *Michigan Teamster*, April 1943; Tom Flynn, letter to Ray Bennett, July 8, 1942, quoted in James and James, *Hoffa and the Teamsters*, 82.

31. *Retail, Wholesale, and Department Store Employee,* July 1, 1943; *Detroit Labor News,* March 7, May 2, August 29, 1941.

32. McMaster interview; John Herling, undated manuscript, pp. 21–22, Box 33, Folder 5, "Who Shot Walter Reuther?" John Herling Collection, Archives of Labor and Urban Affairs, Wayne State University.

Among the ex-Teamster lawmen was Russell Gregory, a former officer of Local 247 who was promoted to Chief of Detectives of the Wayne County Sheriff's Department in 1943. See *Michigan Teamster,* December 1943.

33. *Detroit Labor News,* August 20, 1943; *Retail, Wholesale, and Department Store Employee,* September 1, 1943; *Michigan Teamster,* November 1943.

34. *Congressional Record,* 1943, A1307, A1450–A1451, 2613, A1548–A1550, 3258–3259, 3370–3371, 3563, 4099–4101, 5681; *Michigan Teamster,* April 1943; McMaster interview.

35. *PM,* October 24, 1943; August Meier and Elliott Rudwick, *Black Detroit and the Rise of the UAW* (Oxford University Press, 1979), 203–205; *Detroit News,* October 25, October 27, 1943; *Detroit Labor News,* October 29, 1943; *Michigan Teamster,* November 1943; *Michigan CIO News,* January 28, 1944.

36. *International Teamster,* September 1942; *Michigan Teamster,* January, April, November 1943.

37. M. A. Clark, letter to Trucking Commission, National War Labor Board, March 18, 1943, "Correspondence with Region XI," Trucking Commission, National War Labor Board, RG 202, National Archives; Report of Joint Labor-Management Meeting with Government Officials, at Stevens Hotel, December 13, 1943, Series 2D, Box 121, Folder 1, IBT Papers; *Michigan Teamster,* August, September, October 1943; Training Program of the Motor Trucking Industry of Detroit and Vicinity, "Correspondence with Region XI," Trucking Commission, National War Labor Board, RG 202, National Archives.

38. *Michigan Teamster,* January, March, April, May, August, October, December 1943.

Seven

The Making of a "Labor Boss"

1. Sigmund Freud, *Civilization and Its Discontents* (J. Cape and H. Smith, 1930).

2. *Michigan Teamster,* January, April, May, September 1943, June 1944. The 1940 census reported that 4.1 percent of trucking and warehousing employees in twelve Midwestern states were female, but it is likely that nearly all of those women were in warehousing. *U.S. Census of the Population,* 1940: Vol. III, *The Labor Force,* Part I, Table 77.

3. *They Drive by Night,* Warner Brothers Pictures, Inc., 1940. Hoffa was described as "George Raftish" in "The Jolly Teamsters—Take I," February 16, 1956, "James Hoffa" folder, B2-60, Daniel Bell Papers, Tamiment Library, New York University.

4. *Michigan Teamster,* June 1944, July 1945. For a similar discussion of the connections between workplace autonomy, danger, ribaldry, and masculine behavior, see Joshua B. Freeman, "Hardhats: Construction Workers, Manliness, and the 1970 Pro-War Demonstrations," *Journal of Social History,* Summer 1993, 730–731.

5. Joseph Franco with Richard Hammer, *Hoffa's Man: The Rise and Fall of Jimmy Hoffa as Witnessed by His Strongest Arm* (Prentice-Hall, 1987), xiii; Sloane, 56; James and

James, *Hoffa and the Teamsters*, 53; Leonard Shaffner, interview with the author, Taylor, Michigan, June 15, 1998.

6. "[Hearing] Before President's Committee on Fair Employment Practice, United States of America, In the Matter of The International Brotherhood of Teamsters, Chauffeurs, Warehousemen, and Helpers of America, Local 299, et al., Detroit, Michigan, June 2, 1945," 222–236, Case No. 84, Records of the President's Committee on Fair Employment Practice, Record Group 228, National Archives and Records Administration, College Park, Maryland [hereafter referred to as FEPC Records, College Park].

7. "Transportation Manpower Survey, Discrimination Supplement," April 3, 1943; "Community Attitudes," August 15, 1944; Festus Hairston, summary of complaint, undated; "Discrimination in War Industries," December 9, 1942; 5-UR-1269, Active Cases, September 1941–April 1946, Teamsters Local 299, A. F. of L., Detroit, Michigan, Records of the Region V Office, Records of the President's Committee on Fair Employment Practice, Record Group 228, National Archives—Great Lakes Region, Chicago, Illinois [hereafter referred to as FEPC Records, Chicago]; "FEP Agency Opens Office in Detroit," *Detroit Labor News*, January 15, 1943; Meier and Rudwick, 32, 45, 114; Maurice Isserman, *Which Side Were You On? The American Communist Party During the Second World War* (University of Illinois Press, 1982), 21. At the 1943 Michigan Federation of Labor convention, Simmons co-authored a resolution as a representative of Local 663. See Michigan Federation of Labor, *Convention Proceedings*, 54 (1943), May 20, Resolution No. 55.

8. G. James Fleming, memorandum to Daniel R. Donovan, February 5, 1943; "Community Attitudes," August 15, 1944; Will Maslow, memorandum to files, October 4, 1944; George M. Johnson, memorandum to G. James Fleming, April 24, 1943; Daniel R. Donovan, memorandum to George M. Johnson, August 18, 1943; all in FEPC Records, Chicago; "Report of Discriminatory Hiring Practices," Dealers Transport Company, August 14, 1944, FEPC Records, College Park. In 1938 the president of the Michigan Colored Mayors' Association complained to Frank Martel of the Wayne County Federation of Labor that Teamsters Local 271 refused to allow black truck drivers to deliver beer. See Reuben J. Patton, letter to Frank Martel, July 23, 1938, "Teamsters International Union" folder, Box 18, Part 1, Series 1, Wayne County AFL-CIO Collection, Archives of Labor and Urban Affairs, Wayne State University.

9. William T. McKnight, memorandum to George M. Johnson, May 8, 1945, FEPC Records, College Park; G. James Fleming, memorandum to Daniel R. Donovan, February 5, 1943; Edward M. Swan, memorandum to William T. McKnight, November 24, 1943, both in FEPC Records, Chicago.

10. George E. Johnson, "complaint," August 3, 1943, FEPC Records, Chicago.

11. "Community Attitudes," August 15, 1944, FEPC Records, Chicago.

12. Michigan Federation of Labor, *Convention Proceedings*, 54 (1943), May 19, Resolution Nos. 43, 44, 45; *Detroit Labor News*, February 20, 1942.

13. *Detroit Free Press*, January 6, 1945; *Detroit News*, January 9, 1945.

14. George M. Johnson, memorandum to Daniel R. Donovan, May 12, 1943, FEPC Records, Chicago; Thomas E. Flynn, letter to Boris Shishkin, July 21, 1943, FEPC Records, College Park; Robert C. Goodwin, memorandum to Edward L. Cushman, August 9, 1944; Emanuel Bloch, memorandum to Malcolm Ross, August 25, 1944, FEPC Records, Chicago.

15. Louis Ruchames, *Race, Jobs, and Politics: The Story of FEPC* (Columbia University

Press, 1951), 56–57; William T. McKnight, memorandum to George M. Johnson, May 8, 1945, FEPC Records, College Park.

16. Simon Stickgold and Frank D. Reeves, memorandum to Maceo Hubbard, May 23, 1945, FEPC Records, Chicago; "[Hearing] Before President's Committee on Fair Employment Practice, United States of America, In the Matter of The International Brotherhood of Teamsters, Chauffeurs, Warehousemen, and Helpers of America, Local 299, et al., Detroit, Michigan, June 2, 1945," FEPC Records, College Park.

17. Hearing, 5–6; Ruchames, 121–136.

18. Franco, 196; Daniel R. Donovan, memorandum to George M. Johnson, August 18, 1943, FEPC Records, Chicago.

19. *Michigan CIO News*, March 10, November 24, 1944; *International Teamster*, August 1944; Daniel Tobin, letter to John J. Conlin, April 7, 1944, Folder 8, Box 11, Series 2A, International Brotherhood of Teamsters, Chauffeurs, Warehousemen and Helpers of America, Papers, State Historical Society of Wisconsin, Madison. See chapter 4 for a history of the Teamsters' first contract with Dossin in 1940.

20. *Ibid.; Detroit News*, March 1, 1944.

21. Tobin letter to Conlin, April 7, 1944; *Michigan CIO News*, March 31, April 14, 1944; *Detroit News*, March 9, April 5, April 9, May 10, May 12, 1944. When the trial of Sniderman and his alleged coconspirators opened seventeen months later, charges against all three were dismissed. *Detroit News*, August 10, 1946.

22. Teamster business agent Jimmy Clift, who claimed self-defense, was acquitted of a charge of assault with intent to kill. *Detroit News*, July 16, 1946.

23. *Detroit News*, May 18, May 19, 1944.

24. National Labor Relations Board, "In the Matter of Detroit Coca Cola Bottling Company and Local 337, International Brotherhood of Teamsters, Chauffeurs, Warehousemen and Helpers of America, A. F. of L.," Case No. 7-R-1753, Certification of Representatives, July 13, 1944, Folder 8, Box 11, Series 2A, IBT Papers; *Retail, Wholesale, and Department Store Employee*, July 1, 1944; *International Teamster*, July 1944.

Tucker Smith, the man directing Michigan operations for the Retail Workers, was actually a pacifist socialist with no affiliation to Trotskyist groups.

25. *International Teamster*, August 1944; A. H. Raskin, Memorandum to the Chief, Industrial Services Division, June 9, 1944, Folder 245, "Labor Relations," Box 1029, Record Group 179, War Production Board Policy Documentation File, National Archives and Records Administration, College Park, Maryland; *Michigan Teamster*, July and August 1944.

26. Melvyn Dubofsky, *The State and Labor in Modern America* (University of North Carolina Press, 1994), 183; Christopher L. Tomlins, *The State and the Unions: Labor Relations, Law, and the Organized Labor Movement in America, 1880–1960* (Cambridge University Press, 1985), 288; *Michigan CIO News*, November 24, 1944.

27. *Retail, Wholesale, and Department Store Employee*, April 1945.

28. Lichtenstein, *Labor's War at Home*, 216–218, and *The Most Dangerous Man in Detroit*, 225; Robert H. Zieger, *The CIO, 1935–1955* (University of North Carolina Press, 1995), 216; Joel Seidman, *American Labor from Defense to Reconversion* (University of Chicago Press, 1953), 205–206. Ironically, and perhaps inevitably, the year following the signing of the charter saw the greatest strike wave in the history of the United States.

29. James and James, *Hoffa and the Teamsters*, 80.

30. The intervention of CIO corporatists and the National Defense Mediation Board

against the United Construction Workers Organizing Committee's campaign in trucking is discussed in chapter 4.

31. Directive Order, February 7, 1944, Case No. 4648, "Central States—Government Inquiries" folder, Box 2432, Dispute Cases, Trucking Commission, National War Labor Board, Record Group 202, National Archives and Records Administration, College Park, Maryland; *Michigan Teamster,* April 1943, July–August 1944; Directive Order, April 26, 1945, Case No. 111-13937-9, "Greater Detroit Cartage Association" folder, Box 2436, Dispute Cases, Trucking Commission, National War Labor Board, Record Group 202, National Archives and Records Administration, College Park, Maryland; Thomas E. Flynn, letter to John Gillespie, June 13, 1945, Folder 27, Box 7, Series 2A, IBT Papers. On the participation of cartage members in the local's meetings, see *Michigan Teamster,* June 1944. On "hate strikes" in the automobile industry, see Meier and Rudwick, 162–174.

Average hourly earnings for automobile production workers increased from $1.240 in June 1943 to only $1.269 in May 1945, while average weekly earnings actually decreased from $59.52 to 57.99 during the same period. U.S. Bureau of Labor Statistics, *Employment and Earnings Statistics for the United States, 1909–66* (U.S. Government Printing Office, 1966), 310.

Hoffa's support among the rank and file of Local 299 is further discussed in chapter 7.

32. Many of the Case bill's provisions, including the ban on secondary boycotts, were in fact contained in the Taft-Hartley Act, which was passed by an override of Truman's veto in 1947. See Joel Seidman, *American Labor from Defense to Reconversion* (University of Chicago Press, 1953), 256–258, 265–267.

33. *Detroit News,* April 23, April 24, April 25, April 26, 1946.

34. *Detroit News,* April 27, April 28, 1946, May 23, 1947. For DeLamielleure's relationship with the Teamsters, see chapter 3.

35. *Detroit News,* April 29, May 2, May 3, 1946.

36. *Detroit News,* May 1, May 3, 1946; *Detroit Free Press,* April 30.

37. *Detroit News,* May 4, May 8, May 11, May 16, 1946; *Michigan Teamster,* November 1944; *Congressional Record,* May 6, 1946, Appendix, A2478.

38. *Detroit News,* May 3, May 4, May 9, May 10, 1946; *Detroit Free Press,* May 3, 1946.

39. *Detroit News,* May 11–13, 1946.

40. *Detroit News,* May 11–13, May 15, 1946; *Congressional Record,* May 10, 1946, 4825.

41. *Detroit News,* April 30, May 8, May 20, 1946; *Michigan Teamster,* May 1946.

42. James Hoffa, letter to Tom Flynn, May 15, 1946, quoted in James and James, *Hoffa and the Teamsters,* 78–79; *Detroit News,* May 13, 1944.

43. *Detroit News,* September 8, 1940; May 15, May 19, 1946; Frank Donner, *Protectors of Privilege: Red Squads and Police Repression in Urban America* (University of California Press, 1990), 57; "Retain Judge George Murphy Recorders Judge," *Michigan CIO News,* October 1941.

44. *Detroit News,* May 28, May 29, 1946; Lichtenstein, *The Most Dangerous Man in Detroit,* 66–68, 80–81, 93–94, 126–127, 306–307.

45. The relationships the Teamsters developed with DeMass and the Sheriff's deputies are discussed in chapters 3 and 5.

46. *Detroit News,* May 7, June 13, July 6–7, July 27, 1946.

47. *Detroit News,* May 2, May 3, May 17, May 20, June 22, June 28, July 27, August 22–23, August 27, 1946, January 22–24, 1947; *International Teamster,* May 1946. In

January 1947, Hoffa invited the scorn of both the AFL and the CIO when he ordered Teamster drivers to disregard pickets set up at seven downtown cafeterias by waitresses affiliated with the AFL Hotel and Restaurant Workers. The waitresses had struck the cafeterias after their demands for wage raises were rebuffed. As the strike entered its sixth week, Hoffa derided the strikers' demands as "silly" and ordered all Teamster truckers to cross the picket lines. The grand jury investigators looked into but dismissed charges made by Frank Martel that a payoff from the restaurant owners through Curran had been given to Hoffa in exchange for breaking the strike. They took more seriously the possibility that Hoffa was attempting to retaliate against Martel, who had recently ordered the cancellation of the AFL charter for the Music Maintenance Workers Union, with which the Detroit Teamsters had a close alliance. The investigators overlooked the fact that in addition to receiving supplies from Teamster drivers, the cafeterias were serviced by milk drivers and bread drivers affiliated with the Dairy and Bakery divisions of the Teamsters' chief rival, the CIO's Retail, Wholesale, and Department Store Employees. In 1942, Hoffa issued a forty-eight-hour ultimatum to all of Detroit's hotels, restaurants, and supermarkets that unless they transferred their milk business from CIO-organized dairies to those with Teamster contracts, they would be cut off from all truck deliveries. *Detroit News*, September 17, September 18, 1942, January 22–24, 1947.

48. *Detroit News*, May 28, July 2, August 18, December 2, December 3, 1946.

49. *Detroit News*, September 25–29, October 1, October 3, 1946, March 19, 1947; Thomas Flynn, letter to James R. Hoffa, March 19, 1947, Folder 5, Box 109, Series 2B, IBT Papers.

50. *Detroit News*, April 14, April 16, May 22, 1947.

51. *Detroit News*, August 13, 1947.

52. *Detroit News*, May 22, October 13, October 27, 1947, March 27, December 2, 1948, January 13, 1949.

Eight

Jungle Politics

1. International Brotherhood of Teamsters, Warehousemen and Helpers of America, *Proceedings of the 16th Convention*, October 13–17, 1952, 292.

2. Petition from the Woman's Society of Christian Service of Christ Methodist Church, May 9, 1946; H. Tom Collord, letter to Edward Jeffries, April 2, 1946; Charles E. Freese, letter to Edward Jeffries, May 7, 1946; Charles Thurber, letter to Edward Jeffries, April 29, 1946; Anonymous, letter to Edward Jeffries, May 12, 1946; all in "Unions (1)" folder, Box 7, Mayors' Papers, 1946, Burton Historical Collection, Detroit Public Library.

3. James and James, *Hoffa and the Teamsters*, 82.

4. James and James, *Hoffa and the Teamsters*, 122–124, 145. Despite having sent 400 organizers to the South during a two-year campaign after World War II, the CIO's "Operation Dixie" folded in 1948, having produced few permanent local unions.

5. International Brotherhood of Teamsters, Chauffeurs, Warehousemen and Helpers of America, *Proceedings of the Fifteenth Convention*, August 11–15, 1947, 439–440; *Proceedings of the Sixteenth Convention*, October 13–17, 1952, 290–292.

The alliance between Gibbons and Hoffa was cemented in 1953 when Hoffa helped the St. Louis Teamster repel a criminal organization's attempted takeover of Local 688. Later, Hoffa promoted Gibbons to secretary-treasurer of the Central States Drivers Council and then vice president of the IBT. See Lon W. Smith, "An Experiment in Trade Union Democracy: Harold Gibbons and the Formation of Teamsters Local 688, 1937–1957," unpublished Ph.D. dissertation, Illinois State University, 1993.

6. *Michigan Teamster*, November 1949; R. J. Bennett, letter to Thomas E. Flynn, March 23, 1949, Folder 6, Box 114, Series 2C, International Brotherhood of Teamsters, Chauffeurs, Warehousemen and Helpers of America, Papers, State Historical Society of Wisconsin, Madison; Leonard Shaffner, interview with the author, Taylor, Michigan, June 15, 1998.

7. *Detroit News*, November 28, 1945; *International Teamster*, December 1946. As in prior CSDC negotiations, a group of employers refused to comply with the agreement and were struck by the union. Approximately 580 firms employing 2,000 drivers were hit with walkouts in January 1946, and most were brought into the fold after a few weeks of the walkout, but at a wage rate seven cents lower than the standard agreement. Central States Drivers Council, "Union Negotiating Committee Demands," October 25, 1946, Folder 3, Box 122, Series 2D; A. F. Hudson, letter to Mel Sokol, January 22, 1946, Folder 2, Box 122, Series 2D; "Salient Features of 1949–1952 Central States Area Over-The-Road Motor Freight Agreement," November 12, 1949, Folder 1, Box 123, Series 2D; "Central States Conference of Teamsters and Southern Conference of Teamsters Makes History," Folder 1, Box 123, Series 2D; all in IBT Papers; *Michigan Teamster*, January 1949; James and James, *Hoffa and the Teamsters*, 330–331, 342.

8. McMaster interview.

9. *Detroit News*, December 17, 1948; *Michigan Teamster*, December 1948; Frank V. Battle, memorandum, November 16, 1953, "Detroit Teamsters" folder, Box 84; unsigned memorandum, November 25, 1953, "Background Info" folder, Box 86; Frank V. Battle, memorandum, November 16, 1953, "Detroit Teamsters" folder, Box 84.

10. *Detroit News*, November 19, November 20, November 22, 1949; "Teamster Operation in Flint, Michigan area," August 25, 1953, and untitled memorandum, August 27, 1953, "Detroit Teamsters" folder, Box 84, Clare Hoffman Papers, Bentley Historical Library, University of Michigan; James and James, *Hoffa and the Teamsters*, 72. As previous chapters have shown, challenges to Hoffa's control and calls for decentralization were constant but nearly always emanated from the chief officers of rival Teamster locals.

11. James and James, *Hoffa and the Teamsters*, 46; U.S. Senate, Select Committee on Improper Activities in the Labor or Management Field, *Investigation of Improper Activities in the Labor or Management Field: Hearings*, 5189; "David Brinkley's Journal: Inside Jimmy Hoffa," NBC Network, April 1, 1963, transcript in Folder 30, Box 10, John Herling Collection, Archives of Labor and Urban Affairs, Wayne State University.

12. *Michigan Teamster*, July–August 1944; *Detroit News*, September 9, 1944; see chapter 3 for a discussion of the 1943 Detroit mayoral campaign.

13. *Michigan CIO News*, February 2, 1945; Robert Zieger, *The CIO, 1935–1955* (University of North Carolina Press, 1995), 182.

14. Teamsters Joint Council 43, letter to Edward J. Jeffries, September 17, 1945, "Unions" folder, Box 7, Mayor's Papers, 1945, Burton Historical Collection, Detroit Public Library; Zieger, 242.

Scholle "was almost alone in the labor movement in his early and consistent recognition of the need to assert labor's interests in the state Democratic party." Dudley W. Buffa, *Union Power and American Democracy: The UAW and the Democratic Party, 1935–72* (University of Michigan Press, 1984), 13.

15. *Detroit Labor News*, October 12, October 19, 1945; *International Teamster*, December 1945.

16. Stephen and Vera H. Sarasohn, *Political Party Patterns in Michigan* (Wayne State University Press, 1957), 48–49, 54; *Detroit News*, December 8, 1946, January 26, February 27, March 1, March 2, 1947; Frank McNaughton, *Mennen Williams of Michigan: Fighter for Progress* (Oceana Publications, 1960), 96–97 ("muscular" quotation); Neil Staebler, *Out of the Smoke-Filled Room: A Story of Michigan Politics* (George Wahr Publishing, 1991), 29–31; Buffa, 16; Richard H. Pells, *The Liberal Mind in a Conservative Age: American Intellectuals in the 1940s and 1950s* (Harper and Row, 1985), 108–109; Americans for Democratic Action, letter to delegates, June 7, 1948, "CIO and Michigan Democratic Party" folder, Box 82, Clare Hoffman Papers, Bentley Historical Library, University of Michigan; Helen Washburn Berthelot, *Win Some, Lose Some: G. Mennen Williams and the New Democrats* (Wayne State University Press, 1995), 25–33; "Wallace Will Gain as Phonies Push Truman," *The Worker*, Michigan edition, July 25, 1948. The ADA was formed out of the remnants of the Union for Democratic Action.

17. "Biographical Sketch of Mr. John W. Gibson," Box 45, Papers of John W. Gibson, Harry S. Truman Library, Independence, Missouri; Staebler, 31; Berthelot, 26.

18. McNaughton, 90–91, 99–100.

19. Buffa, 14, 17; "State Locals Hear Victor Bucknell," *Michigan Teamster*, May 1948; *Detroit News*, February 27, 1948; Walter P. Reuther, letter to August Scholle, March 12, 1948, Folder 2, Box 60, Walter P. Reuther Collection, Archives of Labor and Urban Affairs, Wayne State University; *Michigan CIO News*, March 17, 1948; J. David Greenstone, *Labor in American Politics* (Knopf, 1969), 120; Tom Downs, "Research Paper #7: The Election of 1946—And the Long Term Results," 5–6, in the possession of Tom Downs, Lansing, Michigan.

20. *Ann Arbor News*, May 3, 1948.

21. Michigan Federation of Labor, *Proceedings*, 59 (1948); *Michigan Teamster*, May 1948; *The Worker*, Michigan Edition, June 6, 1948; *Detroit News*, May 27, 1948.

22. *Detroit News*, June 20, July 4, July 6, July 8, July 11, July 15, 1948; *Detroit Free Press*, September 8, 1948; *The Worker*, Michigan Edition, July 25, 1948; Buffa, 17–18, 30 [Fitzgerald quote on 18]; Staebler, 31; McNaughton, 103.

23. Zieger, 266–273.

24. Sarasohn and Sarasohn, 56; Fay Calkins, *The CIO and the Democratic Party* (University of Chicago Press, 1952), 118; Tom Downs, interview with the author, Lansing, Michigan, June 18, 1998.

25. See chapter 3 for further discussion of Hoffa's approach to politics.

26. Buffa, 18–21; McNaughton, 111; *Detroit News*, August 29, 1948; *Detroit Free Press*, September 24, 1948; Mildred Jeffrey Oral History, 30, Michigan Labor and Politics Collection, Archives of Urban and Labor Affairs, Wayne State University; Adelaide Hart, letter to Arthur Elder, July 10, 1953, "Hoffa" folder, Box 6, Adelaide Hart Papers, Bentley Historical Library, University of Michigan.

27. *Detroit News*, September 18, September 24, September 26, November 16, 1948, February 6, October 28, 1949; *Michigan Teamster*, November 1949; Lichtenstein, *The Most Dangerous Man in Detroit*, 307.

28. *Detroit News*, February 9, February 26, 1950; Michigan Federation of Labor, *Proceedings*, 61 (1950); *Michigan Teamster*, June 1950; *Michigan Democrat* quoted in "George Fitzgerald" file, Box 26, Neil Staebler Papers, Bentley Historical Library, University of Michigan.

29. Sarasohn and Sarasohn, 59; *Detroit News*, September 3, 1950.

30. Berthelot, 58–62; Buffa, 31–33; Sarasohn and Sarasohn, 60 [quote]; Downs interview.

31. CIO-ADA partisans claimed Rothe's club was his wife's kitchen pestle, which he brought to the convention because he couldn't find his regular gavel. The Teamsters, as well as several of the Detroit newspapers, described the club as a "sawed-off baseball bat."

32. *Detroit News*, September 21, September 29, 1950; *Detroit Free Press*, September 21, September 23, 1950; *Detroit Times*, September 21, 1950.

33. *Detroit Times*, September 21, 1950; *Detroit Free Press*, October 17, 1950; *Detroit News*, February 3, 1951; McNaughton, 115; Buffa, 35.

34. *Detroit News*, September 23, October 4, 1951, May 9, 1952.

35. *Detroit News*, July 2, August 1, August 4, August 12, 1954.

36. *Detroit News*, June 2, 1940; *Detroit Labor News*, October 25, 1940; *Detroit Free Press*, June 13, 1953; *Detroit Free Press*, May 24, 1954; Leiter, 50; Democratic State Central Committee, "James R. Hoffa and the Republican Party: A Chronology," Democratic Program Service, September 16, 1958, "James Hoffa" folder, Box 29, Neal Staebler Papers, Bentley Historical Library.

Nine

The Enemy Within

1. Lee Adam Bernstein, "The Greatest Menace: Organized Crime in U.S. Culture and Politics, 1946–1961," unpublished Ph.D. dissertation, University of Minnesota, 1997, 119–121; U.S. Congress, Senate, *Third Interim Report of the Special Committee to Investigate Organized Crime in Interstate Commerce* (U.S. Government Printing Office, 1952), 4; Moldea, 52.

2. *Detroit News*, March 21–23, March 30–31, 1953; Gustav Peck, letter to Clare E. Hoffman, March 25, 1953, "CIO and Michigan Democratic Party" folder, Box 82; William P. Rogers, letter to Clare E. Hoffman, June 10, 1953, "Detroit Teamsters" folder, Box 84; Hobart C. Harris and James Gentry, Detroit Police Department inter-office memorandum to Commanding Officer, March 24, 1953, Box 84, "Detroit Teamsters" folder; "Juke Boxes" folder, Box 20; Memorandum submitted by New York City Anti-Crime Committee, January 9, 1953, "Paul Dorfman" folder, Box 86; all in Clare Hoffman Papers, Bentley Historical Library, University of Michigan.

On the origins of the alliance between the Teamsters and the Bartenders Union in Detroit, see chapter 3.

3. As earlier chapters have shown, the Teamsters paid for favors from various Liquor Control Commissioners.

4. The Detroit local of the Brewery Workers affiliated with the Michigan CIO Council in 1942. See chapter 5.

5. *Detroit News*, July 24, July 2, July 4, September 14, 1946. On the affiliation of the Brewery Workers with the CIO and the IBT's reaction, see Daniel J. Tobin, letter to

R. J. Bennett, April 23, 1946, Folder 5, Box 109, Series 2B, and Daniel J. Tobin, letter to Allan S. Haywood, September 27, 1946, "CIO" folder, Box 3, Series 4, both in International Brotherhood of Teamsters, Papers, State Historical Society of Wisconsin, Madison.

6. Leiter, 90–91; *Detroit News*, May 24, May 25, May 30, June 9, 1947; Lester P. Condon, memorandum to William F. McKenna, April 16, 1953, 5, "CIO and Michigan Democratic Party" folder, Box 82, Bentley Historical Library.

7. United States Congress, House, Education and Labor Committee, *Investigation of Welfare Funds and Racketeering, Report of a Special Subcommittee to the Committee on Education and Labor,* 1954, 6–7.

8. McClellan Committee chief counsel Robert Kennedy agreed with his investigator, Walter Sheridan, that pressure had been applied by Ratner, but ultimately sided with Pearson's thesis. See Sheridan, *The Fall and Rise of Jimmy Hoffa* (Saturday Review Press, 1972), 65–67; Robert F. Kennedy, *The Enemy Within: The McClellan Committee's Crusade Against Jimmy Hoffa and Corrupt Labor Unions* (Harper and Brothers, 1960), 45–49; Frank McNaughton, *Mennen Williams of Michigan: Fighter for Progress* (Oceana Publications, 1960), 117; Drew Pearson, "Hoffa's Interests Present Problem for AFL-CIO," *Detroit Free Press,* June 7, 1956; Democratic State Central Committee, "James R. Hoffa and the Republican Party: A Chronology," Democratic Program Service, September 16, 1958, "James Hoffa" folder, Box 29, Neil Staebler Papers, Bentley Historical Library.

9. United States Congress, House, Government Operations Committee, *Investigation of Racketeering in the Detroit Area, Joint Subcommittee Report* (U.S. Government Printing Office, 1954), 2. Among the other issues uncovered by Hoffman's committee was Hoffa's relationship to the Test Fleet company, which is described in chapter 7.

10. Sheridan, 18; Kennedy, 75–80; Budd Schulberg, videotape interview, *The Mafia— La Cosa Nostra: An Exposé: Hoffa,* Madacy Entertainment Group, 1997.

11. *On the Waterfront,* Columbia Pictures, 1954; Budd Schulberg, *On the Waterfront: The Final Shooting Script* (Samuel French, 1980). See also Stephen J. Whitfield, *The Culture of the Cold War* (Johns Hopkins University Press, 1991), 108–113.

Elia Kazan, the film's director, admitted using the story to justify his recent testimony before the House Committee on Un-American Activities, in which he named several Hollywood colleagues as members of the Communist Party. Schulberg, though, was primarily interested in the corruption in labor unions. "It is true that the subject had fascinated me from my high school days," he relates in the introduction to Walter Sheridan's book on Hoffa. Schulberg later wrote a fictionalized biography of Hoffa entitled *Everything That Moves* and worked with Robert Kennedy on a film version of *The Enemy Within.* See Elia Kazan, *A Life* (Da Capo Press, 1988), 500, and Schulberg's introduction in Sheridan, *The Fall and Rise of Jimmy Hoffa,* xi–xvii.

12. *New York Times,* April 11, April 12, April 14, April 26, 1956; *U.S. News and World Report,* June 15, 1956, 124.

13. Various letters in Folder 7, Box 38, Series 8, George Meany Memorial Archives, Silver Spring, Maryland; *New York Times,* April 29, May 12, June 6, 1956; *U.S. News and World Report,* June 15, 1956.

14. *New York Times,* May 6, 1956; AFL-CIO Executive Council Minutes, June 1956, 15, Meany Archives; *New York Times,* June 10, 1956.

15. Robert H. Zieger, "George Meany: Labor's Organization Man," in Melvyn Dubofsky and Warren Van Tine, eds., *Labor Leaders in America* (University of Illinois

Press, 1987), 329, 331, 334; *U.S. News and World Report*, June 15, 1956, 124; *New York Times*, June 6, 1956; AFL-CIO Executive Council Minutes, August 1956, Meany Archives.

16. Clark Mollenhoff, *Tentacles of Power: The Story of Jimmy Hoffa* (The World Publishing Company, 1965), 124; Kennedy, 4, 7–8; Arthur Schlesinger, Jr., *Robert Kennedy and His Times* (Ballantine, 1978), 151; Stebenne, *Arthur J. Goldberg, New Deal Liberal* (Oxford University Press, 1996), 377.

17. Schlesinger, 18, 152; Murray Kempton, "The Uncommitted," *The Progressive*, September 1960.

18. *New York Times*, December 2, December 17, 1956; Leiter, 113–119; George Meany, letter to Dave Beck, February 29, 1956, and Spruille Braden, letter to George Meany, March 2, 1956, both in Folder 18, Box 12, Office of the President, Meany Archives; Kennedy, 80–81.

19. Kennedy, 5, 12, 32, 41–42; Sloane, 138–139.

20. Kennedy, 29; AFL-CIO Executive Council Minutes, January 28, 1957, 41–42, Meany Archives; Joseph C. Goulden, *Meany* (Atheneum, 1972), 236; Robinson, 193.

21. Frank Cormier and William Eaton, *Reuther* (Prentice-Hall, 1970), 341–342; Walter Reuther letter to George Meany, January 21, 1957; "Resolution on Congressional Investigation of Racketeering and Corruption," UAW International Executive Board, January 18, 1957, 3, both in Meany Archives, Office of the President, Box 62, Folder 14; *New York Times*, January 25, 1957.

22. After McCarthy's death in May, he was replaced on the committee by fellow conservative Carl Curtis of Nebraska.

23. U.S. Senate, Select Committee on Improper Activities in the Labor or Management Field, *Investigation of Improper Activities in the Labor or Management Field: Hearings* (hereafter cited as *Hearings*), 2–3; "Racketeering Inquiry," *New York Times Magazine*, August 11, 1957; Bernstein, 191.

24. Kennedy, 256; *Hearings*, 99–100.

25. *New York Times*, February 3, February 7, February 24, February 28, 1957.

26. Walter Sheridan, *The Fall and Rise of Jimmy Hoffa* (Saturday Review Press, 1972), 30–33; Mollenhoff, *Tentacles of Power*, 144–145; Kennedy, 29–30; Schlesinger, 158–159 [Lahey quote, 158]; *Hearings*, 1664.

27. Goulden, 239; Robinson, 193–194; *New York Times*, March 29, April 2, 1957.

28. Quoted in Schlesinger, 164.

29. Kennedy, 36, 40–44; Hoffa, *Real Story*, 97–98; Schlesinger, 164–165; Hoffa repeated this account in a videotaped interview with four historians at Cornell University, April 1975. The videotape is held by the Kheel Center for Labor Management Documentation and Archives, Cornell University.

30. Kennedy, 55–56; John Bartlow Martin, *Jimmy Hoffa's Hot* (Fawcett World, Crest, 1959), 20–21.

Ten

Remaking the American Working Class

1. Cormier and Eaton, 342; Schlesinger, 166; C. David Heymann, *RFK: A Candid Biography of Robert F. Kennedy* (Dutton, 1998), 127. Even in Detroit, where Hoffa's insistence on strict segregation in his locals had received wide coverage during the

FEPC investigation in 1944 and 1945, the black newspaper *Press Facts* had by 1959 come to identify with the Teamster leader. In an article claiming that Hoffa was "just too busy to think about being prejudiced," the newspaper compared "his lot to that of the American Negro." See Ulysses W. Boykin, "Is Jimmie Hoffa Prejudiced?" *Press Facts,* July 1959.

2. Kennedy, 55–60.

3. *Hearings,* 3595–3596.

4. *Hearings,* 5107–5108.

5. *Hearings,* 5262–5263.

6. Kennedy, 72; Martin, 9.

7. *Wall Street Journal,* October 3, 1957; *New York Times,* October 3, 1957; Sloane, 88–91, 93–95; Martin, 64. According to Kennedy, "No question has ever been raised about John English's integrity." See *Enemy Within,* 5.

8. "Acceptance Speech by James R. Hoffa," Folder 15, Box 353, Walter P. Reuther Collection, Archives of Labor and Urban Affairs, Wayne State University.

9. *Ibid.* (emphasis in transcript); Sloane, 95.

10. Kennedy, 118; Martin, 66.

11. A lawsuit filed by thirteen rank-and-file dissidents did result in a consent decree by which a Board of Monitors was established in January 1958 to oversee the union's affairs. Owing to internal conflict and disruptive intrusions by Hoffa, the board proved to be largely ineffective and was dissolved in February 1961. See Sloane, 105–113, 151–153, 167–169, 171–173.

12. *New York Times,* October 11, 1957; A. H. Raskin, "Why They Cheer for Hoffa," *New York Times Magazine,* November 9, 1958.

13. Quoted in Goulden, 246.

14. Stebenne, 387; Goulden, 250.

15. *Proceedings of the Second Constitutional Convention of the AFL-CIO,* December 5–12, 1957, Volume I, 73; Sloane, 103.

16. Jacqueline Brophy, "The Merger of the AFL and the CIO in Michigan," *Michigan History,* Vol. 50, No. 2 (June 1966), 139–157.

17. John Murray, letter to John Swainson, July 24, 1956, "Hoffa" folder, Box 6, Adelaide Hart Papers; "James Hoffa and the Republican Party: A Chronology," "James Hoffa and the Republican Party," press release, October 7, 1958, John B. Swainson for Lt. Governor Committee; press release, August 20, 1958, "Executive Office"; and various newspaper clippings, "James Hoffa" folder, Box 29, Neil Staebler Papers, all in Bentley Historical Library, University of Michigan; *Detroit Free Press,* November 17, 1958.

18. The composition of the committee changed somewhat in 1958. Patrick McNamara resigned in protest over what he considered the Republican members' unfair attacks on the UAW. He was replaced by Frank Church of Idaho. Irving Ives was replaced by Homer Capehart of Indiana. McClellan, John Kennedy, Sam Ervin, Karl Mundt, and Barry Goldwater remained on the committee throughout its existence.

19. See Kennedy's roster of criminal Teamsters, 327–329.

20. Kennedy, 104–106.

21. Kennedy, 108–114; U.S. Senate, Select Committee on Improper Activities in the Labor or Management Field, *Second Interim Report,* 109.

22. Kennedy, 75.

23. Kennedy, 252–253; *The Mafia—La Cosa Nostra: An Exposé: Hoffa* [videotape], Madacy Entertainment Group, 1997.
24. Kennedy, 75; *Hearings,* 13636–13637.
25. Schlesinger, 204; Kennedy, 323–325.
26. Kennedy, 277; Cormier and Eaton, 347–348; Lichtenstein, *The Most Dangerous Man in Detroit,* 185; Fraser interview.
27. After the war Reuther did adopt a Keynesian strategy of increased consumption, but only with increased work-time and only as a means of improving production and national strength against the Soviet Union. To Reuther, workers were duty-bound to work longer hours for the good of the country, not for their own well-being.

Lichtenstein, *The Most Dangerous Man in Detroit,* 197–198; Cutler, "A Slacker's Paradise," 88–106, 146–173; Cormier and Eaton, 396–397, 399.
28. Lichtenstein, *The Most Dangerous Man in Detroit,* 185, 355–356; Schlesinger, 205.
29. *Time,* September 29, 1958; *The Jack Paar Show,* July 23, 1959, National Broadcasting Corporation, Museum of Broadcasting, New York, New York; *Newsweek,* May 12, 1958, 28. During the summer and fall, Hoffa further provoked the McClellan committee and the press by announcing plans to organize the nation's policemen and to merge under his leadership all transportation unions in the country. Neither plan was enacted. See Sloane, 133–136.
30. Schlesinger, 197; Goulden, 295–299; James and James, *Hoffa and the Teamsters,* 149–152; Anthony V. Baltakis, "Agendas of Investigation: The McClellan Committee, 1957–1958," unpublished Ph.D. dissertation, University of Akron, 1997, 398.

For an explanation of "hot cargo" clauses and their significance in Hoffa's organizing campaigns, see chapter 7.
31. Schlesinger, 198.
32. Alan K. McAdams, *Power and Politics in Labor Legislation* (Columbia University Press, 1964), 163–164, 301–302. Scholars who view the ban on coercive organizing tactics as merely the product of right-wing opportunism include James Green, *The World of the Worker: Labor in Twentieth-Century America* (Hill and Wang, 1980), 222; Burton H. Hall, "Law, Democracy, and the Unions," in Burton H. Hall, *Autocracy and Insurgency in Organized Labor* (Transaction Books, 1972), 112; and R. Emmett Murray, *The Lexicon of Labor* (The New Press, 1998), 104.
33. Fraser, 136; Lichtenstein, *The Most Dangerous Man in Detroit,* 111, 162.

Eleven

Crucifixion of an Antichrist

1. Jerry Rubin, *Do It! Scenarios of the Revolution* (Simon and Schuster, 1970).
2. Hoffa, *Real Story,* 150; Victor S. Navasky, *Kennedy Justice* (Atheneum, 1971), 394; Schlesinger, 299–301; Walter Sheridan, *The Fall and Rise of Jimmy Hoffa* (Saturday Review Press, 1972), 193.
3. Hazel Gaudet Erskine, "The Quarter's Polls," *Public Opinion Quarterly* 24 (Winter 1961), 660–661.
4. Quoted in "Report of John W. Livingston, Director of Organization," AFL-CIO Executive Council Minutes, February 1960, Appendix A-1, 45.

5. Sheridan, 177–179; *New York Times*, July 7, 1961; International Brotherhood of Teamsters, *Proceedings of the 18th Convention*, 1961, 44, 51–52, 113–114.

6. Matt Gelernter, "Rank-and-Filer's View of Hearings," *International Teamster*, September 1958, 17; "British Writer Hits Kennedy Technique," *International Teamster*, April 1959, 16; "David Brinkley's Journal Special: Inside Jimmy Hoffa," April 1, 1963, NBC Network, Museum of Broadcasting, New York, New York, transcript in Folder 30, Box 10, John Herling Collection, Archives of Labor and Urban Affairs, Wayne State University.

7. James and James, *Hoffa and the Teamsters*, 135.

8. *Ibid.*, 194–209. One of Hoffa's means of exerting control over local employers and rank and file union members was the "open-end" grievance procedure—unique to trucking and construction—which did not include terminal arbitration and gave the union the right to strike if joint agreement on a grievance claim was not reached through negotiation. As in Philadelphia, when Hoffa needed to appease the local rank and file he used the procedure to win concessions from employers through the threat of a strike. See James and James, *Hoffa and the Teamsters*, chapter 11.

9. Working conditions and fringe benefits had already been standardized in Teamster contracts pre-dating the national agreement. James and James, *Hoffa and the Teamsters*, 345; Sloane, 290.

10. See chapter 5 for a discussion of Hoffa's centralization of trucking negotiations in Michigan during World War II.

11. James and James, *Hoffa and the Teamsters*, 208.

12. See chapters 4 and 6; Martin S. Estey, "Some Factors Influencing Labor Organization in the Retail Trades," unpublished Ph.D. dissertation, Princeton University, 1952, 23–24; Ronald D. Michman, "Unionization of Salespeople in Department Stores in the United States, 1888–1964," unpublished Ed.D. thesis, New York University, 1966, 162–164; "Retail, Wholesale and Department Store Union (RWDSU)," in Gary Fink, ed., *Labor Unions* (Greenwood Press, 1977), 332; James and James, *Hoffa and the Teamsters*, 43, 128.

13. The membership of Local 299 increased from 2,000 in 1938 to a peak of 14,000 in 1953 and gradually declined into the 1960s. Local 337's membership grew from 1,000 in 1938 to just under 7,000 in 1947, reached its high of 10,000 in 1957, then remained steady through 1961. James and James, *Hoffa and the Teamsters*, 82.

14. Text of Landrum-Griffin in Alan K. McAdams, *Power and Politics in Labor Legislation* (Columbia University Press, 1964), 331; Robinson, 198–199. To his other biographer, Joseph C. Goulden, Meany similarly argued that the hope of deposing Hoffa rested not with the older members of the IBT but with the younger members who "know what Hoffa is, and hate him." Goulden, *Meany*, 254–255.

15. For details of the trials, see Sloane, 288–312.

16. Sloane, 313; 2 John 7–12.

17. *Ibid.*, 264; Sloane, 343–344.

18. A. H. Raskin, "What the 'Little Fellow' Says to the Teamsters Is What Counts," *New York Times Magazine*, May 30, 1971; Jerry Rubin, *Do It! Scenarios of the Revolution* (Simon and Schuster, 1970).

19. Sloane, chapters 13–15, *passim;* Moldea, chapters 10–12, *passim.* There is a general consensus among the many who have studied Hoffa's disappearance and apparent murder that it was engineered by Provenzano and Giacalone and that Fitzsimmons was probably informed of the plan beforehand.

Epilogue

Resurrection

1. Some interesting connections between the producers of *Hoffa* and some of Hoffa's supporters are revealed in Sean Wilentz, "Tales of Hoffa," *The New Republic*, February 1, 1993. An interesting exception to the generally heroic portrayal of Hoffa in popular culture is his depiction in James Ellroy, *American Tabloid* (Ballantine, 1995).

2. Teamsters for a Democratic Union was the principal labor project of the International Socialists, a revolutionary socialist organization which had a few hundred members in the 1970s. The IS subsequently split into two organizations, the International Socialist Organization and Solidarity, the latter of which retains strong ties to TDU. See Aaron Brenner, "Rank-and-File Teamster Movements in Comparative Perspective," in Glenn Perusek and Kent Worcester, eds., *Trade Union Politics: American Unions and Economic Change, 1960s–1990s* (Humanities Press, 1995), 111–139.

3. *New York Times*, June 28, 1993; *Labor Relations Week*, June 9, 1993; *Business Week*, August 30, 1993; *Labor Relations Week*, August 4, 1993; *Detroit News*, December 7, 1993; *St. Louis Post-Dispatch*, December 17, 1993; *Labor Relations Week*, December 8, 1993; George Geller, interview with the author, Detroit, Michigan, June 16, 1998; Jeffrey Goldberg, "Jimmy Hoffa's Revenge," *New York Times Magazine*, February 8, 1998.

4. *New York Times*, July 19, December 4, December 18, 1996.

5. *Wall Street Journal*, December 23, 1997; Barbara Zack Quindel to David N. Edelstein, June 9, 1997, http://www.angelfire.com/ga/careywatch/bzqtoed.html; Geller interview.

6. "The NewsHour with Jim Lehrer," August 4, 1997, http://www.pbs.org/newshour/bb/business/july–dec97/ups_8-4.html. I am indebted to Jonathan Cutler for calling my attention to this.

7. George Geller, one of Hoffa's chief advisors, admitted this in an interview with the author, Detroit, Michigan, June 16, 1998.

8. See Brenner, 125–128, 138n56.

9. *New York Times*, December 22, 1996.

Index

Index

Index

Index

A NOTE ABOUT THE AUTHOR

Thaddeus Russell is Visiting Assistant Professor of History at Barnard College in New York. Born and raised in Berkeley, California, he graduated from Antioch College and received his Ph.D. in history from Columbia University. He lives with his wife in New York City.

A NOTE ON THE TYPE

This book was set in Janson, a typeface long thought to have been made by the Dutchman Anton Janson, who was a practicing typefounder in Leipzig during the years 1668–1687. However, it has been conclusively demonstrated that these types are actually the work of Nicholas Kis (1650–1702), a Hungarian, who most probably learned his trade from the master Dutch typefounder Dirk Voskens. The type is an excellent example of the influential and sturdy Dutch types that prevailed in England up to the time William Caslon (1692–1766) developed his own incomparable designs from them.

Composed by
North Market Street Graphics
Lancaster, Pennsylvania

Printed and bound by
Quebecor World
Martinsburg, West Virginia

Designed by
Soonyoung Kwon